GPS FOR LIFE:

GUIDANCE OF A PERSONAL SAVIOR

Brandy Ann Coffee Marks

Published by Doctrine of the Cross
3829 E 18th Street
Vancouver WA 98661

www.dotcross.org

Printed in the United States of America

ISBN: 978-9841522-5-4

Coffee Marks, Brandy A

GPS: Guidance of a Personal Savior

1st ed. – Vancouver WA: Doctrine of the Cross

ISBN: 978-9841522-5-4

DEDICATION

Thanks to everyone who listened, read the books and encouraged me while I pursued the continuing journey writing and publishing ideas.

To every person with dreams that have yet to be fulfilled may you find your dreams renewed and the motivation to pursue them.

To God for whom these book are written, may you say, "Well done".

**INTRODUCTION**

"The Spirit of the Lord is upon me... he has anointed me to preach the gospel to the poor... to heal the brokenhearted, to declare freedom to the captives, to open the eyes of the blind, and to set at liberty the oppressed;" (Luke 4:18)

There came a day when I desperately needed to be set free however turning to Jesus was not my first but my last choice. Determined to live life on my own terms, I soon found myself in a whole lot of trouble.

"Coffee, you have a visitor" the guard shouts. Surprised, I wonder who could be visiting (Attorney's usually visit us outside the cells). Curious to see, I walk to the window in the wall. It opens to another world, then, I see my mother on the other side. She's not alone but her face is all I see and the tears come. I want to reach out and feel her arms holding me, but the walls hold us back, safe from contact. Later I'm in court —where I've been at least a hundred times over the past six months —but this time, I get to go home!

On April 10, 1989, thirty years to-the-day after my release at age seventeen, again I leave jail. Back in 1959, I just wanted to get out and stay out of jail but two years earlier I had rejected God and became an atheist. Nothing about *that* had changed in 1959 yet by 1989 the change I was seeking was more radical than merely staying out of jail. My life was hell and I wanted freedom from *all* the misery. Thus, I went looking for and found not only freedom in Jesus Christ, but the love and acceptance I had been seeking.

GPS for Life was written to share the lessons I learned in becoming a disciple of Christ. As such, it offers a place for new believers to start and learn about the Lord and grow in his Word as a disciple. Not only for new Christians, but for anyone who desires to renew their relationship with God, and anyone else enslaved by whatever controls their heart, mind, and emotions.

To be set free, in your search of answers there are four stages:

1) Awaken: You awaken to what it is you want or need to change in order to have the life you desire. Having a friend, mentor, counselor or sponsor to confront faulty thinking and keep you focused is vital.

2) Awkward: Learning new ways is uncomfortable. In time, with practice, like learning to walk or talk, using the skills becomes less awkward.

3) Awareness: Practicing new skills and with increased awareness, we begin to make better choices thus, we become a more mature person.

4) Assurance: As our mental, emotional, and spiritual maturity develops this new way becomes as natural as walking and talking. Developing maturity takes time, commitment and knowledge of Scripture.

MEDITATION

We learn best by hearing and meditating upon the Word. King David learned that meditating on Scripture had one great benefit, among many.

"Your word I have hid in my heart *so as not to sin against you*" (Ps 119:11).

Thus, we learn Scripture so thoroughly and with such good understanding that it makes it *nearly* impossible to sin against God.

HOW TO MEDITATE

- ☐ Read the verse and consider it

- ☐ Write it down and look at it often

- ☐ Speak it out loud to yourself, repeatedly

- ☐ Discuss the Word, post it, and teach it at home

"You will carefully teach [the Scriptures] to your children [or anyone else who will listen], talk of them when you sit in your house, walk by the way, lie down, and rise up" (Deut 6:7)

So turn off the TV. Put down your magazine. Grab your Bible. Go for a walk. Trust that God will meet you along the way.

"Draw near to me," God says "and I will be near to you" (James 4:8). God wants to be near, *no matter who you are;* so he meets you where you are.

Meditating on his Word, we gain knowledge and our lives are changed.

You will not watch the same television and may even turn it off and your interests and friends will change as you draw closer to God. Your attitude and behavior will change so much that everyone who sees you will know the love of God is in you. Some will admire you and some will hate you and some may want to know how you did it so they can have their lives, homes, and marriages changed. So, study to be a true worker in Christ not needing to be ashamed, but rightly discerning the Word of Truth (2Ti 2:15).

The following eight chapters take you on this eight step life-altering journey to become a disciple of the Lord Jesus Christ.

1. First is Faith, our hope in Christ and the foundation of all that we do.

2. Jesus was born for a purpose. We each have a god-given purpose, thus, awareness of your personal purpose and its pursuit is needed.

3. Jesus believed in his god-given purpose. Our purpose or dream may seem impossible, at times, but believing in God makes all things possible.

4. From the start, Jesus verbally confessed his purpose to the people and we must also confess our faith in Christ and faith in our purpose.

5. Having thus begun our journey, discipline is needed to achieve our goals and to be a delight to the Lord so we are truly blessed.

6. Now you will learn to express yourself in love in your attitude, behavior and communication, so that others can see the love of God in you.

7. Jesus was without sin and therefore, he did not need to be forgiven, but we cannot say the same and must learn to forgive and be forgiven.

8. The Grace of God goes with us as we share Jesus' message as disciples. What this means for each person differs, and that understanding is vital so you follow God's guidance throughout your journey.

∞

You may be wondering how you can apply these eight steps within your life. On the next page, I will share a brief understanding of the eight steps and their application to real life.

REAL LIFE

Here's how I apply these step in life. Shortly after inviting God into my life in 1989, I began to read a Bible. The first Scripture —one that I remember still today —was from Luke, and introduces what is known as the Song of Mary.

> *"You are blessed because you believed that the Lord would do what He said he would."* (Luke 1:45)

I too hoped that if I believed God then he would fulfill his promise to me.

> *Hope [in Christ] is what saves us. If we already have what we hope for, there is no need to keep on hoping* (Romans 8:24). But, anyone who responds by faith to a promise has hope in its fulfillment.

While this speaks of our hope in Jesus Christ, we can hope in anything else. For example, we hope that a certain dream will come true. In faith, then, we take the next step, which is to Aim for our dream or the next goal we desire. Of course, we also 'hope' that this is God's desire for our life because, then, we are all the more assured that it will come to pass. We Believe in God and trust that he gave us the dream or set us upon this path. Walking by faith, we now trust that he will fulfill it. If it does not happen then we have faith that God has another path for us to take, which he will reveal.

Having confidence that God's will is being done, we now Confess our faith in the fulfillment of our dream, and do so in our attitude, how we behave, and our communication, the words of our mouth. Thus, everything we think, say, and do is directed toward faith that God will fulfill our dream. However, we must also do our part to be a delight to God. Now we discipline our lives to achieve the goal, and express ourselves in love, so that others know the love of God is in us. Because we are human and imperfect, failure is inevitable. Therefore, Forgiveness becomes necessary.

We not only forgive others when they fail us, but because we have forgiven, we can go to God, and with a pure heart, ask his forgiveness for our failures. Finally, having completed these steps, as a disciple of Christ, we share the Grace of God with others and pass on Jesus' message of hope because we understand what having that in our life means for other people.

As you can see, this eight-step process helps to have a deeper more intimate relationship with God so that you have the kind of life you desire. Now that you know how, you can by faith pursue the dream. God bless.

 HOPE A FOUNDATION OF FAITH

"You formed me in my mother's womb; I praise you for the wonderful way you created me. Everything you do is absolutely marvelous! I have complete faith that this is true" (Psalm 139:14)

The writer of this above psalm was no agnostic or doubter but knew the truth and the wonderful nature of God with absolute assurance and faith. From experience he knew that the Lord does amazing and marvelous things while completing his designs with and for us. If we are made so marvelously before we are born imagine that God does even more astounding things as he directs our path throughout the journey! A doubter and an agnostic for most of my life, as I read Scripture that changed as I developed a deep and profound relationship with Jesus Christ.

When I first began to read Scripture I didn't believe in anything but I *hoped* that the Word of God would show me a better way. For several years, I had tried various beliefs (witchcraft, astrology, astral projection, tarot cards, and a host of religions) but none offered anything of lasting value. However, in reading the story of Jesus Christ, his life, what he said, how he lived, and the way he loved people but more so, was his sacrifice –it was amazing –the Scriptures came alive for me as 'the truth' was revealed.

While it is marvelous to imagine this, there are many who like me –or the person I use to be –who place their emphasis on education, money, and other pursuits rather than the pursuit of God and his will for their life. God however wants our lives to be spent in pursuit of him and his will so that the way we live our life glorifies him.

When Jesus began his ministry, after leaving the wilderness he began to teach and to heal, then, in the synagogue he faithfully stated his purpose. After Paul was struck blind, then had his eyes opened, and was baptized he immediately went about proclaiming the faith. So being chosen and now followers of Christ we too must proclaim or tell about our faith. Paul taught that as believers we must first proclaim the *faith,* then, grow in *knowledge* of the truth, which then is illustrated by our living *godly lives.*

Through this process, we learn and grow by sharing our faith and become mature in the faith rather than seeking after things of the world, which leads only to despair and hopelessness. One woman lamented_

> *Despair seeps in as I lay in the dark considering. College degrees, many talents and skills −a successful life − yet, it is an empty one. Nothing that I thought would bring peace has. I've tried everything I know how; what's wrong with me; what's missing?*

These age old questions we all ask. How would you evaluate your life? What brings happiness? Do you look to your accomplishments to see how well you've done or to your relationship with God? Does your life show clear evidence of Christ? If you were to describe how you are living, and to what you are devoted what would it be - God or something else? If, like this person above, you have done everything you know how and did your best then nothing's wrong with you. As to what's missing …

> *I once thought (education, power and prestige] gave me worth/value; now I see they are worthless because of what Christ has done for me. Everything is worthless when compared with the inestimable value of knowing Christ Jesus my Lord. For his sake I have discarded everything, counting it all as garbage, just to gain Christ (Phi 3:7-8).*

There is nothing wrong with having college degrees because knowledge and discernment bring wisdom, but faith in Jesus Christ is what gets us through life and the tough times. Faith is the substance of things hoped for and the basis of God's promises, and though the world bring troubles yet Jesus said, "Take heart; for I have overcome the world!"

> *In the past, as an atheist, my choice when life became unbearable was to turn to drugs and suicide. Now these sinful ways have been*

replaced with faith in Christ when life is difficult and rather than fear and despair, I turn to Scripture to strengthen my faith.

So, you have a choice to either give into despair or be faithful to see Gods purposes and plans fulfilled. Rather than doing as Israel did who wavered between the Lord's promises and pagan gods, turn to God. There will be many times when you are tempted to pursue things in life that promise pleasure, comfort, or security apart from God –God gave us freewill—yet if we want the good life, we must refuse and remain faithful:

"Wait on the Lord; have courage; he will strengthen your heart; wait, on the Lord!" (Psalm 27.14)

Yet sometimes it seems God takes forever. The Lord gave Abraham and Sarah a promise and they waited a long time for it (twenty-five years). They also tried to bring it to completion and paid for their faithlessness. In spite of their disobedience their dream came true as God promised for he always fulfills his promises.

God gave me a promise that I could barely wait to see fulfilled. But time moved on and the days passed and weeks became months then years, yet I wait – at times impatiently. However, I know that God is working all things together for the good of all concerned in its fulfillment. It's not just about me!

Waiting for God is not easy and our prayers may seem unanswered or that God does not understand our situation. Lamentations calls us to wait for the Lord *with hope* because God uses our waiting times to refresh, renew, and teach us. Reading Scripture that says to wait patiently sounds great and we idealize that in our minds but it's not always easy when we want a dream so much that we think we cannot live without it. However, Gods uses these waiting times to teach us lessons (Psalm 25:9). Rather than watching for the pot to boil, so to speak, spend time with God and his teachings and learn of his love and how to be patient.

Jesus commanded the people to love God with all their heart, mind and soul, and to love their neighbor as their self" (Luke 10:27); that's a whole lot of love! To know that God loves us, though we are sinners, and then wholeheartedly accept his love makes it easier to love others. To realize God gave his son as *a sacrifice so our sins were forgiven* is monumental. But to know that Jesus *chose* the cross and to sacrifice his self out of love is even more astounding because of the sacrifice. Would you sacrifice a child or your own life for someone who repeatedly offended you?

The question is "do I love, even my enemy a sinner"; "am I willing to show this enemy love": and, "will I sacrifice my selfish desires to love them?"

Oh. It's easy to imagine this love. I myself love the sound of those words, but find that unquestioning obedience to God in loving even my enemies requires greater faith than I seem to possess at times. There are people and situations that I flat out rebel against when it comes to love! At least, until I read this Scripture, which forces me to reconsider my attitude.

> *"As the Father loved me, so have I loved you. Now trust in my love. If you obey my commands, you will remain in my love, just as I have obeyed my Father's commands and remain in his love. I have told you this so that my joy may be in you and that your joy may be complete. My command is: Love each other as I have loved you."* [No matter how stubborn, foolish, or sinful] (John 15:9-12)

Jesus made it clear. The Father loves the Son. The Son obeys the Father. God loves us therefore we obey God as did Jesus, by living as did Jesus. This is not an "I'll love you as long as you love me"; it is love without limits or expectations. Can you imagine putting aside all your expectations for a relationship? "I give 110% in this marriage" as you ruminate on the hurts, you complain "and I'm lucky to get half that back. It's not fair."

To genuinely know – deeply believe in our heart –God loves and always will love us no matter how foolish our behavior creates a loving heart and brings complete joy. Can you imagine that kind of love? Do you deeply believe this is true? To deeply believe is vastly different than having an intellectual knowledge of God's love from simply reading it. Who would not want to live in God's love? Faith alone makes this possible.

My journey can help you to learn and grow in the Lord. Yet these steps are meaningless without a relationship with God through knowledge of him and his ways and following in the footsteps of his son Jesus Christ.

Peter told people, "Everyone (believer and unbeliever, alike) should know for certain that God has made Jesus both Lord and Christ". (Acts 2:36)

When those he taught asked, "what should we do?" (v37) Peter replied,

> *"Turn to God! Be baptized in Jesus name so your sins are forgiven, then he gives you the Holy Spirit who teaches all things; this is for everyone our Lord chooses"* (v38-39).

"You did not choose me" God said. "I chose and sent you to produce fruit that will last. [When you do this] my Father will give whatever you ask in my name" (John 15:16). The fruit he speaks of is joy and peace of mind.

Consider this, are you at peace, and if not, are you ready to turn to God? Would you like to know all things and have a genuinely peaceful life? Wouldn't it be great to have a life of peace and contentment simply by believing in and trusting God? Better yet, is it not amazing that God has chosen you to have this kind of life? Do you hope this is true? It is!

So, if you ready to accept God and make Jesus your Lord and Savior then simply admit that you are a sinner and ask Jesus to come into your life. Instantly God forgives all your sins and though your sins are as scarlet he washes you whiter than snow (Isaiah 1:18). Now that God has called and you have chosen to follow, you may be wondering, "What's next?"

1. THOUGHT FOR TODAY

There are so many people here. But there is a man, standing separate from the rest. John turns toward him. He sees him too, among the reeds. Sunlight reflects off the water and plays over his face, light and shadows, the eyes, sparkling amber, flecked with gold. He lifts his hand in greeting and I see that John does know him. "Jesus", he exclaims. "It's been so long since I last saw him - "Eighteen years!"Then, John smiles and shakes his head in wonder, as Jesus moves toward him. He says to his disciples. "Look. There is the lamb of God."

Then face to face Jesus says, "Baptize me." But John seems confused and does not understand. "It is I who should be baptized by you" he said. But Jesus sinks into the waters and in a single moment John recalls all he heard about this man. Then, remembering Jesus beneath the water he slaps the surface and cries "Arise!" Jesus comes forth from the water and the heavens split and a dove of blinding whiteness alights on him. "This is my beloved Son" John hears "In whom I am well pleased" (John 1).

Do you believe John's story?   **YES**   **NO**

Do you know that Jesus is both Lord and Christ?   **YES**   **NO**

Have you accepted Christ as your Savior?   **YES**   **NO**

If not, what's holding you back?

Do you believe God has called you as his own child?   **YES**   **NO**

As Napoleon was talking to a group of high-ranking officers, his horse got spooked and bolted. A quick-thinking private saw what was happening and went after the horse, returning it safely to Napoleon.

"Well done, *Captain*," said Napoleon upon his return.

The *private* saluted, and said, "Yes sir." He then went to the supply tent and got a captain's uniform, and moved into the officer's quarters.

He could have said, "Surely he didn't mean what he said. "Instead, he took Napoleon at his word and said, "Yes, sir" then acted on it.

The Lord calls us "Friend," All we need say is, "Yes!" then walk alongside him as his friend and companion. Are you a friend of Jesus?   **YES**   **NO**

What does it mean to you to be a friend of Jesus? Describe

THE WAY TO GOD

Once we make the choice to follow Jesus he showed the way by leaving his childhood home to begin his ministry [later his family followed him]. The books of Matthew and Luke tell the story of Jesus' childhood, his baptism, his wilderness journey, and his ministry as it unfolded. So too, each of us must leave our childhood, our immature self-seeking ways to become mature men and women of God - to be prepared for ministry. Jesus was in the wilderness a mere forty days while the Israelites were there forty years. Developing spiritual maturity, we see, takes time. How much time it takes depends upon each person and what they are willing to sacrifice.

Leaving our past, we enter the unknown. Often we are tempted to return to our former ways. Jesus was tempted just as the Israelites were, after leaving their bondage in Egypt. When tempted in the wilderness, Jesus overcame by relying solely on God's word; "Man does not live by bread alone" he said, "But by every word of God" (See Luke 4:4).

When entering the unknown on my journey to healing, I found a safe place to live, and avoided those who tempted me to return to that life. I read books on the Bible (Chuck Swindoll's 'Come Before Winter'), and bought a Bible. I focused my attention on knowing God by listening to pastors, and reading the Bible. In the process, I learned to discern the truth of man from that of Scripture. I gained understanding by looking up verses and reading commentaries; I studied the Word.

No one should blindly accept everything anyone else says. The Holy Bible is the only book that is the authoritative Word of God! Yes, it is difficult especially if you are not gifted as a student to learn by reading. However, there are tapes and CDs available, and books that can be downloaded can usually be listened to for those who learn best by hearing. Scripture does say that belief comes by hearing the Word. Start simple. Go to church and take a note pad with you. Write down the scripture references given and write whatever comes to mind, questions or comments.

If you want to know God and understand Scripture you will soon discover that is like getting to know anyone. Other people can tell you about God and you get some idea from their opinion. However opinions come with personal experiences and resulting presumptions. So, the way to really know God is to meet him yourself as he speaks through his Word. Once you gain certain wisdom and discernment and can separate the wheat from the chaff, so to speak, you will be able to discern biblical truth from other.

After Jesus' wilderness journey and after the 40 days and the temptations of Satan had ended, he set out to fulfill his life purpose. He first began to teach and heal and in the synagogue, boldly stated his life purpose: "the Holy Spirit anointed me," he read from Isaiah, "to proclaim the Gospel to *the poor*, heal the brokenhearted, deliver the captives, give new sight to *the blind*, and to set free those who are oppressed..." (Luke 4:19; Is 42:7). Thus Jesus committed himself outwardly to his purpose and fulfilled it living a life that was well-disciplined in complete obedience to God.

Jesus made it clear that to follow in his footsteps and to have God's grace in our lives and his promises fulfilled we must deny our selfish interests and take up our cross (Luke 9:23); be an example for others to follow. Our cross can be whatever challenge we face and in obedience to God, show our love towards others even our enemies in whatever we think, say or do - our attitude, behavior and communication.

As we follow in Jesus' footsteps, we learn that all things are acceptable but not all things are profitable. There is nothing wrong with a beer or a glass of wine occasionally. However, if you are not a disciplined person and you are unable to tell yourself 'no' after one or two beers, then the obvious choice for you may be abstinence.

> *Upon entering recovery from drug addiction I also stopped drinking alcohol. Then I began to have a glass of wine in the evening. Pretty soon I was having a glass of wine every night. One night I had a dream where I fell through the floor of an outhouse. Immersed in liquid poop to my neck, I was terrified and called for help. Instantly there was a ladder and I climbed out. I stopped drinking wine!*

A funny story, yet true. Discipline is vital to a healthy life. Twenty years later, I live a more disciplined life and as a result, there are occasions when I drink. It took a long time to learn to say no to chocolates by the box however, I still love cheesecake; that's a work in progress!

When speaking of the successful athlete Paul referred to the person who was "wholly self-controlled" or "self-disciplined."

> *Those who compete ...are moderate in all things. [Athletes do it] to gain a perishable [trophy], [Christians do it] to gain an imperishable crown (1Corinthians 9:25).*

So, we learn to live in moderation. We learn that we can have times of great joy or sorrow but those should not dominate our lives. Moderation may be boring to some, but being undisciplined is not the answer either. To strive for continual highs or immersed in sadness or depression continually is sin.

To believe and obey God –that Jesus came so that we might have life –and a joyful one at that –we avoid the highs and lows of sin. Thus, in obedience to God we choose the life Jesus chose though that life at first takes extra effort to achieve through study, prayer, meditation, and making conscious choices to discipline or moderate our attitude, behavior and communication.

In spite of all our efforts, at time it seems we fail miserably. Like an infant learning to walk and talk, we fall down while learning to stand on our feet and stumble over words. Yet that too is part of the learning process.

Where it all Leads

In Genesis 46:1-7 we see Israel choosing to leave Canaan and go to Egypt. Yet it also shows that God wanted this to happen; he had plans for them and this bondage was part of the plan. While they did not realize the trip to Egypt would lead to bondage that is exactly what happened.

Can you imagine God allowed your bondage so you would return to him because he has a purpose and he is using this situation to get you to back on track or move you to another place, to pay attention? Of course, this means that God has a way to set you free too, just as he did the Israelites. Nonetheless, you have to be willing to call on God and when he answers, leave that dependent life you are living.

Leaving my addictions was not easy however, going to jail and losing my freedom made it easier. Yet it was harder to leave the man I had come to depend on. Leaving was a learning process that brought me a lot of grief before I finally trusted God's love, and gave up the man.

It was by God's power that the Israelites left Egypt, generations after they left Canaan. In their minds, they were likely Egyptian and did not want to leave, though they hated their slavery. We too love the *idea* of freedom, but as we leave our bondage we hunger for the quick fix that seems to make life more endurable be it drugs, sex, gambling, or any number of *things*.

One man described the experience of leaving as a deep depression, at first, followed by a tremendous euphoria that gave way to despondency. During this third phase, feeling downcast he was sorely tempted, but rather than return to his bondage, he asked himself, 'Why are you downcast, O my soul? Why so disturbed?' He says to himself, as did David, 'Put your hope in God, for I will yet praise him, my Savior and my God'. (Psalm 42:11)

OUR LIFE STYLE

Often our bondage is to whatever life-style we have become accustomed (anger, control, gambling, drugs, pornography, alcohol, even prison life) and we do not realize that our true life is with God in heaven. Jesus said "the Kingdom of Heaven is within" [if we just take hold of it]. Heaven is within our grasp but we must grab hold, refuse to look back, and move on toward or into the promised-land.

Like the man above, you may feel very depressed at first, then, find yourself extremely euphoric, feeling nothing can defeat you and re-enslave you. But that is when Satan will use his best resources to defeat you as you sink into a mire of misery and even despair of life itself. Nonetheless, like King David and this man you too can turn to God in your despair and find a way out.

If God does not lead you along the shortest path, follow him anyway and trust that he will lead you around unknown obstacles and always into ways that help. God doesn't always work in the way that seems best to us but goes a roundabout way. Like the Israelites God may take you on a longer route to avoid conflicts because he can see the end of your journey too, from the beginning so he knows the safest and best way. Trust him!

2. THOUGHT FOR TODAY

Saul rages at Jesus' followers. *I will kill those heretics*, he fumes. *Perhaps the high priest will give me what I need*, and at once he sought him out. "Letters" He insists. "Give me permission to arrest the followers of *Jesus*". Scorn in his voice, his eyes flash with righteous indignation.

Having the papers, Saul rides off in a blaze of fury heading for Damascus, intent upon murder. Suddenly a brilliant white light surrounds them and blinds the eye. His horse rears in terror and Saul is thrown to the ground. Before he can right himself a voice pierces him like a sharp sword, "Saul! Saul! Why are you persecuting me?" Fearful he demands "Who are you?" and casts about, seeing no one but his companions. He hears the voice; again, "I am Jesus, the one you are persecuting."

Pierced with the truth Saul's mind is a blank. Not knowing what to do, he is told, "Get up and go into the city; and someone will tell you what to do." Blinded by the light Saul cannot see to walk one step, so his companions take his hand and help him onto his horse, and then, lead him to Damascus. For three days darkness surrounds him and fear lurks nearby.

Blind and terrified by his helplessness all he can do is trust that someone *will* tell him what to do. Yet anger seems to overwhelm Paul at times; he has never felt so helpless. Paul is always in command, leading with his anger. So he turns to the One he does trust and prays to God. (Acts 9:1-12)

∞

Imagine what it must have been like to become blind then to see again.

Describe what it would be like (for you to be literally blind and set free but also to be blind to your shortcomings and sins then set free)?

Has God ever knocked you off your high horse to the ground (humbled you) before you saw the light and changed your sinful ways?

Describe

Great is the difference between a man's being frightened at [his sins], and humbled for his sins [which brings repentance or change]. Thomas Fuller

What does it mean for you to be humbled? Describe

FREE AT LAST

To be freed of our bondage is an experience difficult to imagine. Yet, we must learn how not to rely on things of the world and turn to God instead. God provides strength to resist temptation to return to our former slavery. When we are prepared to live on God's terms, not our own, we seek God, knowing he provides everything that we need.

God provides for our needs but this learning takes time as our faith builds. Had the Israelites needed to get to the promised-land by going through the land of the Philistines, they may not have made it. Fighting battles along the way might have quickly discouraged the Hebrews. As it was, their hardships had them longing for Egypt and the safety of the known, many times.

Living in bondage for long [relationships, institutions, or addiction behaviors] can degrade our minds to where we are incapable of any great exertion on our own part. An enslaved or dependent mind makes it hard to think right. Unarmed and ill-equipped, life itself is a battle doing whatever to takes to survive and get from one day to the next. Help is needed!

Social creatures people do not do well alone (See Genesis 2.18). When alone and isolated we can become depressed and ill, mentally and emotionally. God saw Adam alone. Perhaps he was sad and lonely with no one to talk to but the animals. While I love my dogs, walking and talking to them, I would be lonely without the companionship of people. We all need someone to communicate *with* not just talk at. Having friends, aside from our household pets to encourage and support us is vital.

Relationships are about oneness. Two cannot walk together unless they are in agreement. The idea is to move from a dependent state (i.e., dependent on parents, welfare, prison, or substances) to a state of independence then finally interdependence (where we work together in relationship).

While some independence is healthy being too dependent, even on God, is not good either, for instance when we do not exercise our faith by doing good works, using our spiritual gifts. Independently we pray for insight, then work with God interdependently to fulfill the plan he has proposed for us. God is our provider but we were created with freewill.

God sends us into the world empowering us with gifts, abilities, skills, and talents given for his purposes but these must be use independently and also interdependently in cooperation with others. As we use these gifts to help others we create more interactive relationships. Often we believe our need is so great that we have nothing to give.

IN NEED

Maybe you are so much in need that you think you have nothing to give. God says 'Those things my hand made and all those things exist, but upon this one will I look, he or she who is poor and has a remorseful spirit, and who trembles at my word. (Isaiah 66:2)

The answer of course is to humble ourselves, spend time in the Word and in prayer telling God our needs trusting he will provide--he already knows--but more important, thank him in advance for having filled your need. In other words, once you ask for something, by faith believing that it has come to pass, if you have asked without selfish motives.

While the time you spend in the Word varies, if you persist in pursuing God then he guides you into a more intimate relationship. Consequently, you will desire to increase your time in the Word. Throughout this process, you learn to let go of self and lean on the Lord instead of yourself and trust in his word, learning and growing in the Word.

WORDS HAVE POWER!

In the natural world, word can hurt or heal. In the spiritual they have the power to change your life, and get you on track with God's Will! Words spoken in faith can heal body, mind and soul, bring financial blessing, and bring the promises of God's Word into the natural to bless you and your family! God's Word has the power to cause what it says to come about. So believe God's Word, use it as intended, in faith and it will be.

"Confess to possess" is to confess with your mouth speak it out loud and the spiritual truth will take place in the present. All we need is faith but we often make excuses for unanswered prayer instead of looking at what we are doing or not doing. In other words, are we obeying God and his commands and loving others; are we walking by faith?

"Anything is possible for you... let your will [Gods] to be done, not mine" (Mark 14:36). Our prayers are motivated by self interest - what we want - not *God's* interests[1]. We walk by fear often rather than faith.

- "Why were you afraid? Don't you have any faith?" (4:40)
- "You are now well because of your faith..." (5:34)
- "Anything is possible – if you have faith!" (9:23)
- "What you ask for will be yours – if you have faith". (11:24)

---

[1] "Mark 11:24" Life Application Study Bible

God created everything by his word and he can change it too! We create the world around us by our word too and we can change it simply by the words we speak. Have you ever tried to change the behavior of another person and by saying things such as "No; that's not the way to do it"; "You never listen to me"; or "Stop getting so angry"? A while back I was teaching a ten-year-old how to paint and found myself saying to him "No, don't do it that way". Old habits die hard and that was one of mine.

He looked confused and unhappy and it took me a few seconds to realize that was the only way he knew. So then, I changed and started saying, "Wait. Let me show you another way, one that may work better for you". This was helpful because then he could choose between the ineffective and the more effective method; he had a choice.

The words we speak can help or hinder and lead to success or failure. But our words are not nearly as important as Scripture that are God's words. So, read the Scriptures and speak the Word into your life and the lives of others to help not hinder! Satan tried to hinder Jesus purpose, tempting him to yield to pride to prove he was the son of God (Luke 4:1-12). Jesus resisted by the Word; he knew God provides for all our needs.

Often God gives us what we ask when it's in line with his purpose, and when we ask without selfish motivation. He considers the other person and their needs too. It's not just about you or me because our actions can affect the entire world to some degree as this story illustrates:

> *In landing on a branch a dragon fly's wings caused a slight breeze that became a stronger wind and after that wind crossed the seas it became a hurricane in Florida that moved up the east coast and the high waves capsized a fishing boat and two men aboard drowned. The drowning occurred two weeks after the dragon fly landed.*

God has all these things to consider when giving good gifts to his children. How will that gift affect his child; how will that person respond to it; and how their response will affect some other person, and so on. Each person is at a different level in their spiritual maturity and so we must be ready, prepared to handle whatever he has given us so the flutter of our wings does not cause a death in some other part of the world.

So when God does not give you want you want right when you want it, ask yourself, "Am I really ready for this; what else do I need to learn, or what do I need in spiritual, mental, emotional or physical maturity before I take on this particular career, relationship, and/or project?"

3. Thought for today

Do you feel too needy at time, and think you have nothing to give? Describe.

Imagine trusting God to care for you as you take time to care for others.

What dream would you like to have come true? Describe.

Now confess with your mouth so that the spiritual truth will take place for "anything is possible if you have faith…"

Jesus said,   "I am the bread – nourishing you"

"I am the way, the truth, the life – that is in God"

"I am the light of the world – lighting the way for you"

"I am the true vine – supporting you as you grow spiritually"

Have you been in a situation where you got what you wanted but it was much later, and you realized that the waiting made a positive difference? Describe

Have you prayed and walked by faith only to be disappointed later in the outcome – your prayer was not answered or not the way you hoped?

Describe

How do you feel about that now?

Our Provider

Often we believe the world provides what we need, or we seek to please people believing they have what we need - love or possessions. Perhaps, we strive for a college degree thinking it will give a sense of competence. Disappointment can turn to depression when the feel good doesn't last; we discover it is short term and despair soon follows.

Focusing on the Word rather than the world brings peace of mind. However, many refuse and remain blind to the truth. My personal belief is that many people simply want to remain in their sinful life. One man told me that he liked the life he was living and to believe in God meant he had to change – leave his mistress and become faithful – and he had no intention of making that change.

Jesus traveled throughout the countryside in every city and village and declared the gospel. Using the Parable of the Sowers, he spoke to those that came to listen and later, he interpreted the parable for the disciples, because those who want to know ask and listen in order to understand:

The seed in the parable is the Word of God; three ways it's lost.

First, Satan takes the Word away so we do not believe and get saved.

I did not get saved until I was over fifty.

Second, some joyfully hear the Word and believe for a while, but when trials come, they return to their sinful ways.

I have a friend who believes in Jesus. But when difficulties arose in her marriage, her immediate response was to get a divorce.

Third, others hear God's Word, but distracted by the pleasures and cares of life they do not grow and mature in the Lord.

A neighbor had a hormone problem. Her hormones raged and tempted by sex she answered, "I can't help myself" and jumped into a sexual relationship instead of jumping into God's word.

Our goal is to have a heart for God so when we hear the Word (the seed is planted deeply in our hearts), we hold fast and patiently mature so our life bears fruit (love, joy, peace and the salvation of others) (Luke 8:1-15).

Therefore, we are saved when God calls and when difficulties arise in our marriage or at work we must get into the Word and strengthen our faith. Because we are firmly in the Word, the Holy Spirit helps us to resist. Also, we receive spiritual gifts that help us to help others.

Spiritual Gifts		
Romans 12:6-8	**Ephesians 4:11**	**1 Corinthians 12:1-14**
<ul><li>Prophecy</li><li>Ministry</li><li>Teaching</li><li>Exhortation</li><li>Giving</li><li>Leading</li><li>Showing mercy (compassion)</li></ul>	<ul><li>Apostolic</li><li>Prophetic</li><li>Evangelical</li><li>Pastoral</li><li>Teaching</li></ul>	<ul><li>Wisdom</li><li>Knowledge</li><li>Discerning of spirits</li><li>Speaking in tongues</li><li>Interpret tongues</li><li>Prophecy</li><li>Faith</li><li>Working of miracles</li><li>Healing</li></ul>

Circle those gifts you know you have or those you would like to have.

There were misunderstandings in Corinth about spiritual gifts. We have our own misunderstanding too when we allow Spiritual gifts to become symbols of spiritual power, causing rivalries. In Corinth, some people thought they were more "spiritual" than others because of their gifts. This was a misuse of spiritual gifts because their purpose is always to help the church function effectively, not to divide it. We can be divisive if we insist on using our gifts our own way without being sensitive to others. We must never use our gifts as a means of manipulating others or serving our own self-interests.

The spiritual gifts are given to each one by the Holy Spirit as special abilities that are to be used to minister to the needs of the body of believers.

As we use our spiritual gifts the fruit of the spirit is more evident in our lives.

These 9 fruits come directly from the Holy Spirit, and not from us.

God's love, his peace, his joy and his goodness is transmitted into us. These attributes and qualities are part of His divine nature. God is allowing us to share in them when His Holy Spirit imparts these into us! Have you thought about this and fully appreciate what God has done here?

When Jesus called each of the twelve disciples, they left their employment (fishing, collecting taxes, etc.) just to follow him. Jesus chose these ordinary fishermen and hated tax collectors to be apostles.

The Holy Spirit calls us to do what God wants and motivates us as well, but like Jonah we have the choice to follow or not. Some will make what they believe are good excuses for not following while others will find other things to do first and never get around to going with God.

"YOU WANT ME TO DO WHAT!"

4. THOUGHT FOR TODAY

The father realized Jeremiah, just a young boy, was no longer listening. For certain, though, he was listening to someone, for he looked up to heaven and shouted out - to who or what the father did not know, "Lord God. I am only a child and know not how to speak!"

Jeremiah covered his brown eyes, rubs them with the heel of his hand, and shakes his head. His father asks. "What's wrong with you?" Jeremiah turns to him with a puzzled look and says with amazement "The Lord put his hand on my mouth; he opened it and closed it" Jeremiah whispers. "The Lord spoke and said he made me a prophet; and that I must speak whatever he commands." (Jer1:4-10)

Jeremiah had been *set apart* for his ministry in a unique and special way.

While most of us are not set apart for the Lord so dramatically, all of us receive gifts of the spirit that go along with the knowledge, wisdom and skills we have gleaned throughout life. So take these gifts seriously for God gave them to you for a purpose.

What gifts are you aware of being given? Describe your understanding of your gifts and how they could be used by God.

See pages 23 for a list of spiritual gifts, and the fruit of the spirit.

We all are servants but maybe you feel led to serve in a specific area. Perhaps as a clear thinker you can teach? Natural encouragers motivate others to achieve, or you have a generous spirit and are able to give financially. Perhaps you can only give of your time or effort or use talents and skills that bring financial blessings to others.

Ask your family or those close to you if they notice any gifts that God may have blessed you. Those closest often can see what we cannot.

Describe

Describe fruit of the spirit in your life. The fruit of the Spirit makes it appearance as we exercise our spiritual gift(s) (see page 23).

Awakening

Our awakening and maturity in Christ arrives as we come to believe. Even so, change takes time and one's life may not bear fruit right away. Paul was brought to his knees and finally realized the truth about Jesus. But because of a difficult start, the apostles had to send him away where the Holy Spirit then taught and prepared him for several years. Finally, Paul was sent on his first missionary journey (See Acts 13:1-4).

Paul's story is one of faith and patience throughout. Thus, our lesson is not to expect too much too soon. Instead, allow God to transform us in his time and for his purposes as we in faith trust that his will be done. This is difficult in our world today where everything is right now and disposable: fast foods, downloadable movies and music at our fingertips. Waiting on the Lord is not something we are inclined to do with any degree of patience.

> *I've been at this for twenty years and just beginning to think I'm getting someplace with my books and painting. But who knows? Perhaps God will keep me waiting a few more years. So I wait on the Lord. What else is there to do? If I didn't, something else would take its place and likely not be that interesting or pleasant. I might as well stay put and keep my peace of mind. Now that's a transformed mind!*

To have a transformed mind, we must change our attitude and how we view the world. God wants to renew our minds and transform us so that our lives honor and glorify him (Romans 12:2). God wants only what is best for us, and for that reason he gave his only Son to make our new life possible. The least we can do is give a little of ourselves. Okay. Whole lot of ourselves!

To give or sacrifice ourselves in his service may seem like an ordeal.[2] Still, in being transformed into the likeness of Christ it gets easier. Concurrently, we address all that tempts us to turn away from the Word and return to the world's ways (drugs, pornography, gambling, and sexual behaviors). These we use as masks to hide our failures, though God sees behind them all.

2Corinthians 3:18 reminds us that with unveiled face [without our masks] we see as in a mirror the glory of the Lord because we are transformed into that same image. When Moses first came down from Mount Sinai with the Ten Commandments, his face glowed from being in God's presence (Exodus 34:29-35). So too will your face glow when you are in the presence of God; everyone who sees you will know there is a difference.

---

[2] "Romans 12:2" Life Application Study Bible in *e-Sword*

But there is also a veiling of our mind that occurs when we allow hardness of heart and pride to stop us from our repenting and being in God's presence. This veil of ignorance keeps us from Christ just as it kept the Israelites from understanding references to Christ in the Scriptures.

Having our lives transformed is frightening for some; it is the unfamiliar that frightens as we are taken out of our comfort zone. Rather than fuss or worry *'instead pray and ask with thanksgiving – knowing that God has provided - let him know your need* (Phil 4:6)

Ask God to provide then praise him that he has already provided though you cannot yet see whatever 'it' is. Find your strength in the scripture. Psalm 23; is where I find my strength.

> *The Lord is my shepherd; he provides everything that I need and gives me green pastures for rest leading me to a peaceful place. He restores my soul and guides me to live to glorify him. Though I walk with death itself, I fear no evil; for God is with me ... (Ps 23:2-6).*

Like David, the Lord is our strength; and he never forsakes us (Heb 13:5). We all struggle with disease, pain and injury—but only God can walk us through the dark valley of death and bring us safely to the other side.

VALLEY OF SHADOWS

We all have fears beyond death and the shadows of night. Sometimes we fear that a dream will not come true or a boogie man in the shadows. But no matter the situation, if we repeatedly turn to God and trust in his will, he is with us always. Of course, common sense caution is a resource God gave us so we recognize danger signals and deal with them appropriately.

Men and women often become involved in hurtful relationships and when common sense says 'leave' they refuse not wanting to be alone, though they may not recognize it as such. Fear of aloneness has us believing we are in love when fear is what actually guides us. Alienation has been found to be one of the strongest motives for suicide as well. A person isolated and alone, feeling that no one cares about them, often attempts or commits suicide rather than live in a state of aloneness.

We are never alone! God has promised never to leave nor forsake us but we must turn to him in our hour of need. When we call upon God and pray, Jesus brings us peace but not of the world by useless compliments, merely a social nicety, rather his peace is from confidence in God's ability and willingness to provide for our needs.

Jesus not only provides for but keeps in perfect peace those whose faith is firm in him (Isaiah 26:3). He has promised to provide perfect peace, except we refuse to listen (Isaiah 28:12).

The times an emotional crisis has come upon me and I refused to turn to the Lord, I cannot begin to count. Why? God alone knows. Perhaps I get caught up in the drama of the moment, raging or tearful and fearful. God shakes his head in wonder (well maybe not; after all, he knows me far better than I know myself). I imagine him waiting for me, patiently, to calm down and call on him, which I do, ultimately.

Therefore, we should not fear, but trust in the Lord. As we trust in God, our life is like a tree, planted by a flowing river, its roots grow deep and strong and flourishes, bearing fruit. So, place your trust in people or God; one is a curse the other a blessing.

Blessings

"Cursed are they who trust in their own strength... like a shrub in the desert they see no prosperity..." (Jeremiah 17:5)

Jesus is the way and a blessing because he teaches the way of God (Luke 20:21). Christ did not look upon the countenances of men [whether their expression appeared to agree with his view]; he also did not judge anyone by their outward appearance [how well they were clothed; nor did he care if they were handsome or not]. Jesus did not care about their riches, honors, learning, et cetera – their situation in the world. Rather, he looked at the person's heart and respected the sincere and upright.

At times I am concerned about someone's opinion and may covertly watch that person to see by their expression if they agree with what I'm saying. If they seem not to agree, I alter my words to gain their apparent approval. It's a struggle to overcome, knowing that God's opinion is the only one that matters and I seek his approval instead.

What concerns you: pleasing looks and being agreeable to others; do you need to have the finest clothes or look more handsome or beautiful to be acceptable? Or are you sincere and upright, moral and honorable no matter your physical beauty or if you win the approval of anyone?

When we first start off, most of what we learn comes from our family and our immediate environment. Our life is either rich and nourishing or poor and impoverished, and to be accepted we need some neighbor's approval. *"Clean your room. What will so-and-so think; their son's room isn't a mess like yours"; "get good grades (so that person won't think you're stupid)"* etc.

We also learn by example to behave a certain way and also accept sinful behavior particularly when we see our parent sin and they justify the sin. I have known waitresses who took home plates and cups from work, saying *just one of the perks of the job*. In hospitals often nurses took medications and dressings and other items. We then learn by their silent consent and may become a thief. Still we do not have to "follow the leader".

Being human our own sinful desires tempt us also. Regardless of what we learn or our parent's sins, a born-again Christian walking in the Spirit is no longer under condemnation for the family's sins but they are responsible for their own sins and those alone.

> *"There is no condemnation to those who are in Christ, who walk not after the flesh, but the Spirit..." (Ro 8:1-2) "If anyone is in Christ, he is a new creation... The old is gone the new has come" (2Cor 5:17).*

Being a believer does not mean we suddenly are free of bad habits; though it would be wonderful to have the past erased and our sin behaviors gone. Such is not the case. While our sins are forgiven we must struggle with our salvation and overcome our past. "I don't feel that I have [been perfected]" Paul says "but [choose to] forget the past [and my sins as did God when he forgave me], and I struggle for what is ahead" (Philippians 3:13).

We have all done things for which we are ashamed, and we live with that knowledge and conflict of what we have been and what we want to be. But because our hope is in Christ, we must let go of guilt and look forward to who God has made us; accept and become. Instead of dwelling on your past, grow in the knowledge of God by focusing on your relationship with him.

Our hope in Christ is God's forgiveness when we repent of our sins with a change of attitude and behavior, making choices not to deliberately sin, but repent and ask forgiveness when we do. Sin easily sneaks in unbidden when we least expect it. So pay attention and do not let unclean thoughts have a foothold. Rather than television and enticing commercials for sex, alcohol, etc., make other choices. Listen to music or read the Bible.

If you watch television and a seductive commercial comes on tempting you in ways you want to avoid, change the channel, until the commercials end. If the music you listen to belittles men and/or women by its tone, language, or in other ways, stop buying and listening to that music. Pray and talk to God throughout the day and listen for his voice and he will guide you.

When you think you *need* something that you know is sin, stop right then and pray over the situation. Cleanse your thoughts; be not double minded. If you are constantly thinking about illicit sex then that is what you will pursue.

"I can't help myself; he touches me and suddenly we're in bed together". When you think you *need* something that you know is sin, stop right then and pray over the situation. Cleanse your thoughts; be not double minded. If you are constantly thinking about illicit sex then that is what you will pursue. "I can't help myself; he touches me and suddenly we're in bed together".

Whatever happened to turning away the minute you set eyes on a man or woman who stirs your lust?

> *Giving into lust or other any temptation never happens by chance just because you cannot help yourself. You lay eyes upon what tempts you and soon, as you begin to think about it; you desire it; you begin to plan to have it; and finally, you jump in and partake. One teaspoonful at a time, you dig the hole, then fill it with water, and ultimately, you jump in and swim. That is how lust works!*

If you continually think about candy, alcohol, gambling or drugs then that is likely what you will pursue. However, if you attend to your heart desire [ideally it's God] and not allow wicked thoughts a foothold, rather replace them with godly thoughts and pursuits then, you walk in the Spirit.

Often we vow to never do such and such again, then those thoughts seem to arrive as on the wind, or other temptation to sin arrives unbidden. We don't have to seek after sin, it seeks us. Those spiritual forces and power are constantly working against us.

Thus we must learn the Word so thoroughly that we are less likely to sin and have friends who confront our sin and encourage righteous behavior. It is not so much what we say as what we do (Pro 20:11-12); our action and conduct reveal our character. It is important not only to listen with one's ears but also to observe with one's eyes what people do (Pro 20:12).

Galatians 6:1 says that if anyone is overtaken by sin, those who are spiritual should restore such a one in a spirit of gentleness. We are not to rejoice in their shortcomings but restore them. Love covers a multitude of sins (1Peter 4:8) it doesn't talk about or draw attention to, but covers sin. So instead of analyzing another's faults, help that person to be strong in the Lord; that shows where we are spiritually. The carnal person wants to reveal whereas the spiritual wants to restore for they understand how close they are to succumbing to a similar temptation.

> *Once I evicted a man for sin behavior. To retaliate, he wrongly accused me of the same; he lied. Hurt and angry, I felt a need to be vindicated and so, I told someone else about it, analyzing my accuser's motives. In Galatians I was convicted of my sin of gossip later, and repented.*

The spiritual person desires to live righteously and walk in the Spirit (Colossians 1:27) so they do right, relying continually on its presence to guide their every thought, word, and deed (Ro 6:11-14). The presence of the Holy Spirit is seen in its fruit: love, joy, peace, being patient, kindness, faithful, gentle, and self-controlled (Gal 5:22, 23).

Thus, when angry, be at peace; when tempted to retaliate, respond with patience; be kind and gentle; manage your attitude and actions with self-control suffering the slings and arrows of affliction.

Paul knew that chains and tribulations awaited him in Jerusalem but "none of these disturb me" he said. "I don't care what happens to me, as long as I finish the work that the Lord Jesus gave me to do... to tell the good news about God's great kindness" (Acts 20:23-24). His testimony was far different than many of ours.

> *One of my greatest sins is being a ruminator and fault-finder. While I can blame my parents and say that I learned it from them I must accept responsibility for my words. Often I find myself repenting to God and apologizing for my hurtful words. My intent is always to be generous and helpful so my witness does not suffer.*

What testimony do you share with the world? Do you whine and cry over every slight, ruminating on the wrongs? Do others see or overhear you when your actions are less than Christian? When someone mistreats you or says something cruel or, worse yet, they lie about you, do you gossip and spread rumors about them to retaliate? Living in the spirit to glorify God is not an easy task but it is one we as Christians are called to.

LIVING IN THE SPIRIT

Living in the Spirit to serve and glorify God in love is a choice every Christian must make, daily. The challenge is to make a conscious choice each day to serve only God. Take a moment to write about your past and the problems that followed you into the present. The intent here is not to blame other people for the problems in life. Rather gain awareness that will help create change throughout your walk with the Lord. Begin to view problems as potential for growth and a turning away from sin.

> *If we sin willfully after we have received the knowledge of the truth, there remains no more sacrifice for sins, but a certain fearful looking toward judgment and God's fiery indignation, which shall devour the adversaries... It is a fearful thing to fall into the hands of the living God* (Heb 10:26-27, 31).

This does not mean that if you struggle with sin there's no hope. We are not struggling against human flesh and blood. We fight against forces and rulers of darkness and powers in the spiritual world. (Eph 6:12) At times you may even wonder in this struggle if you are forgiven; is there anything needed to gain God's blessing" But God says, "No. It's is done; it is all by grace". There are no do's or don't; it's all about love!

What is legalism? Many people today seem to think that legalism is just about anything! If they don't want to do it, then they cry out, "legalism". Some of **the things you might hear are.**

> **"You are being legalistic telling me I *have to* do such and such!"**
>
> "You live by the rules of the Bible. That is so old school. I'm happy living the way that I want to – my way."
>
> "You live in an ivory tower while the rest of us live down on earth. We shouldn't have to live your way. It's freewill. Remember?"

Legalism is living "the letter of the law" so God will be *pleased* with you. If you have a list of do's and don'ts or have-to's that help you feel 'spiritual' then you are legalistic and being self-centered.

Spiritual discipline obeys the laws of God but the motivation differs. You obey God because you love him and are willing to do all that you can to please him no matter what others say or think! Spiritual discipline is a relationship with God and not a list of do's and don'ts.

So, do not be upset by legalisms you can never fulfill. Legalism is defined by dictionary.com as "strict adherence, or the principle of strict adherence, to law or prescription, esp. to the letter rather than the spirit [of the law]. In *Theology it is* the doctrine that says salvation is gained through good works and that the judging of conduct in terms of adherence to precise laws."

Rather than placing yourself or others under the letter of the law, legalism, try to understand that, on the basis of the finished work of Jesus Christ you do not *have* to study, pray, or worship. Belief in Jesus Christ is what matters. Christ encourages us to confidently come to God by faith (Ephesians 3:12). So, don't drive yourself crazy with vain striving instead, trust the Lord with all your heart and if you *choose* to study, pray or worship so as to know God, then do so, and *enjoy* your salvation and the journey.

5. THOUGHT FOR TODAY:

There are three degrees of faith in the Scriptures: those with no faith; those with little faith; and those with great faith.

Faithless:

"Oh *faithless* and perverse generation, how long will I be with you?" Jesus asked "How long will I bear with you?" ((Matt 17:17, Mk 9:19, Lu 9:41)

Jesus' disciples were given the authority to heal, yet had not learned to use God's mighty power. Jesus' frustration was with the [faithless] and unresponsive generation, yet his purpose here was not to criticize the disciples but to encourage greater faith.

Little Faith

If God clothes the grass of the field so beautifully, which last a moment, will he not more clothe you, *O you of little faith*? (Mat 6:30)

Peter sank in the sea; immediately Jesus reached out his hand and caught him, saying, *you of little faith*, why did you doubt? (Mat 14:31)

We start with good intentions but lose sight of our goal (seeking the Lord) then our faith falters as did Peter's. Yet, when afraid, he reached out for Jesus the one who could help. When your faith fails, remember, Christ is always with you and is the only one who can really help.

Great Faith

A Roman captain had a servant who was on his deathbed, whom he prized highly and didn't want to lose. He sent leaders asking Jesus to come and heal his servant. Jesus went and when he was still far from the house, the captain sent a friend to say, "Master, don't go to all this trouble. I'm not that good a person. ... Just give the order and my servant will get well. ... I give orders and tell a soldier 'Go,' and he goes; another, 'Come,' and he comes;'..." (Lu 7:2-8) This man understood authority and the result of immediate obedience.

Jesus marveled and said, "I tell you, No greater faith have I found, even in Israel [where they learn about God and faith as a child]!" (Luke 7:9)

How's Your Faith, Reader?

How low do you have to sink before you cry out to Jesus?

Describe a situation that illustrated your faithlessness

Describe a situation that showed you had a little faith

Describe a situation that revealed your great faith

Matt 17:20 "…you have so little faith, but honestly, the faith of a mustard seed will move a mountain. With faith *nothing will be impossible for you.*"

- *You say, "He didn't mean it literally!" What did he mean?*

Mark 1:16-18 Simon and Andrew were casting a fishing-net into the sea and Jesus said to them "Come, follow me. I will make you fishers of men." And *immediately* they followed.

- *Would you have followed if you had not known who Jesus was then? Would you have obeyed his voice of authority?*

Mark 4:3:32 speaks to the shallow faith like that of rocky soil that is uncertain faith whereas good soil is sound faith.

Mark 9:19   Jesus said, "Oh faithless perverse generation… (Mk 9:19)

Gal 5.6   We are saved by faith, not by what we do however, our faith is clearly seen by what we do for others in love.

Eph 2.8   We are saved by faith in God, who treats us better than we deserve. This is God's gift to us.

2 Cor. 5:7   Faith means we believe what we have not seen; the reward of this is to see what you believe. (Saint Augustine)

 **DREAM FULFILLED**

I know my plans for you, of success not failure, the future you hope for [I gave you the dream]. When you pray and want me more than anything, you will find me and be restored. (Jeremiah 29:11-13).

Marjorie McBride, The administrator noticed my interest in art and cared enough to give me oil paints. Great was my delight and right away I began to paint. Since a small child drawing figures had been a passion that consumed my time, when I was not reading anyway. Sometime after the paints arrived, a dream followed. Then my uncle came to visit me. "What do you want to do when you leave here?" He asked. "Be an artist" I responded with enthusiasm, to which he cynically replied "You can't and expect to make any kind of living." As the dream arrived, so it vanished just as sudden.

While there are always people who can destroy our dream, try to imagine a future filled with hope rather than despair and that all God requires is for you to want him more than anything in the world. He has a purpose for you that will provide a future of success and not suffering. Oh I know. There are people whose dream has already happened; they've made their millions, so what now? Well, that would depend upon how joyful is your life, truly.

Those who believe that money brings joy, or sex and drugs a feel good, or that stealing gets them what they want may soon discover that their joy or feel good is only temporary; it does not last. While celebration is good, our true joy is found in the Lord; that is our strength! (Neh 8:10)

Money may provide some things that make life pleasant, but those things do not always bring lasting peace of mind. You can be poor or rich and still be miserable. Maybe you believe in God and even prayed and hoped for something but your prayer was not answered and you begin to think that God doesn't care. Or your sins mount up higher than heaven itself but God does nothing so once again, you think he doesn't care.

For years I blamed God and everyone else for my misery, and I became a success by my own will, or so I thought. College degrees, a house, and I raised my children alone not trusting anyone to do what I could do myself. Of course no one warned me about Nebuchadnezzar's pride and the result; not that I would have listened. It took thirty-five years for me to realize my sin and turn to God. When I started to care about something besides myself and looked to God he moved in my life.

We all have challenges to face, but the real challenge is to believe in God and remain faithful. Giving up is always an option, but, throughout the Old and New Testaments God repeatedly calls his people back. And when we do return, Christ shows us that what we once thought had value was actually worthless, garbage as Paul said.

"Nothing is as wonderful as knowing Christ Jesus my Lord" (Phil 3:7-9).

Satan would prefer that we give up and turn away from God but, those who remain faithful no matter how dismal life becomes have a reward. And Psalm reminds us that our weeping or grief may endure for a night, but joy *comes* in the morning (v30:5) because we have confidence that with God we can accomplish anything.

God has everything under control because he knew everything about us when he first formed us in the womb, before we were even born.

"You saw me when I was in the womb. All the days ordained for me were recorded" (Psalm 139:16).

God accepted us from the beginning; he knows everything about us and in spite of everything we have done and might yet do God knows, loves, and accepts us regardless, though he may not like what we do.

Many find it difficult to accept God's unconditional love and reject it and the love of others. Some view life's traumas as evidence of a hateful God, particularly if they were rejected and never felt real love as a child, being abandoned and/or mistreated. To accept God's love is both a choice and an act of faith! That acceptance is more than mere intellectual knowing but is a heartfelt response.

ACCEPTANCE

Everyone wants love and acceptance for themselves. Nothing has such an enduring effect as the experience of not being accepted. Countless persons, deeply wounded by the experience of rejection, feel unloved and unwanted. There is no single reason for feeling rejected. You were given up for adoption; you were left by one or both parents; another was preferred over you; you have physical or mental disabilities; your spouse left you for another; you are not pretty or handsome enough; your body is not well formed—at least not by social standards of the day; and other reasons too numerous to recount.

Parents may be critical instead of discerning and helpful. They may do the best they know how and generally do. But when their best is worse than what can be imagined, we who are wounded end up rejecting ourselves and others for not living up to some impossible standard. While it may seem simplistic, the solution is love and acceptance. To accept and love those persons who have in the past rejected us or who may still reject us seems impossible at times. However, with God nothing is impossible.

To love and accept a person does not mean accepting their behavior. But instead of hating and rejecting them, we love them, regardless of what they have done. We can pray for them to change but when that change does not come, then pray and allow God to change them. Our task is not to seek love, but find within ourselves those barriers we have built against love, then, remove them. *That was my goal, to discover all the barriers built between my mother and me, and then take them down, stone by stone.*

> *My mother was not outwardly affectionate. Her father was not very affectionate and her mother died when she was very young. Thus, she had not learned to show affection. I wanted her to love me but she didn't, not in a way that I equated with love. Convinced that she did not love me, I was angry and resentful. My sister said, "Brandy, Mom may never change. So, are you going to be angry forever?"*

I realized she was right. So, I changed rather than be miserable. The barrier was our discomfort showing affection; it was unfamiliar. So, each visit to see Mom, I hugged her and said, "I love you". That was one of the hardest things ever. Yet that was the first stone down.

Over the next three years, all but one stone came down. I forgot to hug her once day. She looked confused and perhaps wondered why. That's when the final stone came down. She came and hugged me! At last, my mother showed affection in a meaningful way but I had to choose to remove the barriers. You may need a different strategy but if you seek you too will find a way.

Having the relationship restored with my mother was a joy. However, not everyone is so fortunate. God provided and I took the opportunity to learn about love and to share my story with others.

WHAT'S LOVE

We usually think of love as a warm feeling, passion, or assigning some value to a person or object. In reality, love is a choice and a behavior. The world thinks that love is what makes us feel good and that it's okay to sacrifice moral principles and others' rights to obtain such "love." But that is not genuine love but the opposite, selfishness. Love is patient and kind, always there for the other person, not selfish rude or inconsiderate; and love never fails (See 1Corinthians 13:4-7)

The Life Application Study Bible says love explains: (1) why God creates—because he loves, he creates people to love; (2) why God cares—because he loves us, he cares for sinful people; (3) why we are free to choose love — God wants us to give love freely; (4) why Christ died—because of his love for us he offered a solution to sin [his sacrifice]; and (5) why we receive eternal life—God's love is expressed to us and through us forever.

Since God loved us this much, we love one another. Real love for others will chase our worries away (1John 4:11-18). But even more, we love now because God loved us first (v19). God's love is the source of all love. In loving, God kindles a flame in our heart that we light in others. In turn, we love others and warm them by God's love through us.

Scripture says "Give and it will return to you in full—pressed down, shaken together, running over, and poured into your lap. The amount you give will decide the amount you get back" (Luke 6:38). Would it not be marvelous she spread love around the world by simply giving it?

While we often think of giving in terms of money, giving can be anything that has value, which is not always money. Yet many prosperity ministries encourage tithing in response to this verse– usually for their ministry. Tithing can be good but that does not mean that what you give will come back exactly the same. You may give away a hundred thousand dollars and end up with hundreds of thousands of people expressing their love to you. Now that's radical and maybe not too accurate but the point is, because you give money does not mean you get money in return.

I gave my time as a volunteer in a counseling ministry for ten years. That experience later netted me a good job and the hours that were required to apply for licensing, which led to an increased salary where I was able to then buy a house and enjoy great freedom from apartment living. Hey, that was a bountiful storm the dragonfly's wings created!

As you see, that Scripture is about giving a talent, gift, skill, or an attitude. So consider giving whatever you want to receive, anger and rejection or love and acceptance, etc. Of course if a person by their own negligence rather than hardship does not pay a debt then you paying their debt may encourage further negligence. Sometimes "No." is the greatest gift.

> *When my children were growing up I had a difficult time saying 'no' just like my mother. My sons would ask for something and I gave an excuse like 'we don't have enough money' or 'you don't need that'. Other times I would say 'let me think about it' and then forget it. So then, they learned to think there was never enough money etc. To this day I have trouble saying no to people but I have learned to do it even the uncomfortable if it means showing love.*

The solution is to give, not as you received or want to receive but love. An eye for an eye went out with the New Testament when Jesus showed up and showed us how to do it. In love, he gave his life for ours. The idea is that we be willing to give ourselves sacrificially too. Not necessarily dying on a cross but dying to self. To love and accept one another may take an act of self sacrifice. Yet when we accept people without accepting their sin then they are more likely to accept us.

In accepting a person without expectation they do not have to be whom they are not, nor do we! This is God's love and acceptance and thus we are free to be ourselves and pursue our own way of life or God's way. One great gifts God gave humans is freewill and with it, the right to enjoy the rewards of obedience and to suffer the consequences of sin. To accept God's will and obey his guidance brings great rewards.

Because God loves us with an everlasting love, and his desire is that we have a future filled with hope (Jeremiah 31:3). Thus, he gives the means to fulfill our dream when we walk by faith. As we call upon God in prayer, he listens and responds. In Acts 18:9, the Lord spoke to Paul in the night.

> *"Do not fear," he said "Speak and be not silent". He opens our eyes so we might see the truth. "I will bring the blind by a way they knew not; I will lead them in paths they have not known; I will make darkness light, and the crooked straight. I will do this and not forsake them"* (Isaiah 42:16).

God guides blind people who need a guide, and he will remove whatever obstacle there is in our way when we trust his leadership Scripture reveals God's assurance that he does love us and he will see our dreams fulfilled. Yet God's ways are not our ways, so the unexpected can cause serious disruptions, if our emotions get out of control.

> *In September 2005 I was awakened from a peaceful sleep at 0530 in the morning and within minutes was standing outside in the cold air watching my house burn down. The house needed a good cleaning and was in need of serious repair, but this seemed a bit drastic.*
>
> *I could have been upset yet I knew God had a purpose and a plan for this seeming disaster. Years earlier my response would not have been so complacent, but time had strengthened my faith. The house was a ruin when I bought it yet God's purpose and plan found a way to get the work done far better than I could have done.*

Abraham trusted God and in faith gave glory to God; he was convinced that what God promised he would do (Romans 4:20-21). Our response to the unexpected or difficulties make a difference. God wants to reassure and have you trust him, so when spiritually bankrupt and you can't see the forest for the tree, so to speak, know that God is still with you.

> *'For all those things my hand has made, and all those things exist,' says the Lord. 'But on this one will I look: those who are poor and of a contrite spirit, and who trembles at my word' (Isaiah 66:2).*

The key to God's favor is a humble and contrite heart. Those who seek him and respond with fear and trembling hearing God's word will find favor while those who call upon fate and look to karma and fortune cookies for their destiny, will perish (vv11-12).

6. Thought for Today

Joseph's Dreams

Joseph at age seventeen feeds the flock with his brothers but he also carries tales to his father about his brothers. Because Israel loved Joseph more than all his children (he was the son of his old age and of his favorite wife) he made him a coat of many colors. It was no huge surprise that when his brothers saw the clear evidence of favoritism, they hated Joseph who enjoyed the favoritism and helps his status along by bringing to his father evil reports of his brothers. But good old Joe also had a dream (later fulfilled in Egypt) and it showed his brothers bowing down before him. A second dream showed the entire family even mom and dad bowing down to him.

"So you're going to reign *over us*?" Snarled his brothers; and they hated him then for the dreams and for his words.' While Jacob didn't care for Joseph's dreams, as a man of God he realized the dreams were of God - not that it helped Joseph; he was sold into slavery out of their jealousy (Gen 37:1-11).

Favoritism in families may be unavoidable, but its divisive effects should be minimized. Parents may not be able to change their feelings toward a favorite child, but they can change their actions toward the others and share their attention and love with everyone.

Did anyone experience favoritism in your family growing up and/or now?

Joseph fueled the fire of envy burning in his brothers with his immature attitude and boastful manner. No one enjoys a braggart. Joseph learned this the hard way. His angry brothers sold him into slavery to get rid of him.

After years of hardship, Joseph learned an important lesson: Because our talents and knowledge come from God, it is more appropriate to thank him for the talents, gifts and knowledge than to brag about them.

Describe an experience where something wonderful was revealed to you and you had to share it with someone a friend or family member. But the story had a backlash, resulting in anger and resentment.

A DREAM FULFILLED

Like Joseph, we all have a dream though perhaps not as prophetic. Mary had a dream and a message from the Lord that changed her world just as our dreams can change the world around us depending upon how we respond to them. Do you respond as did Joseph during the ancient days, or as did Mary and Joseph of Jesus' day?

MARY'S DREAM

Betrothed to Joseph, Mary doubtless had a dream of being his wife and a mother one day until God unexpectedly intervened in her life. The angel announced that Mary would be the mother of the savior (Luke 1:24-41), which she fully accepted.

Can you imagine! I would have a tough time with an announcement like that even from an angel and would likely think I was hallucinating. But, Mary came from a family with generations of believers and her faith likely contributed to her acceptance of God's will. [3] No one I knew in my family had that kind of faith and so to be told something of that magnitude, there is no way I would have believed it. Clearly, God chooses people for certain tasks wisely. He knows what we are capable of, what we can and cannot do.

Mary was about age thirteen when visited by the angel who brought her God's message. She would have a son, but not just any baby. This child would be the Son of God, and he would save the world from sin. While an honor there could have been serious consequences for Mary.

In that culture then, a woman pregnant out of wedlock could be stoned. Mary likely felt a bit anxious hearing the angel, yet, knowing that God was guiding the situation, Mary submitted: "As the Lord's servant! Let it be done as you have said." And the angel of God left (Luke 1:38).

Mary was faithful and committed to God throughout her life, and so, the lesson we learn here is to trust God no matter what the situation, and not allow fear of the known or unknown stop us from living for God.

---

[3] See Matthew 1:1-18 details Old Testament history that demonstrates the Israelites faith may have contributed to Joseph's and Mary's faith and their ability to believe in God's purpose for their lives.

JOSEPH'S DREAM

Joseph's life is another illustration of great faith. He listened to God and saw his dream fulfilled. Joseph dreamed of Mary becoming his wife--until she became pregnant. Joseph did not want to embarrass Mary in front of everyone –thinking she was pregnant by a man—so he decided to quietly call off the wedding. God intervened in that situation too and Joseph obeyed God's directions (See Mat 1:18-25), not just this one time, but throughout his life on several occasions.

Ultimately, both Joseph and Mary realized their dream, but not the way they may have imagined. Joseph and Mary became husband and wife, and Mary a mother, according to God's purposes and methods. God's dream was the same but Joseph and Mary were chosen for a higher purpose so the result occurred in a way that gave it greater significance.

CHOSEN FOR A PURPOSE

When chosen for a purpose, God often finishes his plans unlike anything we expect. But if we accept the changes, including any disasters, unexpected pregnancies, and other unforeseen events, and trust that God is fulfilling his purpose, life becomes so much easier. Most of us have experienced situations that caused us to wonder, why such and such happened and there seemed to be no reasonable answer. So, again, the simple answer is, faith, and know that God's purpose will be fulfilled.

God's timing may also differ from ours, or he may call us to a different path, one to strengthen us for a journey more difficult! So, when God calls and your life heads in a new direction, consider how you will respond. When your house burns down or your company bankrupts, will you look for God's guidance or become distraught and emotionally volatile? Disasters that bring insecurity may be only an impending change wherein God is altering your course.

Many hear, and say, "Here I am; send me", but how many go?

> *Years ago, when one certain song was sung that echoed God's call to Jeremiah, I would sing out "Here I am Lord, I will go" but I sure did drag my feet at times when God wanted me to do certain things.*

Jeremiah answered, "Lord. I do not know how to speak; I *am* but a boy" (1:6) God encouraged him saying, "Do not be afraid; I *am* with you" (v8).

As Mary, Joseph, and others[4] faith not fear is what God desires. And, as with Jeremiah, God gives us encouragement or whatever is needed to prepare us for the journey, and does not allow temptation to destroy our faith.[5]

> *"God is faithful; he will not let you be tempted beyond what you can bear. But when you are tempted, he will also provide a way out so that you can stand up under it [resist it]"*. (1Corinthians 10:13)

No temptation takes you but that which we all experience (1Cor 10:13). You say, "I'm embarrassed to share (a weakness, temptation, problem)"; "no one else understands; no one thinks that; no one struggles as I do." These thoughts and struggles are common to everyone. Not only are temptations common to all, but it was common to the Jesus Christ.

> *Human, Jesus understands all of our weaknesses, because he was tempted in the same ways we are. Yet he did not sin! (Heb 4:15).*

Tempted as we in *all ways* yet, Jesus does not look with anger or disgust at the one who struggles with sin saying, "How could you?" He looks on us with compassion saying, "I know what it's like." (See Heb 2:17-18)

Jesus did not take on the nature of angels nor is he Satan's brother. Jesus chose to be human like *us* to know, to understand and be merciful. And he says. "I understand your struggle; I know what you're going through."

While Jesus never sinned he experienced temptation and so understood, not because he was God but because he wanted to understand us.

---

[4] Eighty-six instances were found in the New King James Version of the Bible that either commands a person to "fear not" or to "be not afraid."

[5] 2Cor 12:9 my grace is sufficient for you: for my strength is made perfect in weakness. Most gladly then will I rather glory in my infirmities, that the power of Christ may rest upon me.

7. Thought for Today

Proverbs 29:18 "Where there is no revelation [dream] the people cast off restraint [perish]. But blessed is he or she who keeps the law."

> *An atheist for 35 years, I lived without restraint not keeping God or man's laws. I moved from one goal to another, succeeding, yet my life was without meaning. As a Christian though and understanding that God had a purpose for my life I felt a sense of peace knowing my life had meaning, not just getting from one point to another.*

God puts a purpose in our hearts, a dream. That dream keeps us moving in a certain direction otherwise we tend to go our own way, walking whichever way the wind blows, rather than follow the leading of the Holy Spirit.

We need to communicate with God so we can hear the direction he gives and helps us understand. Richard Poole[6] says God speaks four ways.

> First, God speaks in the world in which and what he has created. Some scientists of course believe that our world just happened, *somehow*. But the creative hand of God is at work in everything. God reveals himself through the world that he has made.

> Second God speaks to us through Scripture. Who he is and what he is like, what makes him angry, his love for us, his patience, purity and holiness, the stories of God's people and their success and failure provide material for those who seek to know the truth about God.

> Third, God came as a man, and taught us about himself, about heaven and about how we should live through Christ's example. He showed his love, the greatest love by laying down his life for our sins.

> Fourth, God speaks directly to us. The Holy Spirit is given to all Christians to help us until Christ returns. But we must be open to his leading, and humbly obedient to the spirit of Christ in us.

> Micah 6.8 challenges us saying: "He has shown you what is good. What does the Lord require of you? To act justly, love mercy and walk humbly with your God". Gods Holy Spirit helps us do that.

---

[6] Richard Poole, "What is our vision?"
http://homepage.eircom.net/~interfriendpublisher/page23.html, accessed 11June 2009

So what is your vision? Even if you've never told anyone, reveal it now. Taking risks develops courage. Courage is not the absence of fear but going for the goal or overcoming the giant in our lives in spite of our fear!

Write the vision as though it is already accomplished: "I am an author with several published books"; "I am a successful artist" and so forth.

What is your personal vision? (Artist, author, teacher, healer, etc)

What is your vision for your community? (Drug free, prosperous)

What is your world vision? (No more war; peace, prosperity, etc)

How do you experience Gods presence?

God speaks to me through the created world (in music, the beauty of a sunrise/set) and/or...

God speaks to me through Scripture when (read and hear his voice sending me in a certain direction, for example) or ...

God speaks to me through Christ when (I read about Jesus' love and strive to love as did he by...) or...

God speaks directly to me when (in some dreams I know God has told me of a change I need to make such as...) or...

A Purpose and Vision

Ideally our vision encompasses our life, family, church, and the world. We may not even have a specific plan yet. What we do not directly know how to deal with however we can actively pray for God's intervention and trust that he is working on whatever we cannot.

How we work towards our vision differs for each one of us. It will depend on circumstances, our resources and the talents and skills, our abilities and spiritual gifts that God has provided. Regardless of how we achieve, faith in God as the director of the plan is vital.

My total vision has not been fully realized, but its reality is guaranteed for as the prophet Isaiah said (9:2):

> *"The people walking in darkness have seen a great light; for those living in the land of death's shadow light has dawned. (Isaiah spoke of Jesus)... The zeal of the Lord will accomplish this."* (Isaiah 9.2)

So, whether or not you know your vision or even know a small part it may be that God has not found the time right for revealing it to you. When he does, be zealous in its pursuit. Remember, Paul was a long time in coming to the Lord and in being readied to be sent into ministry but when the time arrived he was zealous in its pursuit.

GOD ENCOURAGES THE FAITHFUL

> God is faithful ... with temptation he will make a way to escape so that you may be able to bear it (1Cor 10:13b).

At Jesus' baptism, a voice spoke, "This is my beloved Son [Jesus] in whom I am well pleased" (Mat 3:17). In the wilderness Satan tempted Jesus him in ways that are common to all of us: pride, power, and possessions.

Jesus was at death's door when Satan came, *"If you are the Son of God ..."* he said, tempting Jesus to doubt God's provision (Mat 4:3).

Have you heard *Satan whisper, "Are you not satisfied? Were you not born again? Why are you still hungry?" "Did not God promise to provide?" "Perhaps he is a liar after all?"*

Jesus answered as can we, "It is written man shall not live by bread alone, but by every word that comes from the mouth of God." Thus, we are not nourished by material things of the world, but by Gods Word.

"*If you are* the Son of God", Satan challenged Jesus, "Take a leap of faith. See if he keeps you safe from harm. Satan left out an important part, for Psalm 91says *"to keep you in all your ways"*[7] — not to do your own thing, but to walk God's way. Jesus said, "I will not test God."

> *Satan entices us, "Take a leap of faith. Name it and claim it. God will fix it. Jump into that relationship. What's wrong with sex before marriage? After all, you have needs and desires. It will be ok."*

But we answer, "If he wants me to, he'll tell me who, when and where". Satan wants us to test God but we must trust God's promises.

Finally, the devil showed Jesus all the world's kingdoms, tempting him with possessions and to doubt God's promise, *"All of this will be yours if you will fall down and worship me"* (see Mat 4:9).

> Has Satan tempted you? *"Maybe God wants you to have that new car; wouldn't it feel great with that red leather jacket wrapping your body in its soft supple warmth. Go on. Use that credit card; what's the big deal.* Jesus said, "I will worship My Father alone, and no one else."

We Answer, "I will follow God and not be tempted to turn from his path; his Word is my strength and my shield. Whom shall I fear?"

To overcome temptation for possessions, lust, fornication, murmurings—anything that can trip us up—stay in the Word. Speak the Word loudly as did Jesus, confess its truth. Satan cannot read either our mind or heart. Therefore, he is defeated by what we *say.*

> *God says, "I will never leave or forsake you." We say, "The Lord is my helper, and I will not fear what man can do"* (Heb 13:5-6).

Finally, we submit *to* the Word and not use it as a ritualized incantation.

> *We use to go to confession and say the Act of Contrition and whatever repetitive prayers to have sins erased: 'Hail Mary's' and 'Our Fathers'. Kneeling on the hard pew bench my only goal was not repentance but 'getting it over with' so I could go play. I like to think God understood the heart of a child and while the priest or nuns might not have, he would have had compassion on me.*

---

[7] Psalm 91:11-12 in this Psalm Satan referred to - God's angels would have charge over [Jesus], to keep him safe. They shall bear you up in *their* hands, lest you dash your foot against a stone.

Instead of repetitive prayer that can be boring and certainly not heartfelt, it is far better to like Jesus, commit to obey the Word and speak it aloud – not the same words repeatedly but as a heartfelt plea to God as did King David to be relieved of the guilt of his sin. Jesus spoke the Word and did what the Word said, and *that* is where the power lies.

We use words when tempted to gossip about our boss or murmur against our spouse or those who cause us problems but, the Word says to bless those who persecute and despitefully use you; instead pray for them and submit to the Word speaking it aloud; *that* renders Satan powerless.

"You did not choose me," says God. "I chose you to bring forth fruit."[8] When we follow Christ, and obey the Word, and follow the path God has chosen for us, we fulfill our purpose and our lives bear fruit. Fruit doesn't exist for itself but for others. The fruit of the Spirit is so *we are* satisfied, or to be fulfilled. But that's not the purpose of fruit.

There are two important things that the Fruits of the Spirit accomplish.

    1.   They give you the power to fulfill your destiny in Christ.

Without the Holy Spirits spiritual fruit, we would be powerless and would not have the *endurance* and *faithfulness* to complete God's calling. We would not have the *discipline* to study the Bible or to pray.

    2.   God uses fruit of the spirit to draw people to Himself.

People who, no matter the situation, always radiate a godly *peace* – that are unshakable, others are drawn to that kind of peace. With all of the chaos in the world, people search for whatever *peace* and *joy* they can get.

We try to fill the emptiness with alcohol, food, and illicit sex, things that numb the pain for a while, but leave us miserable. You say, 'I am rich. I have everything I want. I don't need a thing!' And you don't realize that you are wretched and miserable and poor and blind and naked (Revelation 3:17).

When they see God's peace and *joy* looking back through your eyes then they want to know what you know to have the fruit of the Spirit of God. When we seek to know him he gives them to set us free from our misery. Jesus exchanges our misery for his peace, our failure to forgive for love, and our sadness and depression for his joy.

Galatians 5 describes the fruit of the Spirit as love, the implication is that joy and peace, longsuffering, gentleness, goodness, faith, meekness, and self-

---

[8] John 15:16

control are all that love is. It comes down to the two commandments Jesus gave, love God and love one another. We find our joy in the Lord; patient in faith we wait on the Lord; Jesus brings us peace when we are gentle, good and kind and longsuffering to those we see as not deserving; and meekly humbly we live a self-controlled life.

We all know people who refuse God; they prefer the addiction, despair, depression, or other sin behavior. Yet, when one chooses God and to go into the world as disciples, God pours his love outward through us, as a preacher like Billy Graham, or an artist, mechanic, or dishwasher.

God knows our faults, depressions, obstinacy, and wandering into sin, but having chosen us, he will prove his choice is right, unless we totally refuse to follow him. When temptation comes knocking, the answer is to let God dominate and not the sin. Let his love replace your misery.

All have a purpose and a dream upon which to build our lives. However the way in which we achieve the dream makes a difference. We either allow despair to depress or we follow by faith, trusting the Holy Spirit.

> *If you leave God's paths and go astray, you will hear a voice behind you say, "No. This is the way; walk here." (Isaiah 30:21)*

DREAM THE IMPOSSIBLE

Often the naysayers, instead of encouraging, may say things such as this, "You can't do that; it's impossible"; "You'll never make it; you don't have what it takes"; "You're not smart enough"; or "You will never be …"

You were created by God as you are for an exact purpose: to glorify him. He reveals his vision of you to you, how he sees you, and he will fulfill his plan for you no matter how impossible it may seem to others. And he will do the same no matter how imperfect you are now. No one is perfect and without sin; we have all sinned and fall short. So trust in the Lord with all your heart and follow that dream.

Consider your dreams then turn from your self-centered life and begin to live with an outer focused on others in a way that glorifies God. Do not be limited by impossibilities. Brainstorm, pray and seek God's guidance and he will reveal your talents, gifts, and skills, the possibilities and whatever compliments you and fulfills your dream.

OUR PURPOSE

Our purpose is to glorify God (Isaiah 43:7) so, whatever our goals, the way in which we pursue them must glorify God. "Fear not, for I have redeemed you; I have called *you* by your name; you *are* mine". If we claim to belong to God, we avoid doing anything that would bring shame to him. Consider your attitude, behavior, and words – the way you behave at school, with friends, and/or work. Do these actions glorify God? Desired changes can be goals to pursue so your life reflects the glory of God.

Recently, someone asked me how do I know God's purpose for my life? There are times when I've wondered the same thing. But the more I pray about it the more as God revealed the truth to provide understanding. God has a myriad of ways to reveal your life purpose and many of those are in line with your talents and gifts. I'll tell you a story to illustrate!

> *A woman on the internet saw my paintings and wanted me to add the 'wow' factor to a mural she had had painted previous. I spoke with her at her home and she had not one nice thing to say about anyone or anything and complained about everything and everyone. I declined the mural.*
>
> *I had been honest with her and suggested she refrain from complaining about the artists and workers but she didn't hear me. She had given them the work under the guise of love, because they needed the work and therefore felt justified in her complaints. Yet, love suffers long...*
>
> *Later, this woman contacted me, apologizing for any misunderstandings. There were none; she simply was deaf to the truth. Nonetheless_*
>
> *Thinking perhaps this was an opportunity from God, I was about to accept her offer - then the phone rang. A woman called whom I had not spoken with in several months. We talked about this situation and after praying over it, decided the 'interruption' was perhaps from God. The instant I sent an email refusing the commission, I felt a tremendous relief.*
>
> *Often this is how I can tell when God is speaking; if it's me I may continue to feel uncomfortable with my choice but when I make a decision that agrees with God's will, I feel a sense of peace.*
>
> *And so, we learn to long-suffering and not cynical or bitter when God says "No. Now is not the time" or whatever else happens.*

Love is long-suffering—and is not cynical or bitter. In the earlier scenario, I simply did not want to work in an environment filled with bitterness and anger. Love doesn't try to prove itself or say, "See how loving I am" rather love works behind the scenes[9] and does not seek attention.

---

[9] "1Cor13:4" Jon Coursan's Application Commentary, NT

8. THOUGHT FOR TODAY

With which of the temptations have you been deceived and how often?

0= Never   1= Rarely   2= At times   3= Moderate   4= Frequently   5= Always

___ I am not a child of God

___ I have not been saved and/or chosen

___ I do not believe completely in the Holy Bible

___ I pursue other gods and sinful ways of the world

___ I am in bondage to a person, behavior, substance, etc.

Use the same scale to rate yourself:

My attitude, behavior, and communication glorify God_

___ At home

___ Toward my mate (or a 'special someone' – a fiancée, etc)

___ Toward my children

___ Toward my friends

___ Toward my extended family

___ Toward my associates at work

___ I show love toward everyone I meet

What does love mean to you?

Agape love as that of 1 Corinthians can be frustrating for many though amazing.

Love that is longsuffering and kind, that neither envies nor seeks its own, that bears all things, believes, hopes, and endures all and never fails is indeed an amazing love that Jesus illustrated daily.

How loving are you?

Rate yourself on a scale of 1- 5 (Place your score in the clear boxes)

0= Never   1= Rarely   2= At times   3= Moderate   4= Frequently   5= Always

Love is or is not the following: Rate and check any needed change	Rate	X
I am kind to others – I overlook slights and am not cynical or bitter		
I am a patient person – I am able to wait on God and put others first		
I am jealous of others – I often covet others looks or possessions		
I am boastful – I always mention my achievements / possessions		
I am prideful – I take credit for what you have or you have done		
I am rude – I am abrupt and impatient and insist on things my way		
I am selfish – do not give to but expect others to do or give to me		
I am easily angered – I get irritated and touchy over small things		
I keep track of wrongs – I always know who did what to whom		
I rejoice in truth – I always confront sin and encourage honesty		
I am supportive – I encourage others and try to be there for them		
I am loyal – I am often accused of being blind or too loyal to people		
I am hopeful – I tend to always look forward to God's provision		
I am trusting – I have been accused of trusting people too much		

1Corinthians 13:4-7

There is no perfect score yet there for most of us there are going to be areas where we have a need to improve upon to be more loving. How important you see the need is between you and the Holy Spirit.

What would you like to change?

What does God desire?

Often, our relationship with the Lord God determines how well we love. The closer the relationship, the higher our score might be, or not.

WHO'S YOUR GOD?

Is your image of God one of an angry, mean-spirited deity? If so, then that is a faulty image that you yourself may reflect. An angry, mean-spirited person or one overwhelmed by guilt, you may feel that you can never measure up to a God's cruel expectations. Yet, the Bible says "God is Love" (1 John 4:8). But how can we even begin to understand that truth? One of the most well known verses in the Bible is John 3:16, *"For God so loved the world that he gave his only Son, that whosoever believes in him should not perish, but have everlasting life."* And the psalmist says the Lord withholds no good thing from those who love him (Psalm 84:11). This does not mean God gives us everything *we* want, but that he gives us the means to walk along his paths. However we must do the walking in obedience him.

So, if you strive to love the best that you know how —God understands what that is for you —then you're likely on the right track. Yet human love is not only conditional, it is mercurial. We love based on feelings, emotions, and lusts that changes from one moment to the next. God's love transcends our human definition of love to a point that is hard for us to comprehend. Can anyone really comprehend God's "unconditional" love? God doesn't love us because we're lovable. God loves us because He is love. Therefore, **God does not withhold a request because he's mean-spirited, but because he knows the meaning of genuine love.**

If your child for example, asked for what you knew from experience was not good for them, would you give it to them? Of if they were being disobedient would you give them a special treat? This may not be a good example for in today's world children are often given things that are not good for them or allowed the time to do what is clearly not in their best interests (fast-food, electronic games or television deep into the night when they should be doing homework and/or then going to bed for a good night's sleep).

The question, especially for parents is, do I love my child; am I doing what is right in God's sight and what is right for that child? God set standards for good behavior so the social order would work more efficiently and so that we would love as he does, unconditionally. He also allows consequences for when we disobey and go our own way. *God does this because he loves us!*

John said "We love because he first loved us" (see 1John 4:19) and when we understand that the love described in 1 Corinthians 13 is God's love and it's the nature and character of God's love toward us then, our love like God's will inevitably overflow toward others.

Taking Action

God's purpose must direct our actions and the way we achieve our dreams. Perhaps, your goal today is to have a happy marriage, home, and family, but your spouse furthers the conflict no matter. Don't ask "Why?" Instead, ask, "What can I learn to be a better spouse, etc.?"

To see and behave as a godly person is a choice. You can be emotionally volatile and out of control, or have a full and well-managed life. Consider who you are as a child of God and if you behave as one. Jesus knew who he was; he knew his calling, purpose, or ministry, and was true to it.

He Said "I AM"

- I am the bread of life. John 6.48.
- I am the good shepherd. John 10.11
- I am the light of the world. John 8.12, 9.5
- I am the door that men may enter. John 10.9
- I am the way, the truth and the life. John 14.6
- I am the true vine; God is the vinedresser. John 15.1, 5

Jesus nourished with Scripture and food; his candle was in the open to light the way for others by living a godly life, by example. He was receptive and compassionate so people could enter his rest and find peace. Jesus was not just a shepherd he was a good one, showing the way to live for God. He was honest, the true vine upon which we can grow our lives, and others can also.

Jesus never let another person's opinion dictate who he knew himself to be, the Son of God. Jesus knew who he was; he knew his purpose; and he did what was needed to finish it. Lest we think, "Jesus *was* God's son"; being human he had all the struggles we all experience.

'I Am' in Action

How would you answer, "I am"?
- "*I am* unloved and I do not let anyone close to me"
- "*I am* starved for love and smother with my neediness"

How would you like to answer, "I am"?
- "*I am* loved and people are close to me."
- "*I am* full of love and give it away by (volunteer etc.)"

Living as Jesus takes belief, commitment, and discipline; we live the Word as godly men and women, fully grounded in faith.

LIGHT OF THE WORLD

You may believe you never measure up or be perfect as you "should be" or you look to another for love, to be there for you, or to light your way. Jesus said while he was here on earth, "I am the light of the world." After Jesus' resurrection, when no longer in the world, this is what he said:

> *"You* are the light of the world. A city on a mountain cannot be hid, nor do they light a lamp and put it under but atop a lamp stand so it shines for all in the house. So *let your light shine* before men, so they may see your good works, and glorify your Father in Heaven" (Colossians 1:10).

How do you feel about being the light of the world? Inadequate! This is a good place to be. God says, "'My grace is sufficient for you, for my strength is made perfect in weakness.' Paul says, "most gladly I will rather boast in my infirmities, so that the power of Christ may be with me ... for when I am weak, then, I am strong" (2 Cor 12:9-10).

Thus, God will use you as a light to shine before all people. God uses all of you, your talents, skills, and gifts for others benefit in spite of any weakness. Consider your past, people, and situations and get to know who you are, the man or woman God has made you to be.

Every grace and trial is an opportunity to strengthen your faith. Jesus said, "In this world you will have trouble. But take heart! I have overcome the world." (John 16:33) In spite of our struggles and failures, Jesus does not abandon or reject us. We can have the peace of Christ at all times by showing others how to be at peace even in times of suffering.

James 5:9 speaks of suffering and the blessings of those who persevered. Yet, often times, in persecution and distress, it is common for victims to turn against one another. So, the warning: 'Do not grumble against one another, lest you be condemned.' To let our light shine before all is to live a peaceful life in the midst of affliction so others see by our attitude and behavior that being at peace with persecution is possible.

"Don't be happy to see your enemy trip and fall down, or else God will turn his anger away from them [toward you?]" (Proverb 24:17). "If your enemy hungers, feed them. If thirsty, give them something to drink. This will heap burning coals on their heads and the Lord will reward you." (25:21-22)

Romans 12:20-21 echoes, "If your enemy is hungry, feed him; if he thirsts give him something to drink; in doing you heap burning coals on his head. Do not be overcome by evil; overcome evil with good".

James says the prophets Moses, Elijah, Jeremiah were persecuted (5:10-11), and faithfully declared God's word. Persecuted, unmercifully they endured (Heb 11:27, Heb 11:32-40).

If we want to be blessed it is reasonable to conclude that we will also be called upon to do similar. Job is another example. Few ever suffered so much in so short a time. Yet he never cursed God, or turned away and God rewarded his faithfulness, revealing his compassion and mercy.

BELIEVE AND BEHAVE

Believe Scripture and behave as though you do! And have faith that God will see you through anything. Faith is the ability to enter fellowship with God so we are able to do whatever he sets before us knowing that it is not we who do them, but God who works in us and through us.

Faith achieves different results. In some, it produces the strength that turns the battle; in others, it produces suffering that endures affliction. Faith uses God's mighty power to achieve any purpose within its reach. But to have that power God wants us to walk in a way that pleases him: *"that you may have a walk worthy of the Lord, fully pleasing Him."*

9. THOUGHT FOR TODAY

Peter, James, and John stood near Jesus on the mountain. Suddenly, it was as if his head had caught fire! A white radiance came and covered the Lord gloriously. His face shone like the suns brightness and his whole being grew even brighter as we stood there.

Two men stood on either side of Jesus, talking as if they had known him forever. A loud thunderclap knocked me to the ground and a cloud covered the mountain, from which a voice spoke, "This is my beloved son in whom I am well pleased. Listen to him!" (Luke 9:35)

What an acknowledgment!

God regards us "You did not choose me, but *I chose and appointed you to* go and bear fruit, and your fruit should remain, and that whatever you ask the father in my name he may give you" (John 15:16)

Is it not marvelous to be chosen by God? Imagine God speaking for you on judgment day, "This is my beloved in whom I am well pleased."

Chosen and we choose God but some are not nor do they choose God. 'From that time on many of his disciples left and no longer followed him' (John 6:66; see also John 6:64-66)

Why do you think these disciples turned away?

Jesus knew people could only understand if the Father had drawn them, had chosen them. Sometimes we try to convince others of God instead of being an example so when drawn by the father, they want to come.

While an atheist, one friend was a Christian. Her life was not perfect but she was one of the few that accepted an unwed mother at a time when it was not accepted by the world—God's love was clear to see in her.

Are you an example of Christ rather than persuade about Christ?

Describe

Jesus shared the simple truth, knowing that the Holy Spirit would help to apply in the hearts of men the lesson of those the Father had drawn.

If you have chosen to follow Christ, how do you show it?

My friend was and is a teacher however she has a gift of discernment also because with her quiet gentle spirit –totally unlike me—she unknowingly helped me change through Christ Jesus.

TALENTS AND GIFTS

Jesus was a carpenter's son. Therefore we can surmise that he learned the skills of a carpenter as a youth, which also included patience and discipline for woodworking was done by hand not power tools. His talents were as a preacher, teacher, and healer and were amazing, yet some believed he had a demon. Others saw his appearance of poverty as a limitation, and he was disrespectful of the traditions, and religious hypocrisy. Despite this, Jesus did not view poverty, disease, or lack of education as a limitation. His standards of righteousness were not the same as the religious hierarchy either.

In his sermon given on the mountain, Jesus claimed certain traits as a benefit, even a blessing: God blesses those who depend upon him! God blesses those who grieve, especially for their own sins and especially for the sins of the world! Someone always seems to comfort people who are grieving a loss, and if we do not grieve our own or another's sins then we are not paying attention or are just hard-hearted and do not care!

God blesses the humble! God blesses those who obey him! Those who are merciful find mercy! Those whose hearts are pure will see God, while peacemakers are called his children! God blesses those who do right and others treat them badly as a result. How would you rate yourself?

1= Often True   2 = Occasionally True   3 = Usually Not True

BLESSED ARE THE:

_____   Poor in spirit – you are sensitive to your own spiritual poverty

_____   Mourn – you grieve for your own sins and those of the world

_____   Quiet and gentle spirit – you are not prideful or arrogant

_____   Seek righteousness – holiness you hunger for but do not have

_____   Merciful – you have compassion for the sorrow and pain of others

_____   Pure in heart - you are genuine and not just lip service - pretense

_____   Peacemaker – you try to reconcile differences not create discord

_____   Persecuted – you live a godly life and are hated for it by others

Aside from our character traits we also possess talents and skills but how we use them is what makes the difference.

Natural Talents

We all are born with talents and throughout life we learn certain skills. But spiritual gifts we receive when we become a follower of Christ. Limitations may be from a simple failure to believe and have faith, and whatever stops you from accomplishing goals. Some limitations are birth-related. These may be physical or mental limitations yet some are consequences of life or life styles we choose. Some limitations reveal God's glory as with the man born blind that Jesus healed but others are a chance to be forgiven and healed.

SPIRITUAL GIFTS

Pray and ask God to reveal your gifts as you read the following:

- The gift of wisdom is the ability to make wise decisions and give guidance that is in accord with Scripture and God's will.

- The gift of knowledge is the ability to receive information and assess it biblically for others understanding of spiritual issues.

- The gift of faith is being able to trust God and encourage others to trust God, no matter the circumstances.

- The gift of healing uses God's healing power to restore the sick, injured, or suffering using extraordinary abilities.

- The gift of miracles is being able to perform signs and wonders that give authenticity to God's Word and the Gospel message.

- The gift of prophecy is being able to proclaim a message from God to people or within the church as a group.

- The gift of discernment is the ability to determine whether a message, a person, or an event is truly from God or not.

- The gift of tongues is speaking a language you do not know to communicate with someone who speaks that language.

- The gift of interpreting tongues is to translate tongues spoken and communicate it to others in your language.

- The gift of administration is being able to keep things organized and direct others in accord with Godly principles.

- The gift of helps is always having the desire and ability to help others, to do whatever it takes to get a task accomplished.

10. THOUGHT FOR TODAY

Lord, reveal our talents and gifts and let our eyes see and ears hear what you desire of us. Help us invest our gifts wisely, using them with our skills and abilities to honor you and bless, encourage and strengthen others (doing so in love for without love, our gifts are nothing!). Amen.

The following steps may help you discern your gifts.

1. **Desire**. If God gave you a desire, he will show you how to use it. You may struggle with the decision to preach, for example, but not able to do so, not because you don't want to; you simply feel inadequate. So, examine your motives and the reason you desire this gift. Many want certain gifts for the honor associated with that gift. But *desire for prestige is not the correct motive.* The desire to serve others is.

2. **Evidence.** Some gifts must be developed and perfected. I had a desire to counsel, for instance, and first earned a masters degree, then, counseled for several years. I encouraged, comforted, confronted, and rebuked sin, exhorting people to godly living. Yet, I was not a patient listener but could talk with anyone (drug dealer or car dealer) face to face.

3. **Openings.** What doors have been opened to you? In college I loved to do creative writing --research writing was difficult --and to clarify teachings to help others understand by writing about the subject. These learning experiences as a counselor and from my personal life became topics for me to write about and I published a book. My books have helped many, and one day God may open that door wider.

Spiritual gifts are always for service to others. Because of this we must ask, "Where can I best serve?" "Where will my gifts be the more effective?" and "What must I be doing to help others the most?"

To answer these questions, first find your gift and then, check your motives.

"This is why I remind you to fan into flames the spiritual gift God gave you, when I laid my hands on you. For God has not given us a spirit of fear and timidity, but of power, love, and self-discipline." 1Timothy 1: 6-7

"Teach these things… Teach others by your life and your words, demeanor, love, faith, and your integrity. Stay at your post reading Scripture, giving counsel, teaching. And that gift of ministry you were given when they laid hands on you and prayed—keep that in use." 1Timothy 4:11-14

ASSESS THE PRESENCE OF YOUR SPIRITUAL GIFTS

For the manifestation of the Spirit is given to each one for the profit of all

5 = Always   4= Frequently   3 = Occasionally   2 = Rarely   1 = Never

Wisdom	You make wise decisions and give guidance that is in accord with Scripture and God's will.	
Knowledge	You are able to receive knowledge and assess it biblically helping another's understanding.	
Faith	You trust God implicitly and encourage others to trust God, no matter the circumstances.	
Healing	You can use God's healing power to restore the sick, injured, or suffering using extraordinary abilities.	
Miracles	You do signs and wonders that give authenticity to God's Word and the Gospel message.	
Prophecy	You proclaim messages from God to individuals and/ or in the church as a group.	
Discernment	You have the ability to know whether a message, a person, or an event is truly from God or not.	
Tongues	You speak a language you do not know and are able to communicate with someone who speaks it.	
Interpretation	You can translate tongues spoken and communicate it to other persons in your own language.	
Administration	You can keep things well organized and direct others in accord with Godly principles.	
Service	You have the desire and ability to help others, to do whatever it takes to get a task accomplished.	
Other Gift (Describe)		

If you are uncertain, ask family and friends who know you well, and who will not mock what you are doing but sincerely help you discover your gifts.

"But earnestly desire the best gifts. Yet I show you a more excellent way." (1Corinthians 12:25-31), which is love (See 1Corinthians 13:4-7)

Now that you have discerned the spiritual gifts, candidly check your motives, then go back, and answer those three questions on the last page.

THE HOLY SPIRIT

The Apostle Paul says that all gifts of the Spirit are equally valid, but not all are of equal value. The value of a spiritual gift is its worth to the body of Christ. Paul used the analogy of the human body. All parts of the body have a function, but some are more important. Our service must be in proportion to the gift that God has given each of us and our level of faith.

All believers, the body of Christ, work together for the body to function (1Corinthians 12:12-26). And all gifts work together to produce the full potential of the church. Since the gifts of the Spirit are gifts of grace, their use must be controlled by the rule of love -the greatest of all the gifts of the Spirit (1Corinthians 13). In fulfilling a gift, we are of one mind and at peace so God is with us (2Cor 13:11). Also, do not worry whether you can finish a task. When you have difficulty finding your way, pray, and trust God's lead and use your gift according to the level of your faith.

When the apostle Paul was having difficulties, the Lord spoke to him in the night by a vision, "Be not afraid but speak, and be not silent;" (Acts 18:9). God encouraged Paul just as he encourages us, and as we should encourage one another and be at peace, content with whatever happens (Psalm 138:7).

God does not want us to be ignorant, but to realize that the church as a body vital to our community as believers. There is a serious battle going on in our society, and culture and Word of God are at variance. Submission and service are not high on our list of priorities, but are two godly characteristics we must cultivate. The godly choice is to humbly submit.

The Holy Spirit distributes the gift to benefit the church. While it is easy to focus on which spiritual gift(s) we have received and only serve in that area, God called us to serve him, not the spiritual gift. Always seek God's will. If we search, we will find for he will reveal it but we must also accept it. The question is; are you willing to accept what God reveals, or does presumption and pride get in the way, thinking you are too good for whatever he has, or that you are not good enough?

To seek God's will is to obey his leading. He always equips us with whatever gifts we need. So, using your talents and gifts serve your community and your church. Do you see a need in the neighborhood? Do what you can to fill it, not counting the cost. Is there a need in community service such as youth agencies that need mentors? Is God perhaps leading you, then go forth with your talents and gifts and put them to good use.

Place your emphasis on God's Word and submit to his leading. I have a gift for dreams and interpreting but that does not mean that all dreams are from God.

> *Not long ago in a dream one of my roommates was talking to me about the upcoming holidays and suddenly she asked me, "Did you have something to say to me?" I did, as a matter of fact.*
>
> *"Yes. You have to move by the first of the year."*
>
> *While this seemed like a dream from God, I still was not able to tell the roommate she had to move, not on the basis of a dream. Thus, I had a conversation with God and said that I needed verification and would tell the roommate if she actually said to me what was said in the dream.*
>
> *A week or so later she and I were talking about the holiday and she turned to me and said, "Did you have something to say to me?"*
>
> *I was so dumbfounded that I sat there with my mouth open not knowing what to say. For two days I agonized over telling her she had to move but then decided to simply tell her about the dream because we talk about this kind of thing all the time. So I told her about the dream.*
>
> *She then told me that she had several dreams lately but there was no end to them and maybe this would open things up. Her family is on their way for the holidays and in the meantime we are allowing God to lead the rest of the scenario. Time will tell whether she actually moves or not, but I suspect she will as God shared with me a while ago that things were going to change for me after the first of the year.*

PUTTING IT ALL TOGETHER

Everyone has natural talents, skills and abilities. Con artists, as an example, often have the gift of gab and the ability to influence people, wisely or unwisely. Many sales persons and great preachers have also had this ability. The way in which each person uses that influence however, makes all the difference. Using talents, skills, and gifts as God intends is the key.

Regardless of how influential our purpose in the world, not allowing pride to get in the way matters. God and man alike prefer the modest person over the braggart. Nothing is quite as annoying as the person who cannot talk about anyone but their self and their own accomplishments. Rarely does this individual give compliments and encouragement to others but instead seeks recognition only for their self.

Jesus spoke of the blessings of humility in opposition to pride; this is a lesson we can learn from King Nebuchadnezzar. He walked about his palace saying, "Is not this the great Babylon *I built* for a royal dwelling by *my mighty power* and for the honor of *my majesty*?" (Daniel 4:30) While he was speaking, a voice from heaven declared, "King Nebuchadnezzar, to you it is spoken: the kingdom has departed from you."(Dan 4:31)

Nebuchadnezzar found himself suddenly without his mental faculties, an animal eating the grass of the field for several years. God humbled him. So the wise remember, "the Lord is on high, yet he regards the lowly but resists the proud" (James 4:6)

God opposes the proud and gives strength to the weak.

> *"Yours, O Lord, is the greatness, the power and the glory, the victory and the majesty; for all that is in heaven and in earth is yours; ... Both riches and honor come from you, and you reign over all... ; in your hand it is to make great and to give strength to all." 1Chronicles 29:11*

We can do nothing on our own and Jesus reminds us that he is the vine, and we the branches (John 15:5). If we stand with him, our lives will be fruitful: "without me", he said, "you can do nothing." Does that mean that we sit back and wait on to God to do everything? No.

To "wait on the Lord: have good courage, and then he strengthens us" (Psalm 27:14) is to help prepare us with patience else wise we wear out with busy work. Being still and waiting patiently can bring peace.

The pool of Bethesda: *A multitude of people, the infirm, blind, and lame, wait for the angel to stir the waters waiting to be healed. They sit or lie about longing for healing, staring into the pool. I've never seen so many, so focused as they wait, not knowing when; they wait patiently. But wait! The waters churn. It's time! How they move, so fast to catch the moment and so they will not lose the opportunity God has offered.*

Waiting on the Lord is not passive but we actively focus our attention; this requires effort: "Blessed is the man [or woman] that hears, watching daily at my gates, waiting at the posts" (Pro 8:34) So rather than wearing yourself out with busy work and perhaps miss whatever God has in store, be still and wait. Not a lazy slug but attentive to the Lord's opportunities while you go about your day.

Place yourself where you can hear God, which is more an attitude than a posture; it is not *where* we stand but *how* we stand, attentive or distracted.

My youngest son used to drive me crazy when he was little and wanted attention. Finally, I came up with a solution. "Stop and place your hand on my arm and hold it there; wait patiently." He did as instructed.

As I became aware of the persistent gentle pressure on my arm I was able to choose the moment to attend to his need. It was a much more pleasant way to gain my attention and was not annoyed by pestering and he got the attention he wanted.

Turn away from distractions. Be aware of the way in which God is leading you. Do not expect God to have every detail written down or to whisper in your ear. God leads by his Word, wisdom, godly counsel, circumstance, other people, and his Spirit. Pay attention to what is happening around you, and as God leads. Don't miss the moment!

GPS: Guidance of a Personal Savior

God always guides us, but we must listen so we know which direction to head. Once you know the direction God is leading, act without hesitation. Our action is shown by our faith. As you go about your life, be aware of God's presence in every situation and have faith that God guides you. Ask, seek, and walk through doors of opportunity. Do not push uselessly at the door that fails to yield; perhaps God is saying, "This is not for you."

As you ask and seek open doors, consider how you can achieve a goal and be as realistic while still open to possibilities. Your goal may be a behavior change something specific for your situation. Paul said, "Put off the old, as regards the former behavior that was corrupted by deceitful lusts, and are now renewed in the spirit of your mind, putting on the new" and

> Do not lie, be truthful; be angry but don't hurt anyone with your anger; deal with it the same day. Stop stealing; get a job; give to those in need. Stop cursing or using filthy language; speak to the need so grace is heard ... Let all your bitterness, anger, wrath, turmoil, and evil speaking cease, and be kind and tenderhearted; forgive as God forgave you... (Col 3:8)

Colossians makes it clear what is acceptable and what is not in God's sight, and the reason for doing what is right. God is the author of all but we must do our part in humble obedience.

11. Thought for Today

King Nebuchadnezzar's pride cut him down to size. Yet even some of God's mighty men had problems with pride and arrogance. Joseph was a youthful dreamer and braggart, became a slave then a prisoner (unjustly accused), a dream interpreter with good management skills. Joseph went from youthful braggart to humble pie yet he learned and grew in wisdom, knowledge and skills needed that made it possible for him to succeed as Pharaoh's second in command over all the Egyptian resources.

David was a humble shepherd, a bear and lion killer, a giant slayer and a warrior, and as Israel's King he was also an adulterer and murderer. David went from humble shepherd to a position of power as king of Israel and then became arrogant and covetous, which led to his sin. When humbled on his face before God, again, he was broken and repentant when his sin was confronted. David was known as a man after God's own heart, for even with and because of his human frailties and sin he never lost sight of God's awesome power nor his grace and mercy.

Describe how pride and arrogance has led to sin in your life.

Do you seek God's will and wait for him to reveal it? Describe

Describe how you sometimes presume that you know God's will in a situation, and only make matters worse for everyone involved.

Describe when you tried to be the vine and other people the branches where you tried to control /manage a situation your way.

How well did that work out for you?

YOUR IMMEDIATE GOALS

Our immediate goals vary depending on a situation and long term goals. You need a GED for instance, before entering college or even some jobs. So, getting the skills such as a GED to achieve that initial goal may need to come first. As to other goals, consider topics we've explored so far and any problem areas and add those to your list of needed change. Are there people that seem to drive you crazy and you think that if a certain person would change, then life would improve. We may have difficulty seeing that part of a problem is within us, and we may need to change first.

"You can see the speck in your friend's [your spouse's] eye. But you do not notice the log in your own eye. How can you say, 'Friend, let me take the speck out of your eye', when you do not see the log in your own? Fools! First, get the log out of your eye. Then you can see to take the speck out of your friends" (Matt 7:3, Luke 6:41).

Notice by comparison the size of a log as opposed to a speck. Often the very things that blind us to our own faults are huge by comparison to the other person's. So, look to yourself and clean up the sin in your own life then you will be better able to help your friend or your spouse.

One thing I know from experience is that what I see in someone else is visible to me only because I recognize the similarity in myself or at the very least it is an area I've visited myself and overcome.

So to begin, first identify the problems in your own life or marriage then, consider how you contribute to the current problem. Now, what can you do to improve the situation? In other words, first get that plank out of your own eye--whatever it is that blinds you to the truth –so you can see clearly to help the other person.

Still having difficulties identifying problem areas? Ask one of your parents or your spouse. Asking that question might should shock them and bring an embarrassing amount of pleasant attention.

Keep things simple; stick with the facts; keep an open mind and listen for the truth in their words. Do your best not to hear criticism but a desire to help you. Maybe they really love you and want you to be the best you can be. Is that so bad?

Let people help you select your target goals.

ACHIEVING GOALS

You may know your vision, dream, or purpose, and needed changes even if they are a bit vague or clear-as-crystal. Brainstorm ideas and ask your family and friends for honest feedback about ideas you have voiced or changes you have talked about making. Now do something about it and take the first step forward!

JESUS' PURPOSE

Jesus' purpose was specific: preach, teach, heal, and to set people free. Marriage and children were not in his future, yet he referred to himself as a bridegroom in Matt 9:15; Mark 2:19; Luke 5:34; John 2:9. Jesus was a leader with extraordinary talent and skills. He chose many of his followers while others came to follow because they liked what they were hearing; he was trustworthy, attentive to their needs and to his own. Jesus was bold and outspoken, and for the most part, lived life in-the-moment.

After bringing a couple of disciples on board one day, Jesus took them to a wedding feast with dancing and feasting, and where he performed his first miracle turning water into wine for the celebration.

He fellowshipped with his disciples, but he also spent time with God. Jesus was employed as a minister, healer, and teacher providing for his needs. He dressed nicely but not extravagantly, and ate well in the homes of the common, the wealthy, and even the religious hierarchy.

Jesus set the example in his ministry. His priorities included marriage, children, fellowshipping (social contacts), food and clothing (a career - may require education), spiritual (a relationship with God), celebration of life (but in moderation regardless and some things not at all, depending). Thus, we can seek opportunities to express ourselves in these ways too.

What goals do you have? I paint, write, and talk and encourage others, and do landscape design. Yet God has closed some door whereas he has opened other doors such as with my art and writing.

OPPORTUNITIES

When seeking to improve the quality of life, we can address these items and other opportunities that arrive unexpectedly. What opportunities are you seeking right now? All too often, we procrastinate in our work and fail to finish the daily goals set before us. It is not proper to celebrate when little or nothing has been accomplished. Problems can creep in and sidetrack us and problems may arrive with certain people. Relationships can create problems and opportunities too. One must learn to avoid certain people and situations that tend to create problems.

First, realize that problems always will be part of life and that people, no matter who they are, have problems too but their problem do not have to become your problem. God brings people into our life but we must be wise enough to discern the purpose, which may be so that both can learn from the experience. Regardless, God has a purpose for their presence in your life. It may be so that you can express your love no matter how you feel at the moment.

People always challenge us to grow and mature simply by their presence. Loving others is a challenge especially even when we do not feel like being loving. Do you think Jesus *felt* like going to the cross? "Father," he cried in anguish, "if you will, please do not make me suffer this way. But I'll do whatever you want" (Luke 22:42) [*I am human after all, and would rather avoid the pain and humiliation*]. Through this experience Jesus completed his purpose, fulfilling God's plan for humanity.

COMPLETION

We too have a purpose to fulfill God's plan for humanity. And over time, God will reveal what will help your understanding and achievement of his purpose for your life. How well we achieve our dream – his purpose- depends upon what we believe: is he in agreement with us, and do we believe the goal is attainable. Jesus said to the blind *"Do you believe I am able to do this?"* They said, "Yes Lord". He touched their eyes, saying *"According to your faith* let it be [done] to you" (Matt 9:29).

In childhood and later on, other person's actions impact us in some way. It depends on the situation and the person, and often our mood at the moment. Comments not intended to be hurtful can deeply wounded one person while another goes unscathed. Words and/or behavior toward us physically, mentally, and emotionally, and how we perceive them, can have a lasting impact on our lives. Thus, our belief system develops in response.

What we believe about God, marriage, family, home, friends, neighbors, our work, career, and our government is based on how we view our parents and other significant persons and their responses to life events, as well as our own emotional and situational events. Depending on life events beliefs develop and behaviors adjust in response. Belief systems will be covered in the next chapter. Complete the "Thought for Today" from this chapter.

12. THOUGHT FOR TODAY

My dream as a young girl was to be an artist. Becoming an author and a friend was not part of that dream. Yet I became an artist and author, and as needs arose, acquired friends as well. Thus, my life is now filled with people and plenty to do that give me great joy.

What's your dream or life purpose?

How can you discover your life purpose?

This is the real reason why you're here — the very reason you exist, so you may want to discover as much as you can about it.

If you do not believe you have a purpose and that life is without meaning you can *change that thinking right now*. Not believing that you have a purpose is like not believing in gravity; it will not stop you from falling or finding your purpose in this case, but it might take a bit longer. However, if you want to give it a try, first forget everything you have ever been told and trust that you do have purpose, meaning, and value.

Now, if you are ready to begin, use the following to start your discovery, or if you want to use a mind map use the example on next page:

- Take a sheet of paper and write

- "My genuine and true purpose in life is ..."

- Good grammar or spelling is *not important*

- Write whatever comes to mind no matter what; just keep on writing, and don't stop!

- Write until you weep or

- Until you feel 'finished'.

On the next page are two examples of mind maps!

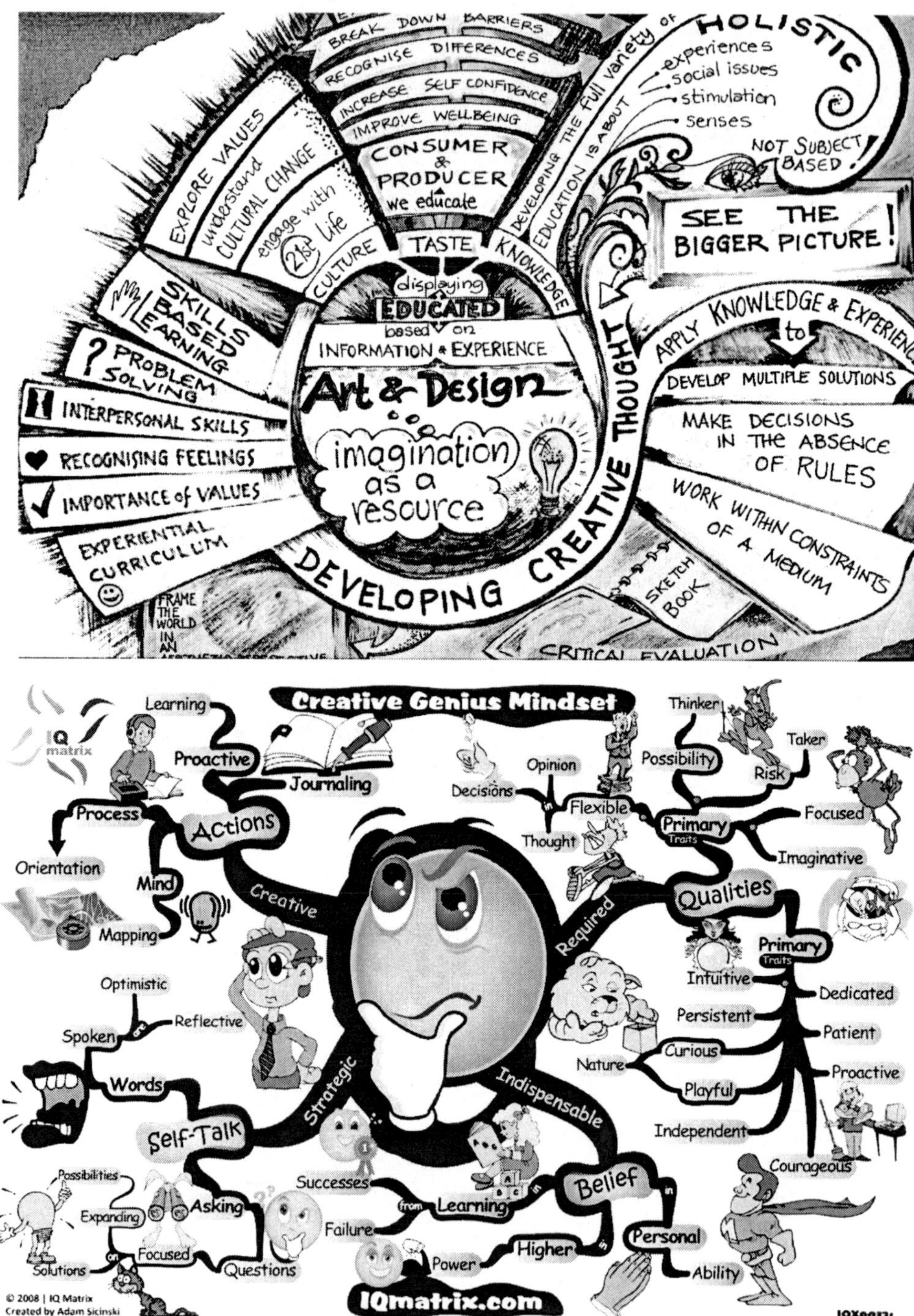

Mind maps can be created anyway you like; anything you do with them is okay!

ELIEVE AND BE SAVED

These are written, so you will believe that Jesus is the Christ, the Son of God, and by believing you will have life in his name. If you believe [then] all things are possible " John 20:31

To believe in Jesus and be saved is more important than any other belief for that alone guarantees eternal life with God in heaven. However, while eternity awaits us, we live here on earth, and what we believe about that decides whether we live in heaven or hell on earth!

Jesus said that beliefs alone decide our lives here on earth and, perhaps, it is the reason he also said "with God all things are possible." So we will believe in more than what we have come to believe is possible. It takes courage and a whole lot of faith to believe in the impossible, or what we have previously thought of as being impossible. Nonetheless, if we believe in God first, then, in the impossible nature of Jesus' birth, his life and the miraculous nature of his ministry and, the events surrounding his death and resurrection, then, we have come a long way in accepting the impossible.

If you can believe in those impossible events, you can believe in almost anything. That alone opens up countless possibilities. In spite of Jesus birth, life, death, and resurrection and the people who profess to believe, there are a surprising number who live with a vast crowd of impossibilities: "You can't do that; it will never work; or don't be such a dreamer" and the litany of unbelief goes on and on from one generation to the next.

When my uncle visited me at the state school, he shot down my dreams from the start, though that was not likely his intention. He was probably just being practical and wanting the best for me. But who's to know what would happen if he had said, "That is a great idea! I encourage you to go for it. But, you might also want to think about a job to support yourself, at least until you begin to make money as an artist."

To have someone who believes in you, who you are, and the possibilities, and express it makes such a difference. So believe in and encourage others to strive for the seemingly impossible, and start seeing dreams come true!

What does it mean to believe? Merriam-Webster's online dictionary defines believe as "**a:** to consider to be true or honest … **b:** to accept the word or evidence of <I believe you> <I couldn't believe my ears>".

Faith is the substance of things hoped for; thus, we read, or see in the Word possibilities, and begin to believe in the impossible!

What we believe and how we respond to life events depends upon what we often have been told by parents or others in authority (i.e. counselors, aunts and uncles, pastors, or teachers). Beliefs arise when we agree to anything an authority figure tells us. We may accept as fact that authority [their influence] without personal knowledge of its truth. Knowledge is the "clear perception of a truth or fact".[10]

Our central beliefs develop from social customs, education, the system, public opinion, and the convictions of family, friend, church, and society. A father, mother, or other family member such as a teacher or counselor is generally a child's authority and that child tends to accept their word as being true and then base their beliefs on the 'truth' of what they are told, which in turn determines the child's conduct.

A child may be told they are stupid and asked "What's wrong with you?" Perhaps all they did was make a simple mistake. Still, if they hear this often enough, they may begin to believe they are stupid and that something is wrong with them, and over time this belief becomes who they are and how they behave, stupid and that whatever they do it is always wrong.

> *Our mother use to say "Why did you do that? Are you stupid or what?" or something similar. As a result, I reacted by going through life trying to prove I was smart and had all the answers.*

---

[10] A. J. Balfour's *Foundations of Belief*

Others, by contrast, assume they are stupid and quit trying, failing in school and often in life. But God uses even these circumstances as a means to mold us so that we use our gifts whether it's intellect or some other.

While we may believe the same as our parents or other authority figures, for whatever reason, we may also reject their beliefs in favor of our own. Or we accept some while rejecting others, depending on other factors. If we do not like a person or disagree with their opinion --it is not reliable because they have lied in the past --we are less likely to accept what they say. By contrast, we may accept some things that make no sense at all.

In the mirror I see my knees, twice the size of others, and their hips small with little butts while mine spread like soft butter, twice their size. Feeling ugly and awkward, disgusted with this body of mine, I hate God for my being this ugly thing. Rejecting, I push people away and God too, hating them and him, believing they judge me just as I judge myself. And so, I live with anger and resentment believing I am ugly and therefore, become an angry and ugly hate-filled person.

At some point reason awakens and our beliefs change. Hopefully good sense takes over and we realize that do not have to agree with what someone says in order for them to like or love us. Nor do we have to accept their negative estimation about us.

Reason about God awakened in me as a teenager (Yet my reasoning was not well-informed], thereby I rejected God and his authority along with that of every other person in authority. This attitude eventually landed me in jail. Thirty-five years later, in going back to jail, I finally bowed to the authority of God - after inviting him into my life and accepting Christ as my Savior. Beliefs about me, as a person in relation to other people changed over time, through reading the Bible.

Other changes also resulted from reading the Bible where we learn what sin is and that we must fight against our mind, for it makes us a prisoner of sin, controlling us, making us miserable (Rom 7:23-24). Believing anything bad about ourselves is sin for God created us and everything in creation. Daily, God reviewed his work and said "it is good" (See Gen 1).

The Bible as the authoritative Word of God is evidence of the truth that is Christ Jesus. But the Bible also offers a history of its people and other information so we can be informed regarding a decision to believe or not. For instance, as a teenager, while having been raised a Catholic, I was taught the Catholic doctrine but not the Bible, and my immediate family did not teach biblical principles or apply them in their own life.

Our father did tell us stories about David and Goliath but not how to assess their value. Thus, I knew nothing about a personal relationship with Jesus Christ.

Yet, even with knowledge of the Bible some people become atheists. For them the decision is not a lack of knowledge but not accepting God's truth. My decision to become an atheist was not well-informed because I lacked certain knowledge. The point is, having accurate knowledge is important but the right decision is imperative.

In reading Scripture, I saw Jesus was disdainful of the religious hierarchy. He rejected their authority because of observed hypocrisy, and he saw them unworthy of respect. This was amazing to me. As children, we were not allowed to question the authority of the Catholic Church or my mother, the family matriarch, both of which were flawed as I saw it, but then, I did not understand human frailty, either.

Because of Jesus' teachings, a new authority emerged, an unfamiliar one but one I could respect. Consequently, I re-assessed my beliefs about God and as such became more discerning of what legitimate authority should or could be - the truth versus a lie, etc.

Jesus knew that our attitude and expressed authority had to be more than lip service; it had to be shown in our actions. Words that say "I love you" but come with an attitude and behavior that is abusive or disrespectful, speak the greater truth. I have been in many a relationship where "I love you" was verbalized yet the person's behavior was critical, even physically abusive.

Jesus taught that our attitude and behavior must agree with our words. In saying, "I love you" we must behave as such!

Teachings such as these, with much study, convinced me of the truth of God's word and as a result my beliefs changed. I accepted belief in God. As a result, my life has experienced more blessings that before becoming a believer when I experienced misery. Do not mistake what I am saying. Life still can be miserable however, because of the Bible's teachings I have learned to respond less emotionally to traumas and as a result have become a better person as I learned to trust God.

BLESSINGS AND CURSES

"Cursed are they who trust in their own strength, whose heart is far from `the Lord. For they are like shrubs in the desert, and do not see when good comes, but inhabits the dry places in the wilderness, a salt land uninhabited. Blessed are they who trust in the Lord, whose hope is the Lord. For they are as a tree planted by the waters, spreading its roots, and see not the heat come, but is unconcerned in the drought, continually yielding its fruit." Jer. 17:5

Often we put our trust in people who disappoint us. When this happens we may become angry, resentful, and distrustful. People inevitably let us down – that's life – and I had to learn to trust in the Lord that he would works things for the good of everyone. Thus, we walk by faith not sight, and believe in what is not as though it were a reality (2Cor 5:7).

Scripture also says that those who do not believe Jesus and refuse faith do so because they prefer the praise of their friends. Alcoholics hang out at the bar with friends who encourage their behavior as do addicts and gamblers. "How can you possibly believe?" Jesus said. "You strive for a friends' praise, and don't care about God's praise!" (John 5:44).

Jesus also said that belief is important to our faith and to healing. He did many miracles in his ministry because of beliefs: Jesus turned water into wine; he healed a nobleman's son; he healed an invalid of 38 years; he fed 5000 people one day; he walked on water; he healed a man born blind; and he raised Lazarus from the dead. These are miracles of faith.

MIRACLE OF FAITH

Miracles and healing are the result of belief. Miracles are not as evident today because of unbelief, as it was in Jesus' day. When we fail to believe in God and/or miracles, we miss the opportunity to experience God's miracles. What we believe makes all the difference. But more whether we live by faith then matters even more.

Jesus emphasized the importance of beliefs: "As you believe, let it be done" and "Whatever you ask in prayer, believing, *you will receive*" (Mark 11:24), which presupposes faith; he also chastised those who would not believe unless they could see signs and wonders" (John 4:48). "The Scriptures are written so you might believe Jesus is the Christ, the son of God, and believing you have life in his name" (John 20:31).

When you know your purpose aligns with God's and doubt creeps in, reject the lie. 'Not my will (ungodly beliefs) but your will be done, Lord.' Thus, we pursue faith in God. John spoke of Jesus and what he believed about him as a person, his beliefs and how he taught others to believe in his sermons and the way he lived his life and fulfilled his god-given purpose.

Paradox of Faith

"Whoever believes in me" Jesus said "is not condemned, but whoever does not believe is condemned not having believed" (John 3:18). While it is easy to say "I believe" often deeply held beliefs deny our words, therefore, we must confess them to be free.

Consider the man who cried, "Lord, I believe; *help my unbelief*". We all experience this paradox of faith versus unbelief, and must come to terms with it "Lord, I believe; help my unbelief!"

We want to believe, yet find it difficult. Hating this contradiction, we seem to fight against it in vain. Childhood voice say: "You'll never be good enough"; "What's wrong with you": or "That's just plain stupid" but you hear, "You're stupid" and we begin to believe it.

When we hear these voices (I like to think of them as my personal demons of despair and hopelessness) we doubt and lose hope. Sight of our dream soon vanishes and we feel defeat overwhelming. Instead, we must keep the dream alive; walk by faith; for God strengthens the hearts of those that hope in Him (Luke 6:41-42).

HELD AGAINST US [FROM REVELATION)

> *"You have some good qualities" Jesus remarked "but you have abandoned your first love. Remember how far you have fallen. Repent, and return to your first love. If not, I will remove what good remains, if you don't change your ways."* (Rev 2:4-5)

A relationship with God is like that of a marriage. The couple begins to take one another for granted after a time. They no longer pay as close attention to each other. Time together as a family becomes limited; intimacy is lost. But God wants us to pay attention and not lose that special closeness we experienced at the first with him or with others in relationship.

"You have some who are married to the world and its ways and teach others the same putting stumbling blocks before the people." (2:14) We begin to cheat on our marriage with the Lord, spending more and more time away from praise and worship, study of the word, and more time earning money and getting ahead in our career.

> *"You tolerate that harlot Jezebel who calls herself a prophetess and misleads my servants into a self-indulgent religion! She has no intention of giving up her kind of god-business"* (2:20-21).

Perhaps your Christian service is outstanding but if impure doctrine is being tolerated with immorality and idolatry and you justify this compromise with the world on the ground that it would allegedly advance the cause of the church then God wants you to repent.

"Wake up! You have a little strength and it is almost gone. Try to be stronger for you are not completely obeying God. (Rev 3:2) Wealth and comfort can lull us" (3:16).

Pride, ignorance, self-sufficiency, and complacency suggest that we need a new boost of the Holy Spirit.

~~~~~~

Have you forgotten what it was to be passionate and vibrant for God? "But I will give you power over the nations, everyone who wins the victory and keeps on obeying me until the end". (Rev 2:26)

Listen! I am standing and knocking at your door. If you hear my voice and open the door, I will come in and we will eat together. (Rev 3:20)

Body builders do not get strong just sitting around looking at the weights, imagining their strength increasing; they gain strength by lifting the weights. So too, with biblical strength, we pick up the Bible and read then exercise or put into practice what we read.

We know when our behavior is questionable, and not perfect before God. Remember the teachings you received, hold fast, cling to it, and repent that you became lazy. Repent of your wrong doing:

"Behold, this is our God; we have waited for him, and he will save us. ...we will be glad and rejoice in his salvation". (Matthew 9:24-29) He gives power to the weak, to those who have no might he increases strength. They will mount up with wings like eagles; they will run and not be weary; they will walk and not faint –John 21:31.

When we decide to turn away from God, not caring whether we sin, God's Spirit no longer constrains us and we are in danger of losing our salvation. We must be very careful that the temptations, lusts of the flesh do not send us scurrying in the wrong direction.

If we sin willfully after we have received the knowledge of the truth, there remains no more sacrifice for sins, but a certain fearful looking forward to judgment and fiery indignation, which shall devour the adversaries [of God] (Heb 10:26-29).
~~~~~~

The warning isn't that if you sin or struggle with sin, there's no hope for you. No, the sin is turning your back on Jesus Christ, the one who gave his life to provide forgiveness *for* sin. Nonetheless, if we pay attention and strive to overcome, seeking to glorify God, the danger passes. We may fail at times but, I John says, "If we confess our sins, he is faithful and just to forgive us our sins and to cleanse us from all unrighteousness." John 14:23 assures us that as long as we keep his Word, we do well.

> *When others rebel because there is no fear of God in them* Romans 3:10-18, *the Lord desires that we not to behave as they do but instead fear God who can destroy both your body and soul* –Mathew 10:28.

As such, you are encouraged to separate and replace unbelief with belief in God by turning to the Word, and strengthening your faith, so that when tempted to give up, instead, persist, and believe, no matter what others do.

> *Tormented with my sins, I am in agony, heart, mind, and soul. God seems so very far away. "Can you not hear me? Why do you not answer! Ah. The pain is more than I can bear; you do not care, for if you did, you would answer and not leave me in such torment."*

> *Voices whisper –or else I imagine hearing them –in the dark of my mind. An evil presence hovers. Sensing the barest hint of a smirk though no face appears, and yet, fear does –of hell and losing God and heaven –strike my heart. Still, all is lost. No matter, unrepentant sinner that I am. Tomorrow what will change, if anything? Likely nothing!*

> *In my distress, I cry hot wretched tears; every fiber of my being throbs in agony; if the pain would only go away. I dare not wish yet to die, for then, hell arrives all the sooner. Rather it was heaven, but that is not to be. No one understands the turmoil and the pain – nor do I.*

> *Yet, a still small voice within finds utterance, is pleading with me, "believe in me and do not fear the enemy's lies. Fear not. I am with you always." Finally, peace comes. In his care, I sleep.*

13. THOUGHT FOR THE DAY

Because she believed she received the promises. The promise from God brought a blessing and suffering. While blessed Mary was also predestined to watch her beloved son suffer and die for his beliefs.

FAMILY VALUES affect what we believe and are based on what we see and hear from our parents and other persons; they include the following.

Who you agree with is suggested by your words and actions being similar			You agree with	
	Dad said /acted toward	Mom said /acted toward	Mom	Dad
Money				
Religion				
Leisure				
Work				
Family				
You				
Future				
Sex				
I must				
I wish I could				
I feel loved when				
I feel valued when				
I feel respected when				
I am significant when				
If I change, the danger is				
If I had courage I would				
To be a success I must				
I am happiest when				
I am unhappy when				
I resist success by				
I encourage this by				
I worked hard to succeed at				
A friend encourages me by				
I want to change for me because				
The one real passion that fires my heart and imagination is				

What you worked hard to succeed at may not be the ideal social behavior but if you were a success write it even if you were a gang leader, a drug dealer, etc.
When reading the first four chapters of Revelations, what does, Jesus speak to the churches back then and maybe the church bodies of today?

What thoughts defeat you and stop you from achieving your dream?

Surely you are aware that we as individuals are the church and therefore, Jesus was speaking to us individually as well as the church as a body. So, consider the voice of Christ speaking specifically to you in Revelations 2-3.

Pray over each of these and let God speak to your heart then describe what it is that you need to change to be pleasing to God?

1. **Ephesus** – The church that left its first love (2:1-7). What have you left and for what? God for …; your home/family for…; your spouse and children, for …; etc.?

2. **Smyrna** – The persecuted church that suffered poverty and martyrdom (2:8-11). If you are suffering remain faithful no matter what; don't give up on the Lord.

3. **Pergamum** – The worldly church; mixed doctrines; needing to repent (2:12-17). Repent is you have experienced pressure and compromised your faith!

4. **Thyatira** – The false church that followed a seductive prophetess (2:18-29). If you remember that sex outside marriage or a marriage bed defiled hurts not only you but God because it shows that you prefer to satisfy self more than God.

5. **Sardis** – The "dead" church that fell asleep (3:1-6). Has wealth or comfort lulled you and self- satisfaction caused you to die spiritually? If God gave you a responsibility to teach, lead, or serve, encourage others to be spiritually awake and morally prepared.

6. **Philadelphia** – The church of brotherly love that endures patiently (3:7-13). During times of suffering and tribulation our souls are protected by Jesus Christ.

7. **Laodicea** – The "lukewarm" church; faith that is neither hot nor cold (3:14-22). Are you lukewarm? To avoid discipline: confess, serve, worship, and study his Word and take a stand for your faith!

OUR BELIEFS

What our parents and significant persons said or how they behaved as we were growing influences our beliefs and how we behave in response. This is a good reason for parents to raise their children in the way they should behave in the Lord so they will not depart from it, even when old (Pro. 22:6). When not raised in the Lord, we choose to believe and behave responsibly.

> *As noted earlier, I was not raised to believe in God and attend to his commands but later, as an adult I had to make a choice to behave in a way that was righteous and approved of by God.*

What we believe matters. Jesus was unable to certain miracles and healing because of people's unbelief. When people did not believe him, and even intended him harm, he left (See Luke 4:28-30).

While our beliefs about self and other people matters to us, belief in God makes the real difference, for it is by faith that the faithful are justified and ones dreams realized (Matthew 10:28). Not sufficient in ourselves, we need God. [We] have no confidence in the flesh (self) but we can do all things through Christ who gives us strength (Phil 4:13) *"He who abides (believes and lives) in me .... bear much fruit"* (Jo 15:1-8).

Research shows that about 60% of all people say they believe in God, though only about 10% regularly attend worship. If the professed believers are asked regarding their beliefs *about* God, they become incredibly vague. Generally, a person's view of God reflects the view they have of themselves.

Most of us are self-indulgent especially towards failings and we prefer to think of God as "infinitely kind, always forgiving, not condemning anyone, even sinners. Or "If God exists, and I do what *I think is right*, I'll get whatever reward there is." Guess what, you're right but you are in for a huge surprise and not one that is very pleasant either!

The Christian religion is a *revealed* religion; the Word of God is for all mankind. It cannot be revealed from man if our belief is to have any power and authority; *it must be revealed* by God himself.

Scriptures message is never presented as coming from any human authority. "The Word of the Lord" comes and the prophet delivers it as is. The Word is written for our benefit. Paul says it is "inspired of God" and "God-breathed" (2 Timothy 3:16). Peter said it "came not in old time by the will of man: but men of God who spoke as they were moved by the Holy Spirit" (2 Pe 1:21). Notice: it is not "by the will of man", but from God by His Spirit.

BELIEVE IN GOD

We change the way we believe and how we behave when we:

Know God by reading the Word of God; talk with him as you would a friend; pray to him and listen while meditating on the Word. Talk to God during the day driving in your car, on coffee breaks, at bedtime, or other opportune moments. There are also times to be on our face before the Lord. While the latter may not be necessary every time, there are moments when simply sitting or standing is not sufficient.

Seek God's will is to listen with your heart and not your head. Look for his will in every aspect of life, a word from someone or a door of opportunity that opens. God speaks in dreams (See Joseph's dreams in Genesis 37:6, 37:7, 37:9, and 37:10) and other means.

God warns us of changes, impending dangers, and future glories, like in Joseph's dreams. However God did not warn Joseph about the dangers that were to come later. Yet, Joseph's dreams and his ability to interpret the dreams of another helped him get out of prison eventually. Still there are certain dreams and prophecies we must be aware of as well.

Deuteronomy 13:4 warns, If a prophet, or one who foretells by dreams, appears among you and announces to you a sign or wonder, and actually takes place, and they entice you to "follow other gods", you must not listen to that person. The Lord your God is testing you to see whether you love him with all your heart and all your soul. It is the Lord God you must follow, and him you must revere. Keep his commands, obey him, serve him and hold fast to him.

So be cautious with dreams, for in dreams words and vanities abound; rather, fear God. Trust the Lord, plan your day to include God in prayer and meditate on Scripture, follow through on what God reveals and assess the strength of your relationship with God continually.

Scientists at http://www.reasons.org/about-us/our-beliefs believe there is "one infinitely perfect, eternal and personal God, the transcendent Creator and sovereign Sustainer of the universe. This one God is Triune, existing eternally and simultaneously as three distinct persons: Father, Son, and Holy Spirit. ... Jesus Christ is both true God (second Person of the Trinity) and true man (Incarnate Son of God).

"[They] also believe in the great events of Jesus Christ's life and ministry: eternal preexistence, virgin birth, miracles, sinless life, sacrificial death on the cross, glorious bodily resurrection from the dead, ascension into heaven, and present work as High Priest and Advocate. And that He will return in glory to resurrect and judge all mankind".

Theirs is a clear and detailed description, though I did not include all. Are you that clear about what you believe when it comes to God?

Belief in Self

When we put our belief and faith in self rather than in God, arrogance and pride can result because we believe it is by our own might that we achieve. But what happens when we run out of good ideas or motivations? Rather than believing in yourself, instead, have confidence that God will lead you and provide whatever you need, especially when life begins to fall apart and there is nothing you can do to make things right.

God knows all our failings, depressions, wanderings into sins, our rebellion and pride, and our weaknesses. But God also knows his purpose for our lives and will justify his having chosen us. Thus we show our confidence our faith in God by our works. But we must also be realistic and remember that God leads, and does so in many ways.

"I, the Lord God, will take hold of your right hand, saying to you, fear not" (Isaiah 41:13). As a father takes a child by the hand, leading and supporting us so we do not stumble or fall, assisting us over obstacles, guiding into the smooth places, so God leads us. If we are conscious of such guidance then as God said, *"My presence will go with you."*

How God Leads

God Leads Leaders

> *He came ...; and a certain disciple was there, named Timothy... 2[who] was well spoken of by the brethren. 3Paul wanted this man to go with him; ... (Acts 16:1-3).*

Barnabas chose to go toward the island of Cyprus, Paul decided to go overland into Anatolia, and visit the churches ... strengthening them. Thus, he came to where he recruited Timothy as a co-laborer because he was already a disciple. God led Paul to Timothy who was a disciple thus he was prepared to labor alongside Paul in the ministry.

God Leads With a Message

4 They passed through the cities, and delivered the decree that had been decided upon by the apostles and elders in Jerusalem, for them to observe. 5So the churches faith was strengthened, and increased in number daily (Acts 16:4-5).

By delivering the decrees, the church was strengthened in its faith and also increased its membership daily.

God Leads through Doors

6 They passed through Phrygian and Galatia, but were forbidden to speak the word in Asia; (Acts 16:6).

Paul and Silas had some open doors on the first mission and others opened on this second missionary journey but Asia's door was closed. The *Holy Spirit had forbid them to speak the word.* Paul and Silas plan to start churches there, but the Holy Spirit said, "No. Not now."

I know your deeds. Behold, I have put before you an open door which no one can shut, because you have a little power, and have kept my word, and have not denied my name. (Rev 3:8).

There was an open door placed before this church this time because God had opened it though when Paul and Silas had come earlier the door was closed to them.

God Leads through Needs

A vision came to Paul at night: a man of Macedonia stood and appealed him, "Come to Macedonia and help us." When he had seen the vision, immediately they went, for they believed God had called them to preach the gospel there (Acts 16:9-10).

Thus, we have various ways to navigate our spiritual life. The first is God's Word; the second is through leaders; and the third is God is speaking to your heart. But you cannot ignore the first two and go solely where your heart may lead for without the first two; our heart can easily lead us astray.

So when finding your way: ask God, seek sound counsel, and knock on doors of opportunity. When a door opens, walk through it! But when a door stays shut, no matter what do not kick or blast it open; storming the citadel by force will not work. Gideon brought down the walls of Jericho with patience and persistence over many days.

So go for the goal, for whoever works (to succeed) will have plenty to eat; those who chase "unrealistic" dreams have lots of nothing (Pro 28:19). Not doing our part --taking action --puts our goals in the realm of the unrealistic. Having friends who support and encourage your success is important as well so ask yourself, which friends are supportive of your efforts?

BELIEVE IN OTHERS

We pray and ask God to bring companions who encourage us and confront our fault ways. Of course, we do the same for them. In choosing disciples, Jesus chose men with potential; they were fishermen who went to sea daily, knowing they might return home in the evening with nothing to show for their efforts. Tax collectors, to do their job had to be able to withstand the scorn of their fellow men. Jesus did not choose just anyone; he handpicked those whom he knew could withstand adversity and, ultimately, those he knew would be there to help fulfill his purpose, according to God's will.

Our heart is in the right place yet, like Peter, we put our foot in our mouth at the wrong time. And then, there are those who have a problem with pride. James and John, as one example, knew all about pride; they asked Jesus if one could sit, "on your right hand and the other your left, in your glory" (1Corinthians 15:33).

Though we may say the wrong thing, or let our pride get in the way, God can and will use us for his purpose. He understands us and will accommodate all our peculiar ways. Regardless, our responsibility is to learn and grow in the Lord and put aside our sinfully peculiar ways.

One way we leave our sinful life is to associate with those who have similar goals, beliefs, and values. In the past, like you your friends did not believe. But, as a believer, now you must turn away from those who undermine your faith and fellowship with people who strengthen your faith with the Word (John 1:1-3). However, we also need friends who will when asked be honest, and not only encourage us but confront our hypocrisy as needed.

Jesus asked his disciple's opinion though not for the same reason. His intent was not so they could decide his next course of action, or be in agreement with them but to see if they were receptive to him.

Jesus chose these twelve men as companions, because they were teachable, and who were willing to share his vision and his ministry. Having friends who support and encourage you and share your vision is important. How do we choose friends for our walk with the Lord? For not all who call themselves a Christian, behave as though they are, Jesus warned.

CHOOSING FRIENDS

Once we have genuinely entered a true Spirit-filled walk with the Lord, God prunes people from our life. He removes those he does not want, and brings in those he does want. God wants us to have healthy people in our life, those who will have a positive godly influence. He did not want immature people in our life, those who merely profess to believe. Of course, one can always choose to involve immature unhealthy people in their life. However, these people may be too flexible in their walk with the Lord; their worldly walk is trouble for you.

God brings people who have knowledge of Scripture you do not have, and you have knowledge they do not have. Thus, both learn and grow in the Lord through one another. God knows who will be best for you and your particular level of spiritual development, so let him guide you.

Several people I know became Christians, after entering recovery. They lost their way when they tried to convert their drug-using-friends when they went back into the drug houses to do so. They were not prepared to deal with the temptation. Perhaps their intention was honest, as to the reason they went there. If so, it was a foolish thing to do.

Don't be misled: "Bad company corrupt good character." (1 Cor. 15:33, NIV)

Therefore, when introduced to a potentially new friend, be cautious, for "The righteous ... choose [his or her] friends carefully, for the wicked may lead astray." (Proverbs 12:26)

Once you turn your life over to God, he will now make sure that you get connected to the right people, so you have genuine godly friends. A true friend in the Lord will always be honest and straightforward. Indeed, we must always be completely honest with one another.

For those without godly friends, in prayer, ask father God to bring someone into your life. Ideally, some suited to your level of spiritual maturity. It will amaze you the people he brings. Be prepared to be honest and accept his gifts whosoever they may be.

When I prayed, it was amazing to me how many people he brought into my life. While not all became my bosom buddy, some did. In others, I could see myself and my own failings and that enabled me to change as well as accept myself far better. Some were so warm, loving and encouraging that they gave me a new heart that was more warm, loving and encouraging.

Unless God is keeping you for himself for a season, as he sometimes does, then there is no reason he will not bring you a friend or two. God did for Adam and in the garden and he will do it for you too.

Let's take a look at an article[11] that gives several good reasons for choosing Godly friends, friends of God.

1. Choose Friends Carefully

"The righteous should choose their friends carefully, for the wicked leads them astray." (Proverbs 12:26)

Many of God's people have lost their way because they hung out with the wrong people. I have known a couple of people who entered recovery and before long went back to the drug house to "help a friend" then ended up back on drugs themselves.

2. Choose Wise Friends

1. The wise are mightier than the strong, and those with knowledge grow stronger and stronger. (Proverbs 24:5)

2. Be sure you have sound advice [from wise friends] before making [any] plans or [especially before] starting a war. (Proverbs 20:18)

3. The wise are mightier than the strong, and those with knowledge

4. Without good advice [from friends] everything goes wrong-- it takes careful planning for things to go right. (Proverbs 15:22)

5. "Where there is no counsel, the people fail; with many counselors [giving sound advice] there is safety." (Proverbs 11:14)

6. Pay attention to [good] advice and accept correction [from friends], so you can live sensibly. (Proverbs 19:20)

7. If you stop learning [from wise counsel or teachings], you will forget what you already know. (Proverbs 19:27)

Once you turn your life over to God to manage, he will make sure you get matched with the right people that will become your true God-friends.

---

[11] Michael Bradley, "Choose Your Friends Carefully", http://www.bible-knowledge.com/bible-friends/ accessed on 19Jan2011

4. Do Not Be Unequally Yoked With Unbelievers

1. "Do not be unequally yoked with unbelievers. For what part has a believer with an unbeliever? ... (2 Cor 6:14)

2. "He who walks with wise men will be wise, but the companion of fools will be destroyed." (Proverbs 13:20)

3. "But we command you, brethren, in the name of our Lord Jesus that you withdraw from every brother who walks disorderly and not according to the tradition which he received from us." (2 Thess 3:6)

All of these warn us to stay away from the bad apples in this life, those who will do nothing but bring us down to their lower way of life. Many Christians have had their lives totally ruined as a result of choosing the wrong kinds of friends to hang out with or marrying the wrong person.

Jesus sent the apostles out two-by-two instead of by themselves. Paul always traveled with a companion in the ministry.

For those of you who have not been matched up with a good friend, go to God in prayer and ask him to bring you the friend(s) best suited for you at your level of spiritual development.

14. THOUGHT FOR TODAY

"One day our father said to the elder of two sons, 'Son, go mow the lawn.' The son answered, 'No. I'm busy right now.' Then, as he thought it over, he decided to mow the lawn. The father later that week asked his second son, who answered, 'Right away, Dad.' But, fooling around, he didn't mow the lawn. "Which of the two did what was asked?" The church-goers Jesus asked said "The first". "Yes" Jesus said. "By the way, crooks and whores will get into God's kingdom before you [so-called righteous] (Matthew 21:28-31).

In this modern version of Jesus' story, those who talk the talk (they say or do what looks pleasing) do not walk the talk and obey God in thought, word, and deed. We do what is pleasing to Christians but are too busy fooling around with the world to get busy and do what God wants.

Is any of this true for you? Describe

What do you believe about God's justice in this story?

Do you walk the talk by doing as God commands?

What does it mean to you - being a witness for Christ?

Describe how you share Jesus' message or demonstrate your beliefs?

If your words are angry, bitter, and resentful, then pray for change:

"Create in me a pure heart oh God and renew a right spirit in me; Restore the joy of your salvation, and uphold me with a right spirit" (Psalm 51:10).

Because we are born sinners (Psa 51:5), our inclination is to please our self rather than God. Right conduct can come only from a clean heart and spirit. Ask God to create a pure heart and spirit in you. God also fills all your needs; so, seek answers; and act in faith, behaving as though you truly believe.

GOD MEETS OUR NEEDS

EMPLOYMENT AND/OR CAREERS

Ask God to bring you the perfect job while being aware of the talents and gifts that God has given you, as well as the limitations that might prevent you from receiving some employment (education, certification). Still, with God all things are possible.

> *A young girl wanted to work in a daycare center but did not have the education or experience needed--childcare centers require special classes in childhood development --yet, the job she had in mind was offered to her with the opportunity to take the classes. She prayed and God opened the door for her and made it possible.*

So, look and expect to find the perfect job, which means you must take risks and step outside your comfort zone. Talk to people you would not ordinarily seek out. Act on faith means to apply or complete resumes. When, when an employer calls, you go to the interview, trust God to give you right words to get the job, or not.

Jesus chastised his disciples for their lack of faith because he was a friend. "But [Peter] saw the wind and the waves and began to sink [he was walking on water]; terrified and he shouted "Save me, Lord!" Jesus immediately reached out and grabbed him "You of little faith." Then he asked "Why did you doubt me?" (Matt 14:30-31) Often we lose sight of our goal and friends like Jesus will reach and take hold, to help us 'keep faith'.

When we fail, Jesus does not withdraw his affection but in compassion, points out the cause and encourages us onward.

A MATE OR TO RENEW YOUR MARRIAGE

Ask God to bring you the perfect mate, or restore your marriage. Seeking the ideal mate, first understand what God desires. Idol worshipers would not be high on his list nor would people that are violent or involved in illegal activities. No matter how good looking a person is, or regardless of how charming they seem, if they are not a godly person and do not walk in the way of the Lord, then be sensible and just walk away.

Look and expect to find the ideal partner by going where you will more likely find a partner. Unless you want to marry an alcoholic, going into the local bars would not be ideal. However you will not always find the right person in church but that may be a good place to start. The best way is to pray, seek

God's will and when you meet that special someone, use wisdom and discernment as you take time to be certain this gift is from God not a temptation of Satan.

Often movies depict couples meeting and having sex right off. Of course, the perfect relationship develops [only in the movies], and they fall in love, get married and then, they live happily ever after. These scenarios set us up for faulty expectations. In real life, these relationships seldom bear fruit, or the fruit is a child. Then both end up in a future filled with anger and conflict, sometimes violence over failed expectations. And both of you and the child suffer for the mistake of being lustful rather than wise and discerning.

> *I am an authority on this matter in that I have two sons, both born out of wedlock, one with a married man. My sons paid for my sinful life and the lust that drove me to live my way without regard for others. My sons both grew up without a father and without God.*

So, act on your faith and trust God to bring it all together in his good time. Fellowship with the kind of person you want for a partner. If there are early warning signs such as irritability, easily angered, or other behaviors and you discover he or she is married, walk away before it goes any further.

Regardless of how much you think you love someone *do not ignore* or *make excuses* for what is clearly sinful behavior. You could easily end up in a marriage with a partner that brings you nothing but grief. Or you could end up in an adulterous affair involved in an expensive lawsuit.

Be not yoked with unbelievers or believers who have a carnal mind. Do not fellowship with men or women just because they look good or feel good filling your loneliness or sexual desires. Pray not to fall into this temptation. We cannot fellowship with God and unbelievers at the same time.

2John says, "Look to yourselves and do not lose the things of God, but that we may receive a full reward. If anyone does not bring the doctrine of Christ and behave as a Christian, do not receive him into your house, nor speak a greeting. For he who speaks a greeting is partaker of his evil deeds." (1:7-11)

Ephesians speaks about believers who are not in fellowship with God and not producing fruit (5:1-14). When not doing work for the Lord they may be involved in a life of sin. The passage exhorts us to imitate God in our walk. Verses 7-12 speaks to the shamefulness of going back to a worldly lifestyle after Christ sacrificed himself so that we would not have to be a slave to sin and suffer eternal damnation, (v. 2). Instead we are to act like a child of light possessing eternal life, (v. 8), rather than like the world and losing one's inheritance in the kingdom of Christ for being immoral, (v. 5)

"Do not associate with a hot-tempered man, with the easily angered, or you may learn and get yourself ensnared". (Proverbs 22:24)

If someone behaves as the world, do not to be friends with them for they will lead you astray and/or give you a bad name by association. An evil that befell me happened as a consequence of renting a room to a Christian man who was in recovery. It was not long before I saw that he was still living in the world, sleeping with a female friend and before long, he was drinking. In time his behavior deteriorated and ultimately, I had to evict him. Also he returned to jail for violating his probation, drinking and threatening behavior. He retaliated by telling people lies about a supposed inappropriate relationship with me.

1Corinthians stresses, "do not be misled: Bad company corrupts good character." 2Corinthians warns not to fellowship with unbelievers: "Do not be bound together with unbelievers; for what partnership has good and evil, or what fellowship has light with dark? Therefore, come out from their midst and be not part of them", says the Lord. As a result of my misadventures, I learned. But what do you do when the one you love wants to marry you but they live a sinful lifestyle? A friend revealed this story to me.

There was a man with whom I had two prior marriage licenses but for some reason we never married. While he believed in Jesus he had not totally given himself over to his lordship and continued in a sin life of drugs, illicit sex, and illegal behavior. Yet I loved him. God understands because I do not. One day he said "Let's get married."

I wondered, 'what is this?' Wanting to be agreeable in case God figured for some reason it was time for us to marry –though I did not believe that for one second –still, I agreed. Off we headed to the department of licensing.

Lest you think I blindly followed, no way; I did not go blindly into that dark night or whatever. Instead on the way I prayed. As we filled out the papers, I prayed. Then, the woman looked at the man and said "I'm sorry but your ID is expired. I cannot give you a license."

To say the least, he was a bit upset. After all, it took him a long time to get to this point where it was his idea. All's well that ends well and my confidence in God was not shaken in the least. He had a purpose.

On the way home, I happened to notice that my driver's license was also expired but they had not paid attention to mine. Looking for an opportunity to strengthen his faith, I shared this information and the fact that I had prayed for the Lord's will to be done.

"You prayed about it?" What, is it a crime to ask for God will? He was offended by that also and seven years later, we are still unwed. Now we could have gone the next day and taken care of the ID business but did not. Perhaps he was willing to honor God, or his flight of fancy disappeared in the night, and eventually he did also. The question is, had we married would he have disappeared? Who knows!

He pops in and out of my life, and perhaps one day, as God wills it.

Restoring Your Marriage?

If you are looking to restore your marriage, it is important that you know and understand your biblical role as a husband or a wife. Once you have that information consider ways to fulfill your role using talents, gifts, and skills that God has given you. Generally, in a marriage each person has strengths that can offset the mate's weakness. Our challenge is to discover how to use our strengths to help our mate, and vice versa. Compliments not criticism and being willing to humble ourselves is the key to love.

Eph. 5:23-32 *...a husband is the head of his wife as Christ is the head of his body, the church; he gave his life to be her Savior. As the church submits to Christ, so a wife must submit to her husband in everything. And a husband must love his wife with the same love Christ showed the church....a man truly loves himself when he loves his wife. No one hates his own body but lovingly cares for it, just as Christ cares for his body... As the Scriptures say, "A man leaves his father and mother and is joined to his wife, and the two are united into one." This is a great mystery, but it illustrates the way Christ and the church are one.*

The picture of marriage expands into something much broader where husbands are urged to lay down their life in sacrificial love protecting their wife, home and family. And in this safe and cherished embrace of a loving husband, what wife would not be willing to submit to his leadership? We could write a book on this topic alone!

The Bible is replete with love stories and marriage. Filled with stories of maleness and expressions of power through love and domination, the one book of the Bible that brings everything down to humanness surrounds the images of a man and woman and erotic love.

One cannot read "The Song of Songs" and not experience the fullness of their most expressive sexual self and what love can mean for both. The Song is an encouragement to genuine love, purity, and passionate sexual intimacy within the bonds of matrimony.

Regardless of problems, I encourage both spouses to sit down and read this book. Talk about it honestly. Get past your past and into a future of marital intimacy, with a biblical marriage counselor if need be.

Starting a Business or Career?

Ask God for opportunities in-league with your natural talents, skills, and god-given gifts; expect it to happen; advertise, talk with others in the business, those with the knowledge, wisdom, and skills and who will encourage your efforts. David was anointed king at age 15 but he was not crowned until he was 30 years of age. He defeated the giant Goliath because of his love for God and his skills with a sling shot and the encouragement of those who supported him in his efforts to take on the task. When his brothers did not, he turned from them.

We all need people who will support and encourage us. David turned away from his brothers and gained not only the encouragement of other soldiers but of the king who listened when he assured Saul that he could get the job done. David had the necessary experience and the courage of his convictions because of his belief in God.

First, he asked for information about the job; he sought out the king and interviewed assuring him that he was capable and competent for God was on his side. When the king offered the opportunity, David took up the tools of his trade, strode in, perhaps a bit fearful but not hesitating, and slew the giant, Goliath.

From the start work was part of God's plan. He did not create man to be idle but to work to support himself and his family. God worked hard to create the world and then he set Adam to work in the garden

> The Lord God took the man and put him in the Garden of Eden to work it and keep it" (Genesis 2:15)

Work was a part of daily activity before Adam and Eve sinned and not a punishment. God created us to be active and useful and we will therefore be most happy doing so. Paul writes:

> "If anyone is not willing to work, let him not eat... such persons we command and encourage in the Lord Jesus to do their own work quietly and to earn their own living." (1Thess 3:10-12)

This does not mean to sacrifice ourselves, our home and family with endless hours at work and little time at home. Balance in all things, including work. Have mercy on your family!

15. THOUGHT FOR TODAY

"After all I've done for you and now you're letting me go. I didn't have to do any of those things for you!" She said. "But you didn't do what was asked. You did what you wanted to do and not what was needed." He explains.

Frustrated, she simply does not understand. She has sacrificed her time and energy doing what she thought was important and not caring for the people who needed the help, what was truly important.

> "I don't want sacrifice. I want mercy—compassion and concern for everyone." Jesus said, (Matt 9:13)

How would you rate yourself on a scale of 1 - 5:

> 1. Never   2. Rarely   3. Sometimes   4. Frequently   5. Always

_____ Do unbelievers, those in need, relate to you well?

_____ Do they look at you as being holier-than-thou, self-righteous?

_____ Do people enjoy your company because you represent life and joy; there's a quality about you that attracts believers and sinners alike?

Matthew said to his friends, "Come on over to my house and meet the One who has shown such grace and mercy to me." We need "Matthew parties," You can start your own and begin anew right now.

"Come, and let us reason together," says the Lord, "Though your sins are like scarlet, they shall be as white as snow; though they be red like crimson, they shall be [white] as wool. [19] If you are willing and obedient, you shall eat the good of the land; (Isa 1:18-19)

The "holiness" God requires of true believers is not of ascetic hermits, or to profess to worship God and "go through all the motions", then manifest a spirit more inclined toward self-indulgence, covetousness and pride rather than the holiness of God.

Samuel told Saul. "You have not kept the command the Lord God gave you; had you he would have established your kingdom forever. [14] Now your kingdom will not endure; the Lord has sought a man after his own heart ..." (1 Samuel 13:13-14 NIV)

David was that man but he was not a man who never sinned or made a mistake. Yet God still called him a man after his own heart. David committed adultery, and had the woman's husband killed to cover up, so God sent Nathan to confront him with his sin. David's response shows his true heart.

Many when confronted with their own sin deny responsibility, and/or blame someone else. But look at David's response:

David said, "I have sinned against the Lord." Nathan replied to David, "The Lord also has put away your sin; you shall not die. (2Sa 12:13)

Can you say you know God as did David?

Are your friends honest like Nathan? Would they confront you?

Do they support/encourage your efforts to demonstrate your faith?

Do your friends encourage you to walk in the way of the Lord?

What do you seek of God, marriage, career, etc.?

Beliefs and Behavior

"In the beginning was the Word, the Word was with God and was God. He was in the beginning with God. All things came into being by him, and without him not one thing came into being that now exists."

God spoke the world into being through his Word, and so the Word of God speaks us into a new way of believing as we study the Word. Then meditate so that God's Word become so much a part of us that we automatically to put off the old way and put on a new - as automatic as dressing for work.

Recognize how *the word, words* spoken concerning you (for good or ill) influenced what you believe and how you behave. The purpose here is not to condemn our parents or any other person; rather, the idea is to gain awareness of those sins that we have chosen to carry, but must now reject.

In our family one key word was 'stupid' preceded and/or followed by questions: what's wrong with you; why did you do that; do you have any idea how stupid that is or sounds? Is it any wonder that I became a scholar looking for answers and trying to understand the world and what was 'wrong' with me and/or other people?

If your father was an alcoholic and womanizer, and someone said you were just like him when you merely looked like him. Later, while you rejected his alcoholism and never drank you did become a womanizer with one failed relationship after another. The key is not to reject the parent or whoever spoke the unkind words, rather we should reject the sins or failings of that person and choose to serve God. Thus, we do not carry their sins forward into future generations.

How do we achieve this aim? You first become a godly person by letting the Word of God dwell richly in you. You read and understand the Word and in time, you become the real you as God created you. By trying new things, we overcome our fears and anxieties. And we gain the courage of our convictions. We believe that God will prosper us, according to his will not ours. We ask God to meet our needs and in faith expect to receive; and we knock on and open doors of opportunity.

What we ask for and whether we believe we will receive it depends upon what we genuinely believe about God and his role in our life.

Jesus said to a father, "If you believe, all things are possible to him who believes" Immediately the father of the child cried out and said with tears, "Lord, I believe. *Help my unbelief.*"[12] The man believed but also recognized that some unbelief existed that might interfere with his son's healing. He was honest enough to admit it and ask for help in overcoming his unbelief.

Realizing there is a potential for problems like this means we pay attention and are honest about our beliefs about God. When bad things happen, what do you believe God should or should not do about it? What do you believe God allowed in your life, good or not so good? What do you believe God is doing? Have you been angry with God for a perceived injustice against you?

Consider the father in the story and his need of healing for his son. Can you respond to a situation by faith where you or someone else needs healing? Perhaps you have been in a situation like this one. How did you respond? Could you ask God in faith or admit to your unbelief and stand on faith? It's not easy not without practice. Yes. Faith and growing a stronger in faith is an art that takes practice.

More than that our attitude of trust and confidence the Bible calls *belief* or *faith* (Heb 11:1, 11:6) is also a gift from God (Eph 2:8-9). No matter what our level of faith, we are never completely self-sufficient but are required to continually renew our trust in Jesus.[13]

MEN AND WOMEN OF FAITH

Job's Story

Job lived before Israel became a large nation. Married, he had seven sons and three daughters. Job was a wealthy man—at a time when wealth was in livestock not money. Job had seven thousand sheep, three thousand camels, five hundred oxen, and donkeys!

One day, the angels gathered around the Lord God and Satan was there. The Lord asked, "Satan, where have you been?" Satan answered, "I have been all over the earth." God asked. "Have you considered my servant Job, that there is none like him on the earth, blameless and upright, he fears me and shuns evil?'"

Satan believed that the only reason Job obeyed God was because he continually protected Job and all his belongings; that he was selfish and only obeyed God because he was getting something in return.

---

[12] See Mark 9:17-29

[13] "Mark 9:17-29" *Life Application Study Bible* in e-Sword

"Take away all of Job's possessions," Satan challenges God. "Then, we'll see how he reacts. He'll likely curse you."

God confidently replies, "'Behold, all that [Job] has is in your hands, only do not lay a hand on his person; you may not take his life."

Later, we see…

Job's sons and daughters were have dinner at his eldest son's home. Someone rushed up and cried, "A gang attacked and stole the oxen and donkeys! Your other servants were killed, and I alone escaped." As he was still speaking, a second one came running up and saying, "God sent a fire that killed your sheep and servants. I alone escaped to tell you."

Before that servant finished speaking, a third raced up and said, "Three gangs attacked and stole your camels! All of your servants were killed, and I am the only one who escaped to tell you."

Astonishingly, as he spoke, a fourth person dashed up and exclaimed "Your children were having a feast and drinking wine at the home of one of your sons when a sudden windstorm blew the house down, crushing all of your children. I alone escaped to tell you."

In his sorrow, Job tore his clothes and shaved his head then he knelt on the ground, and said: "We bring nothing at birth; we take nothing with us at death. The Lord alone gives and takes. Praise the Lord!"

If you knew God had responded to a challenge from Satan and helped bring disasters upon you (God sent the fire that destroyed his flocks) how would you feel about God, and could you maintain your faith in such a situation? Would you and/or have you been angry with God for disasters like these [death and financial loss] in your life?

JOHN THE BAPTIST

Jesus said of John the Baptist: "Among those born of women there has not been one greater than John the Baptist".

John dressed similar to the prophet Elijah (2Kings 1:8) to distinguish himself from the religious leaders, whose flowing robes reflected their great pride (Mk 12:38). John's striking appearance reinforced his remarkable message. "I am t*he voice of one crying in the wilderness: 'prepare the way of the Lord; make straight his paths'*" (Mk 1:3-4)

John was a recluse who came neither eating nor drinking (socializing), and yet was accused of having a demon (Matthew 11:18). To some, his ascetic life-style appeared almost demonic, like those possessed by evil spirits who frequented the desolate areas (cf. Mark 5:2-3). Yet he did not seek out the people; they sought him out.

John baptized hundreds. His purpose was to prepare the way for the coming Messiah. John came to bear witness of Christ and emphasized that he, John was *not* the messiah, but the fulfillment of a prophecy, the voice crying in the wilderness of the coming Messiah.

John's message of repentance necessitated a deep awareness of the sinner's offense to God, and a required life change. Those who were void of any radical change, he rebuked them: "You offspring of vipers, who warned you to flee from the fiery wrath to come? Therefore, bring forth fruit worthy of repentance." Worthy fruit is the expression of a deep inner conviction and not superficial lip service.

"People," He admonished, "Prove your purity and reveal your heart by the work of your hand. Stop robbing the people, either by violence or false accusation."

Looking out over the crowd, and lifting his voice to heaven he said, "Be generous. If you have two coats, give one to someone with none. Share your food with those who have none. And as to tax collectors, take no more than what is appointed."

Boldly amazing he was. If someone said, 'your purpose is to go into the streets and highways and prepare the way of the Lord's coming, as did John', would you do it? Think about the belief and faith in God, and commitment of purpose required to stand out from the crowd and openly criticize the religious of today and demand change.

MARY'S STORY

After John's mother Elizabeth became pregnant, God sent an angel to Mary who was engaged to Joseph. He was of King David's family. The angel, Gabriel, greeted Mary, "You are truly blessed! The Lord is with you."

Confused by the angel's words, Mary wondered what they meant. "Don't be afraid!" the angel reassured. "God is pleased with you, and you will have a son. His name will be Jesus. He will be great and called the Son of God Most High. God will make him king, and he will rule the people of Israel forever, and his kingdom will never end."

Mary asked, "How can this be? I am not married! [I am still a virgin]"

"The Holy Spirit will come," The angel informed, "and God's power will cover you. Your child will be called the holy Son of God. Elizabeth your relative is going to have a son, though she is old and everyone thought her barren, but in three months she will have a son. Nothing is impossible for God!"

Mary said, "I am the Lord's servant! Let it happen as you have said." The angel left. A short time later, Mary hurried to a town in the country of Judea to see Elizabeth. Later, she and Joseph married.

Emperor Augustus ordered a census to be taken about the time the baby was due to be born. Everyone had to go to their hometown to be listed.

Joseph had to leave Nazareth for Bethlehem, King David's hometown and Mary went with him. While there, she gave birth to her first-born son, Jesus. Mary dressed him and laid him in a manger.

In the nearby fields, angels on high told the shepherds of the baby, and they sought Mary and Joseph, and the baby lying in the manger. The shepherds told Mary and Joseph what the angel had said. Mary's role in Jesus' life was as a mother during his childhood but entering his ministry, at age thirty, he was no longer under her authority.

Consider your beliefs about God and if you could accept a message such as Mary received. How you might you respond in this situation? Have you ever had a dream or prophecy that foretold something for your life that seemed highly unlikely if not impossible?

JOSEPH'S STORY

Joseph was from King David's family, and engaged to Mary, Jesus' mother. Before the marriage, he learned she was pregnant. Joseph did not want to embarrass Mary, so he decided to call off the wedding.

While Joseph thought about it, an angel of the Lord came in a dream, telling him to marry her. Joseph and Mary were married, as commanded.

Later, the Lord appeared to Joseph in a dream once again and said, "Get up! Take the child and his mother to Egypt! ..." Joseph took them to Egypt.

Again Joseph was told to go in a certain direction - back to Israel - and he went then later to Galilee. Joseph obeyed God even when he may not have understood the reason. Nevertheless he responded with obedience to God's authority. Can you say the same?

16. Thought for Today

Mary and Joseph were from King David[14] a man after God's own heart (Acts 13:22). While David's life was filled with trials, temptations and treachery God found him praiseworthy.

How praiseworthy would God find you?

What is it you need to change to be worthy of praise?

Your word is a lamp to my feet and a light to my path. (Psalm 119:105)

David understood that without the Scriptures before him on his path, he would stumble aimlessly toward destruction. David knew *there is a way that seems right to a man, but its end is the way of death.* (Prov. 14:12) David was wise to place his trust in God's Words.

What seems right to you but you know it goes against God?

What is it you need to change to be on the same track as God?

Do you take pleasure in doing God's will with heartfelt obedience? Describe

Teach me your way, Lord; I will walk in your truth; unite my heart to fear your name. I will praise You, Lord my God, with all my heart, and I glorify your name forever. (Psalm 86:11-12)

Do you have a teachable heart or do you rebel and continue to repeat the same sin behaviors over and over? Describe

Now to Him who is able to do exceedingly abundantly above all that we ask or think, according to the power that works in us, to him be glory..., forever. Amen. (Eph 3:20-21)

---

[14] King David> Nathan-Mattatha-Menna-Melea-Ekiakim-Jonam-Joseph-Judah-Simeon-Levi-Matthat-Jorim-Eliear-Joshua-Er-Elmadam-Cosam-Addi-Melki-Neri-Shealtiel-Zerubbabel-Rhesa-Joanan-Joda-Josech-Semein-Mattathias-Maath-Naggai-Esli-Nahum-Amos-Mattathias-Joseph-Jannai-Melki-Levi-Matthat-Heli >*MARY (Jesus' birth mother). Genealogy from Luke 3:23-28*
King David> Solomom-Rehaboam-Abijah-Asa-Jehoshaphat-Jehoram-Uzziah-Jotham-Ahaz-Hezekiah-Manassheh-Amon-Josiah-Jeconiah-Shealtiel-Zerubbabel-Abiud-Eliakim-Azor-Zadok-Akim-Eliud-Eleazar-Mattham-Jacob->*JOSEPH (Jesus' legal father) Genealogy from Matthew 1:1-16*

VOICES OF AUTHORITY

These Bible characters were successful because they obeyed God even when they did not understand what was asked of them. As you were reading these stories, what came to mind? Did you hear the voice of doubt and disbelief, or that of your family or friends who disbelieve?

Imagine if one of God's angels showed up in a dream and claimed a purpose for your life just as he did for Joseph and Mary. What do you think your initial response would be? What do you believe about God and your purpose? What is the difference in God's voice of authority and that of other people or Satan?

Scripture is the authoritative Word of God who is the author (2Tim 3:16). God ensured the message of his Son would be known and reinforced by him. So, we can obey or reject God and his authority. God's Voice of Authority is heard in the Sermon on the Mount (See Mat 7:24-29 and Luke 6:47-49).

SPEAKING WITH AUTHORITY

Authority usually means some person's opinion that settles an issue in our mind. This authority may come from a parent who decides for a child. Courts often decide the guilt or innocence of people under their authority. The Pharisees lived by the Mosaic Law's authority while the pope is the Catholic churches authority.

Some believe they are their own authority; they do not realize that other authorities influence the decisions they make. There is one authority that no one can defy except at great peril and that is God's authority, which requires us to change. Ultimately, we must come to terms with God's authority, and all will one day.[15]

God's authority does not change; he is the same yesterday, today, and tomorrow. What we believe about God invariably shows in our actions and attitudes, our choices. To change your life, believe in God first, though belief alone is not enough, for even Satan believes in God.

---

[15] Romans 14:11 "As I live, says the Lord, every knee shall bow to me, and every tongue confess to God." Each person is accountable to Christ alone. While the church must be uncompromising in its stand against activities expressly forbidden by Scripture (adultery, homosexuality, murder, theft), it should not create additional rules and regulations and give them equal standing with God's law. Often Christians base their moral judgments on opinion, personal dislikes, or cultural bias rather than on the Word of God. When we do this, we show that our own faith is weak; we do not think that God is powerful enough to guide us. When we stand before God and give a personal account, we won't be worried about what our Christian neighbor has done (see 2Co 5:10). LASB

James asks, "What does it profit, beloved, if someone says he has faith but does not have works? Can faith save him?"(2:14). If a man is starving and you know he needs food but you fail to feed him, he will die of starvation. So, faith by itself is dead as well, if you do not express that faith. Faith is vital for salvation [by faith we believe in Jesus' and his death and resurrection]. Yet genuine faith requires obedience to God, which is shown by our works. Abraham obeyed God by offering his son, Isaac, by faith. All things are possible when belief leads to action and we put our faith into action.

TAKING ACTION

Now, we put our trust the Lord with all our heart, and lean not on our own understanding. In all our ways, we acknowledge God, and ask him to fill our needs, and he will bring it to pass. Thus, we walk by faith and believe in those things that are not a reality as though they were, like walking blind. Can you imagine walking blind? This is so unnatural for us; we could easily stumble. Such is the way of following God except he keeps us from falling.

Those who "walk by sight" depend on their experience in the moment. And when we rely on experience we become uncertain and often need reassurance. Those who "walk by faith" walk as God directs them. Peter denied Jesus as did Judas yet, unlike Judas Peter chose to follow not blindly but with eyes wide open knowing his future and serving Christ.

The question then becomes whom do you serve? Many are concerned with wealth and self-esteem more than God because they can see money, what it does, and offers, the brief feel good or false sense of security it brings. God is our ultimate security.

Nonetheless, the problem is not one of money but that it never satisfies no matter how much we have while God provides what we need. Therefore, God is who we should pursue because there is no guarantee that the wealth of today will be there tomorrow.

Paul told Timothy to warn the rich not to "fix their hope on the uncertainty of riches," which can cause our destruction." Those who "walk by faith" do not have to feel anxious in this uncertainty because God promises to supply all their needs so all they need is to have the faith and put him first.

"I have learned to be content whatever circumstances I am in" said Paul for "I can do all things with Christ Jesus who strengthens me" (Phil 4:11, 13). Can you lose everything and still be content with your circumstances?

Paul was a realist who came to terms with his suffering. He did not despair for he did not lose heart ... for the momentary, light affliction produces an eternal weight of glory ... while we look not at the things which can be seen, but at the things which are not seen" (2Cor 4:18). Paul hoped in his suffering for sights were set on heaven, not this world.

The Bible challenges all of us to "walk by faith, not by sight. As we do, we become more confident in God and in reaching our destination. Renewed by the transforming of our mind, our attitude and behavior is less inclined to be worldly and sinful and we lean more toward God and his ways. This is not true for everyone, however.

Some people simply enjoy their sin and do not want change. There are many who also have an excuse for failure and/or blame their sin on other persons. It may be dad's fault because he drank too much; or mom's because she was never home; or being bi-polar, their mind or emotions are unmanageable. Yet, Jesus said there was no excuse for sin, but when we do we must repent. Have you or someone else you know been diagnosed with a mental disorder and used that as an excuse for sinful behavior?

Instead of excuses, repent and change. Discipline what you think, say, and how you behave and manage emotions. Jesus did not excuse sin behavior or accept anyone laying blame on another. When asked whose fault it was that a certain man had been born blind, Jesus said that it was no one's fault; it was to reveal God's glory. In other words, anyone who believes in God and consequently changes their actions, in spite of problems that before had controlled their lives they make it evident that God is at work in their life, thus they glorify God.

We can remain blind to the truth, or allow God to open our eyes and reveal his glory through us. When we rely on Jesus, we find the peace of mind we desire. Jesus asks:

"Are you tired? Burned out on religion? Come with me and discover a new way to live. I'll show you how to rest. Walk with me and see how I do it. Learn the simple grace. I won't place any heavy burden on you. Come alongside and learn to live a carefree wonderful life." *(Matthew 11:28-30).*

Jesus desires that we obey God's will, saying. "I seek not my own will, *but the will of him that sent me" (John 4:34)* and "I came from heaven not to do what I want *but what the one who sent me wants" (6:18).*

So persuasive was he that Simon Peter and Andrew left their father; James and John left their fishing nets; and Matthew left his tollbooth to be Jesus' disciples. Women left their sins and men their ambitions to follow him. Saul, the Pharisee, heard Jesus and left everything he had previous believed just to fellowship with Christ.

FELLOWSHIP

Fellowship requires that we agree with one another or have a mutual purpose; "Can two walk together if they are not in agreement?" Our will may not align with another's and conflicts occur. Yet, when our will does not agree with God's and our agenda gets in the way, more problems surface. Until we humble our self, and come into agreement conflicts persist.

Agreement is to not be double-minded, unstable in all our ways (James 1:9), stuck between two opinions. We are not to be undecided about what we do, or ask of God, but sincere and straightforward. Rather than ask for one thing and meaning another we are to ask with confidence (James 4:3). Nor do we ask God as mere lip service, praying because it's the latest thing to do, while our heart is far from him (See Mark 7:5-8). No wonder we never get what we ask from God. Rather than undecided or faithless, simply make a choice, then step out in faith, trusting that the choice is God's will and, if not, he will set us on the right path.

To have the correct outcome means to ask the right question and answer it honestly. And is the end-result worth the price? Is loss of freedom worth breaking the law? While not a Catholic, these questions remind me of the Act of Contrition. "Lord, I confess my sins because I dread the loss of heaven and pains of hell, but *most of all - because I have offended thee my God*".

Is the pleasure of an adulterous affair worth the misery that is certain to follow? Is the loss of heaven worth the pains of hell in rejecting Christ? What consequences will your sin bring?

What is the reward for doing what is right? Are the consequences or the reward worth it to you?

Sometimes the end-result is less obvious but you still have a choice, to be a man or woman after God's own heart or not. To have fellowship with Christ we must have a heart for God.

17. Thought for Today

Voices of Authority

"The authority of Scripture means that the Scriptures are God's word ... to disbelieve or disobey any of Scripture is to disbelieve or disobey God."[16]

420 "Thus says the Lord" are in the NASB[17]. When the prophets said, "Thus says the Lord," they were claiming to be messengers from God himself, and were claiming that their words were the authoritative Word of God.

Paul says "the people who aren't spiritual can't receive these truths from God. It all sounds foolish to them and they can't understand it; only those who are spiritual can understand what the Spirit means" (1Cor.2:14).

Do you accept the authority of the Holy Scriptures, God's word?

Do you live as though you believe the authority of God's word (see quote at the top of the page)? Describe

Think about situations you have been in and any ungodly thoughts and ways that were not loving, patient, kind or considerate.

Whom do you serve, God or self? Describe

How will you serve God after seeking forgiveness - this time?

---

[16] Wayne A. Grudem, Jeff Purswell, Bible Doctrine: Essential Teachings of the Christian Faith, Zondervan, 1999

[17] "NASB" is the New American Standard Bible

ONFESSION OF FAITH

Whoever confesses me before men, the Son of Man will confess him before the angels of God. Whoever denies me will be denied. (Luke 12:8)

Is it not a terrifying thought to imagine ourselves standing before the Lord on judgment day and hear these words? "Depart from me, I never knew you!" To follow Jesus is to confess not only our faith but hope in him so we need not fear that awful denial. Do you follow and confess your faith in thought, word and deed? When called, men and women left everything to follow Jesus. "He said, 'Follow me' and Matthew followed.

Matthew would not have praised himself so, nor would any of the apostles because they chose not to seek recognition for their work. This is not true of many evangelists today. It seems that most seek after fame and fortune. Yet rather than fame, Christ's apostles sought to praise God and communicated by attitude and action, their love of Christ. They knew their purpose was not about serving themselves, but serving Jesus' purpose.

"My sheep hear my voice, and I know them, and they follow me," and later Jesus said, "If anyone loves me, he will keep my word...."

Again Jesus commands "You shall love the Lord your God with all your heart, with all your soul, and your whole mind." Jesus also said, "whoever does not bear his cross (communicate his faith by action) cannot be my disciple. For who intends to build a tower without first counting the cost...?" It seems to me that those who refuse to build their life on the Christ's salvation do so because they *have* counted the cost and refuse to pay the price.

Jesus taught that confessing faith was important, and Paul too proclaimed it: "For to me, to live be Christ, and to die is gain" (Phil 2:21) and "I count all things loss for the excellence of knowing Christ Jesus my Lord, for whom I have suffered *the loss of all things*, and count them as [worthless], that I may gain Christ and be found in him..." (Phil 3:8).

He emphasizes, "you are not your own... but you were bought at a price; therefore glorify God in your body and your spirit, which are God's." Later he instructs in saying, "... do not conform to the world, but be transformed by renewing your mind that you may prove what is good and acceptable and the perfect will of God...." (Romans 12:2)

CONFESS YOUR FAITH

Now how do we confess faith and communicate our commitment to the Lord? The choices we make, of course are important and we must be realistic in that choice, put energy or effort into its pursuit, and communicate Christ in everything we say, think, and do. King David as a young boy had reason to believe he could defeat the giant, Goliath. David lived by the courage of his convictions, which he communicated by his words and by his actions.

"The Lord has rescued me from the claws of lions and bears," he confidently proclaimed "and will keep me safe from this Philistine." Then, David went forth and defeated the giant with nothing but faith in God, and his skills with a slingshot, learned as a shepherd boy.

When David left home to see his brothers in King Saul's army, he didn't know what awaited him. God did and had prepared David for the encounter. Born into a family where he had learned to use a slingshot to protect the sheep to drive away bears and lions, David had courage but he also believed that the situation he faced now was in God's plans for him.

"Has not God sent me for a reason?" He challenged his brother when they tried to send him home. David saw an opportunity and asked other soldiers, "What reward is there for the man who slays this Philistine?" (1Sa 17:26)

The men gave a respectful answer, saying that if any man overcomes him the king will give the man great wealth, and his daughter in marriage, and his father's family will be free, meaning no more taxes. Clearly, David had plenty of motives for killing the giant but his most important motive was his love of God; he was a man after God's own heart (See 1Sa 13:14).

God's purpose for David was as future king over Israel (1Sa 16:1) anointed king as a youth --this may have fueled his brother's jealousy. David's motive, aside from taking away the shame of his people, was the great reward. All of which suggests that no matter God's purpose, personal motivation is important. Similarly, Jesus left his childhood home and family and in the wilderness overcame temptation to fulfill his purpose though his motives were different than David's.

While we often look to earthly rewards but Jesus' desire was that we receive heavenly rewards. Yet, he promised to provide for our needs so our joy would be full here on earth too, and later in heaven.

In his Sermon on the Mount, Jesus spoke of blessings for living right: Blessed are the poor in spirit, for the kingdom of heaven is theirs; Blessed are the pure in heart, for they shall see God; Blessed are the peacemakers, for they shall be called sons of God"; and Blessed are those who have been persecuted for righteousness, for theirs is the kingdom of heaven. Thus, a heavenly reward is for those who follow Jesus and fulfill their purpose.

Jesus declared [as written in the prophet Isaiah's scroll] "The Spirit of the Lord is upon me, having anointed me to preach the gospel to the poor, to proclaim release to the prisoners, give sight to the blind, and to set free those who are oppressed, and proclaim the acceptable year of the Lord" (See Luke 4:17-21) Jesus chose to do as he said; and he fulfilled his purpose, even in difficulties when it might have been easier to simply walk away.

When you left your past to follow Christ, did you leave or do you carry the burdens like a sack of rocks? What choice did you made for Jesus and how do you communicate that choice?

COMMUNICATION

Confessing faith requires communication. The way we communicate our faith is important so that people understand what we have to say though they may not agree with us. Jesus was a communicator who could easily make a point. He knew what was in a person's heart even when a persons' words or actions didn't reveal it (Luke 9:47, John 6:15). Jesus wasn't afraid to rebuke someone when he knew there was a need.

Trey Morgan wrote on how Jesus preached...

JESUS TOLD STORIES AND PAINTED PICTURES:

> *Jesus was a master storyteller. There are some instances when he uses scripture, however, the overwhelming majority of the time he told stories and painted pictures. He taught with a towel, a bird, a flower, a shepherd, a son, a coin, a child, a plank, and other things to make his point. Jesus did not preach many expository sermons. [Though he did preach when it was relevant in-the-moment]*

When 'preaching' so to speak, I often tell stories from my own life that illustrate the point I want to get across; this is what Jesus did only he was more prolific and likely more relevant with metaphors.

Jesus was a communicator:

> *There seems to be two kinds of teachers in this world ... communicators and intellectuals. Communicators take something difficult and make it simple. Intellectuals take the simple and make it difficult. Unfortunately, there are far too many intellectuals trying to communicate the Gospel today. Jesus was a communicator. Preaching must be clear not complex.*

Jesus talked about contemporary things:

> *Jesus was relevant with the things he taught. ... I love the fact that Jesus taught on significant things that people needed to know... like eternity, death, how to treat one another, how to forgive and enter the Kingdom of God. He covered topics like adultery, anger, worry, debt, doubts, faith, giving, greed, honesty, hypocrisy, joy, kindness, lust, marriage, money, parenthood, prayer, sex, slander, speech, stewardship, taxes, trust, unkindness, virtue, wisdom and zeal.*

Jesus' teaching was applicable.

> *You could apply Jesus teachings. He did not just tell you what was wrong he told you how to fix it. Too many sermons are about what-is-wrong.*

> *Instead [how about hearing] the specific steps for getting better? What people need today are not what-you-ought-to sermons and more how-to. When you exhort without giving an explanation it leads to frustration. The fact that you could apply what Jesus said left people challenged when Jesus finished preaching.*

Scripture is the authoritative Word of God but a story or parable often helps other people to apply those teachings, thus, encouraging greater learning.

PARABLES

Parables use images or stories to illustrate a truth or lesson, and a principle being taught; the story is built on words that create a picture describing the point or principle being illustrated. It helps the listener discover the deeper meaning in the illustration such as a comparison: i.e., *"the kingdom of God - is like a mustard seed" (Luke 13:19, 21) or a* figure of speech.

The illustration we use today might differ in some respects from those Jesus used. In suggesting counseling to a friend, I used a car that breaks down and needs expert mechanical help, as an example. So, when a relationship falters and needs help, so one might seek out a Biblical counselor (mechanic).

Jesus often used conflicting dilemmas, situations with a double meaning, to illustrate his point or the principle being taught. First the literal meaning is given, this is apparent to almost anyone, followed by the deeper meaning -- one subtle and less obvious (i.e., a camel going through the eye of a needle versus a person entering heaven – possible but extremely difficult – we must become very small in our humility).

Jesus' word-pictures were taken from daily life so people understood his message. Matthew, Mark, Luke, and John share Jesus' parables who reached the heart of his listeners through their imagination thus, moving them to respond to God's love and truth. A picture can be worth a thousand words if it is relevant to the event, thus it speaks loud and clear, saying what words alone cannot. Jesus used the ordinary to point out the hidden message but only to those who had "eyes to see" and "ears to hear".

So the reading or teaching by way of parable is effective, but we must avoid the details and focus on the facts. While details may be clear, some are obscure. For example, why would a rich man allow a dishonest steward to care for his inventory? (Luke 16:1-8).

Every detail need not fit perfect. However, a parable should present a single particular point. Look for the main point and avoid the details (car repair versus marriage repair). Stories with a contrasting view offered a challenge to the listener and invited them to reflect on what they have heard. Jesus meant for his parables to provoke reflection and a response. To listen with faith and not suppose that we know the answer, then we are more likely to hear and understand what God is speaking to us.

Lest we think that Jesus' teachings were all just stories to amuse people remember his teachings often confronted faulty thinking and brought not only conflict but change. Jesus understood the potential in conflict and he often stirred up conflict to for the purpose of promoting transformation toward a deeper reality and a deeper relationship with God. Confronting and challenging sin and hypocrisy can bring about needed change.

The distinction between *recognizing* behavior that's ungodly and *passing judgment* on others is the state of our heart. Are we aware of another's sins because, in trust they have confided in us, or have we appointed ourselves the "moral police" to justify examining sins in everyone else? Is our goal to help restore or redeem the person's relationship with Jesus, or do we have a hidden agenda to elevate ourselves by condemning others?[18]

Scriptures says in regard to confronting someone else's sin:

> *You can see the speck in your friend's eye but don't see the log in yours. How can you say, "Let me take the speck out of your eye," when you don't see the log in yours? Hypocrite! First, get the log out of your eye. Then you can see how to take the speck out of your friend's. (Luke 6:41-42)*

> *"If a fellow believer sins against you, go and tell him in private what he or she did wrong. If that person listens to you, you have helped to restore the person. But if he or she refuses to listen, go again and take one or two other people with you. ... If he or she refuses to listen, tell the church. If he or she refuses to listen to the church, then treat that person as one who does not believe in God or like a tax collector" (Mat 18:15-17).*

> *"If anyone is caught in any transgression, you who are spiritual should restore him in a spirit of gentleness. Keep watch on yourself, lest you too be tempted. Bear one another's burdens, and so fulfill the law of Christ"* (Galatians 6:1-3, ESV).

While these examples encourage clear dialogue regarding ungodly behavior, they also clarify ways in which those conversations should take place.

In view of our own saved-by-grace stories—when the Holy Spirit impresses upon us a need to confront someone, we do so with honesty, mercy, and humility. Our motive is one of restoration instead of self-righteousness.

∞

---

[18]Lisa Harper "Confronting Sin Versus a Critical Spirit", 8/05/2009, accessed 20Jan2011 from www.christianitytoday.com/biblestudies/questions/friendship/confrontingsin.html?start=2

18. Thought for Today

Have you ever used stories of your own to illustrate a Bible teaching?

Were you able to use the stories effectively? Consider Jesus and imagine how you can share your faith. Write on a separate sheet if needed.

Jesus told stories and painted pictures:

He taught with a towel, a bird, a flower, a shepherd, a son, a coin, a child, a plank, and used other elements from life to make his point

What story from your own or someone else's life might illustrate an idea that you want to get across to another person?

Jesus kept it simple:

Good communicators take something difficult and make it simple while intellectuals (they tend to over-think) take the simple and make it difficult.

What have you tried to communicate and it ended up too difficult for others to understand?

How could you communicate so that it is easier to understand?

JESUS TALKS WERE RELEVANT TO DAILY LIFE:

Jesus taught on: eternity, death, how to love, how to enter God's Kingdom, and also adultery, anger, worry, debt, doubts, faith, giving, greed, honesty, hypocrisy, joy, kindness, lust, marriage, money, parenthood, prayer, sex, slander, speech, stewardship, trust, forgiveness, virtue, wisdom and zeal.

Which of these topics are relevant in your life to discuss with family and learn about from the Scriptures? (Circle those that apply)

What story or parable might you use to make your point?

Jesus' teaching was applicable.

Jesus teachings he did not just tell you what was wrong, he told you what you could do about it (believe; get up and walk; etc.).

Think of a problem and what is wrong (something you talk about all the time but do nothing about). Describe the problem

Now, think about how you can and/or will actually do something about it rather than just talk.

CONFRONTATION

Confrontation is important to change yet we hate it. However until confronted and we understand the problem a solution is not likely. Most of my life, I had many problems and knew there was a problem, but I often had no idea what it was or what to do about it. Suicide was one answer, anger another, and also drugs; a catch 22.

"They know they have a problem!" some say, and that is often true. But, when we do not know or even if we do, confrontation still has the potential to promote the needed change. "Family Interventions" are used to confront addicts and bring about needed change. Change occurs when we know that the other person cares enough to confront in love!

> *When I read in the Bible what Jesus said about sin – the Word confronted me, making me aware that there was hope but I was also ready for change. Thus I readily accepted it. Not everyone is looking for or is ready for change but, until they are confronted, you never know.*

Not everyone wants change; they want the other person to change. Yet, we must learn from confrontation and not avoid it. Rather, embrace what we know is true, do not deny it.

Today the church tolerates all kinds of sin. Often the fear is that if a person is confronted they will leave the church. Paul confronted sin and hypocrisy in the church. Paul insisted the church cast out a sexual sinner until the person repented. Conflict is necessary to help bring about change in those we love. And Jesus commands us to love everyone.

> The Pharisees asked, *"Why do your disciples not live by the tradition of the elders, but eat with unwashed hands?"*
>
> *"Isaiah prophesied correctly about you hypocrites, as it is written: 'This people honor me with their lips, but their heart is far from me. They worship me in vain, teaching the commandments of men as doctrine.'*
>
> *"Listen to me, everyone, and understand. There is nothing outside a person that can defile him by going into him. It is what comes out of a person that defiles him"* (Matt 15:2-11).

Communication involves more than one person and is done in love, which is patient and kind, persistently standing by the other person listening until you have heard their message and they know they have understood even though you may not have agreement. We all know how to communicate but often we do not take the time to listen or honestly express ourselves.

Biblical Guide to Good Communication

An entire class could be taught from social theories of communication but the Holy Bible says it all so we must listen to Jesus who said, "Blessed are your eyes, because they see; and your ears, because they hear" (Matt 13:16). Read, think or consider and meditate on each of these verses.

1. Be a Willing and Careful Listener:
    a. "Be quick to listen and slow to speak or to get angry". Jam 1:19

2. Don't Interrupt a Person Who Is Speaking – Listen Completely:
    a. "Shooting off your mouth before hearing the facts is shameful and foolish. Proverbs 18:13

3. Think Before You Speak
    a. "Good people think before they answer, but the wicked speak evil without thought" Proverbs 15:28
    b. "Fools vent their anger but a wise person holds back". Pro 29:11
    c. "See someone that is hasty in words? There is more hope of a fool than for that person." Proverbs 29:20

4. How You Say Something Is Just As Important As What You Say
    a. "A word fitly spoken is like apples of gold in pictures of silver." Proverbs 25:11
    b. "Let your speech be always with grace, seasoned with salt, that you may know how you ought to answer every man." Col 4:6

5. Timing: There Is A Time To Keep Silent and A Time To Speak
    a. "A time to rend, and a time to sew; a time to keep silence, and a time to speak;" Eccl 3:7
    b. "A man or woman has joy by the answer of his or her mouth: and a word spoken in due season, how good is it!" Pro 15:23

6. Speak The Truth
    a. "Stop lying, speak every man truth with your neighbor: for we are members one of another." Ephesians 4:25
    b. "Lie not one to another, seeing that you have put off the old man with his deeds;" Col 3:9

7. Speak The Truth In Love
    a. "Speaking the truth in love, may grow up into him in all things, which is the head, who is Christ:" Eph4:15

8. What You Say Must Be Sound, Accurate, & Untainted
    a. "Keep your tongue from evil, and your lips from speaking guile (sly or craftiness)." Ps 34:13

9. Avoid Filthy Language, and Language Laced With Innuendos
    a. "No filthiness, foolish talk, jesting, which is not fitting: but give thanks." Eph 5:4

10. Do Not Quarrel or Nag
    a. "Avoiding a fight is a mark of honor; fools insist on quarreling". Proverbs 20:3
    b. "Let all bitterness, and wrath, and anger, and clamor, and evil speaking [against your spouse], be put away from you, with all malice: 32 and be you kind one to another, tenderhearted, and forgiving, as God for Christ's sake forgave you." Eph 4:31-32

11. Don't Get Angry Or Respond In Anger, Keep Cool & Be Gentle
    a. "Those slow to wrath are of great understanding; those of hasty spirit exalt folly." Pro 14:29
    b. "A gentle answer deflects anger but harsh words make tempers flare." Proverbs 15:1

12. When Verbally Attacked or Criticized, Do Not Retaliate
    a. "Do not render evil for evil…: rather blessing; knowing you are called to do so, that you inherit a blessing." 1Peter 3:9

13. When Wrong, Admit and Ask Forgiveness, Do Not Blame Shift
    a. "Confess your faults one to another; pray for one another…" James 5:16
    b. "And the son said unto him, Father, I have sinned against heaven and in thy sight…" Luke 15:21

14. When You Forgive, Choose to Not Remember as does God!
    a. "Be kind one to another, tenderhearted, forgiving one another, even as God for Christ's sake has forgiven you." Ephesians 4:32

19. THOUGHT FOR TODAY

COMMUNICATION FROM PROVERBS

For each of the Proverbs below that you have experienced then, give an example from your own life as shown in the first instance.

1. Our words (what we say and how we say it) have an effect.
    Proverbs 11:9 Pro 12:18 Pro 15:4 Pro 18:8 Pro 18:21

    (Pro 18:8) A man spread an untrue rumor about me that was very hurtful and I retaliate by telling true yet hurtful stories about him.

2. Words come from our heart, so to deal with communication we must also deal with our heart and repent before God. Proverbs 4:20-23 Pro 6:12 Pro 6:14 Pro 6:18 Pro 15:28

3. Too much talk leads to sin. Be sensible and be silent. (Pro 10:19)
    Proverbs 10:19 Pro 11:12 Pro 13:3 Pro 17:27-28 Pro 18:2

4. It's better to live alone in the desert than with a quarrelsome, complaining woman [or man]. Proverbs 21:9

5. A gentle answer deflects anger, but harsh words make tempers flare.
    Proverbs 15:1 Proverbs 25:15

6. Think before you speak.
    Pro 12:18 Pro 14:29 Pro 15:28 Pro 16:32 Pro 21:23 Pro 26:4

7. Losing your temper is foolish; ignoring an insult is smart. Pro 12:16 Pro 19:11

8. Healthy correction is good, and if you accept it, you will be wise.
    Proverbs 15:31 Pro 18:13 Pro 18:15 Pro 19:20

9. Speak the truth, and not what makes you look good or what you think the other person wants to hear.
    Proverbs 12:17 Pro 12:22 Pro 19:5 Pro 26:18-19 Pro 28:23

Share any other communication that comes to mind and how Scripture is helpful in changing your communication and bringing healing.

This chapter on confessing, choices and communication gives guidelines for good communication however in effective expression we will address the emotional issues involved in communication. Thus, learning how to communicate in a respectful way now will help when you learn how to manage your emotions more effectively. Nonetheless, what we say or how we say it involves choices.

Making a Choice

How well we communicate is a choice. Some choices are risky and move us out of our comfort zone but we gain greater freedom. God gave us freewill from the beginning. Adam and Eve used their freewill to eat from the tree knowledge and in doing, gained the ability to know both good and evil. Yet that knowledge destroyed their close relationship with God. God intended from the start that we have choices and accept consequences for he told Adam and Eve the consequences before they chose to disobey. You see, freewill does not exist without choice. God warned them not to partake yet they both chose to disobey and thereby suffer the consequences.

Lot's Choice

When given a choice, Lot looked over the well-watered land and chose the plains of Jordan, what looked like a good place to live, and pitched his tent toward Sodom a wicked city, while Abram went to Hebron and built an altar to the Lord. Lot made his choice based on what looked good, and paid dearly. When at a crossroad, rather than going for the looks good, first seek God and ask him to show you the correct direction then, follow his guidance.

Samson's Choice

Before he was born, God chose Sampson to help deliver Israel from the Philistines. Given great strength, he made bad choices, which led to his downfall. Samson's lust enticed him away from his god-given purpose.

Marriage is an important event and we should choose a partner based not on looks alone, but on Godly wisdom. Paul warned "be not unequally yoked with unbelievers, or believers who are live in sin: "what fellowship does righteousness have with unrighteousness?" (2Cor 6:14)

As a result of Samson's choice, he lost God's favor, was taken prisoner by the Philistines and died tragically, though ultimately, his relationship with the Lord was restored. So before you go in the wrong direction on your own path in life, pray and seek God's will but even more, listen to his guidance.

Ruth's Choice

Naomi's husband and sons had died so she returned home to Bethlehem, and urged her daughters-in-law to return to their families. One returned, but Ruth insisted on staying, and said, "Please don't ask me to leave you! I will go where you go...; your people will be my people, your God my God (Ruth 1:16)

Once you have made the choice for God don't turn back but press on and don't turn back. "A man who puts his hand to the plough and looks back" Jesus said "is not fit for the kingdom of God" (Luke 9:62).

When we choose God but then continue to return to our sinful ways and make excuses, "I couldn't help myself" like disobedient children we suffer the consequences. Ruth by comparison was rewarded for following and for obeying Naomi. Consequently, Ruth married a godly man, had a son, who had a son, whose son was David future king of Israel. Ruth was the grandmother of King David.

The Apostle's Choice

Now as he walked by the Sea of Galilee, [Jesus] saw Simon and Andrew his brother casting a net for they were fishermen. Jesus said to them, "Come follow me, and I will make you fishers of men". Immediately they left their nets and followed.

When he had gone a little farther, Jesus saw James the son of Zebedee, and John his brother, who were in the ship mending nets. He called them and immediately they left their father, and went after him.

These men followed Jesus as did many others, yet there were many who turned away after a time. Of the twelve men chosen to carry his message, ultimately one of the twelve made a poor choice and paid with his life. Peter and Judas both made a poor choice but the end result differed.

Judas' Choice

Judas Iscariot "man of Kerioth," one of the twelve, was their treasurer. His priorities were confused. He thought it was a waste of money when Mary anointed Jesus' feet with expensive oil. But Judas also dipped into their funds for his own use, and did not care about helping the poor.

When Jesus went to Jerusalem before his crucifixion, Judas betrayed him for thirty pieces of silver. After Jesus' arrest, remorseful, Judas returned the money then hanged his self rather than repent. Remorse is not the same as heartfelt repentance, which was Peter's choice.

Judas was not a backslider; he just did not believe; he never knew what it meant to truly be saved or he might have repented. Even so, Jesus chose him knowing the end result, for it was prophesied. Judas knew the Lord intimately, often listened to his teaching, yet he chose suicide and eternal death over Christ and eternal life. (John 5:40).

Being in the right place at the right time, hearing the Bible's teachings, even sitting with the Lord does not always produce a change of heart. Still, Jesus was so patient with Judas! How patient and loving has Jesus been with you? How have you responded? Do you truly believe?

MARY AND MARTHA'S CHOICE

Jesus came to a certain village and a woman named Martha received him into her house. Her sister named Mary, sat at Jesus' feet, and heard his word. Martha was worried about all that had to be done. Finally, she went to Jesus and said, "Lord, doesn't it bother you that my sister has left me to do all the work by myself? Tell her to come help me!" The Lord answered, "Martha, Martha! You are worried and upset about so many things, but only one thing is necessary. Mary has chosen what is best, and it will not be taken away from her." (Luke 10:40-42)

Martha wanted to serve the Lord but got caught up in the nuisance of life rather than taking time out to sit at the Lord Jesus' feet. Mary however sat at the feet of Jesus and listened to the Lord. Do you pay attention to God, or are you busy-busy-busy? Maybe you simply cannot make up your mind; you get stuck and cannot decide which way to go. Is that you?

OUR OPTIONS

> *"Elijah asked the people, 'How long will you stall in making a choice? If the Lord is God, follow him: but if [your god] is Baal, then follow him. The people answered him not.'" 1Kings 18:31*

The people did not answer Elijah for we people often have difficulty making choices. For example, I want God to point me in a clear-as-crystal direction so I do not make a mistake. But that is irresponsible and unfaithful behavior to not trust God. Not doing anything until someone else decides is choosing to be irresponsible. We all run the risk of making the wrong choice even when we do nothing. Those who trust God make choices knowing that God works all things together for good; this is not the same as to deliberately sin.

Nonetheless, there also are times when we must make a choice to follow the Lord, or our own and sin. "No one can serve two masters: either she will hate the one and love the other; or he will be true to one and despise the other. You cannot serve God and money [lust]" (Luke 6:13). Choose today, lust and the acquisition of wealth over your desire for God.

Those who are lost think the Scriptures are foolish and a decision is not necessary, that they can continue on their own selfish way. But Jesus said, "You must be born *of the spirit* to see the kingdom of God!" (John 3:5) and "Those who believe are not condemned but those who refuse to believe are condemned already" (Mark 16:16) Being born of the spirit is not the same as being born of water, which is an analogy for our first birth. We must become of the spirit to even understand about heaven.

Thus, the choice is not simply deciding what we eat or wear today, it also decides who we are and how we live, whether we follow Jesus and make a difference, or more important, where we spend eternity. The choice to serve God or not decides all this for all time. When our heartfelt choice is to follow God we know deep within our heart when our choice is of the flesh (of human nature) as opposed to the spirit (of Gods nature). If we indeed follow Jesus we have Gods nature within us.

Are you prepared to totally follow Christ? If so, your faith, talents, abilities, and skills will all be used by God. Even simple skills can help you fulfill your god-given purpose and find joy in its attainment. This spiritual growth takes place slowly, one day at a time. God created the heavens and earth one day at a time; then he looked and "saw that it was good" at the end of each day; he found pleasure in the accomplishment.

God created the world and all that is in it over a six day period with a seventh day for rest. We also need a plan to work on six days a week with one day of rest. But we must have the skills to achieve. Then, having the courage of our convictions fear does not dominate. Fear comes from our Adamic (human) nature—faith comes from the Christ (spiritual) nature. To truly believe and follow Christ he in us and we are of the spirit. This takes more than courage; faith is required and fellowship with people of faith.

The people we choose as friends, those who encourage make a difference. Thus, a wise person seeks those who encourage them as did young David, and avoids those who discourage. Winners hang out with winners! Thus, like David, good friends encourage and that helps us build courage.

David spoke with King Saul and offered to kill Goliath. He had courage. After convincing the king that he could do it they finally agreed to let him. Saul gave him his own armor and sword, but he did not know how to use them; they were too heavy and David was unskilled in their use. He took them off and went to fight with what he knew how to use, a simple slingshot. David chose his friends wisely, as well as the tools needed to get the work done that he agreed to do. In this instance it was to kill a giant.

CHOICE OF FRIENDS

Jesus selected several men as his disciples, men persistent in even the face of adversity, men willing to believe and follow him. Even so, while Jesus' disciples understood hardship and believed in him, it was difficult for them to understand and always be there for him; as in the Garden of Gethsemane, they ran away.

In spite of their failure, Jesus did not reject or condemn these men, rather he forgave them. He knew their heart was in the right place, yet recognized their frailties and forgave. Recognizing that the spirit indeed is willing but the flesh is weak, Jesus gave his disciples a plan of prevention; he said, watch and pray (Mark 14:38).

Jesus knew that being part of God's family was important; those who do the will of God are God's family (John 1:6). So we fellowship with those who help us overcome our sin as we struggle to live rightly remembering that "We wrestle not against flesh and blood but against principalities and powers and spiritual wickedness."(Ps 37:5)

Knowing our limitations we win the battle with God on our side. And as David, focus on your strengths not your weaknesses for the battle ahead. David's knew he was limited in soldiering skills, and that he did not have the support of some family members, yet the skills he had learned and practiced over the years worked for him, in spite of his limitations. David's strength was in his love for and faith in God. He illustrated the courage of his convictions even when those around him did not believe in him by winning the battle.

My neighbor is a lover of animals. Recently her older dog developed a reoccurring illness. Living on a very limited income, three years ago she charged over three thousand dollars for surgery on the dog. Now the illness has returned and to add three thousand dollars to her credit for more surgery is beyond her financial means.

As a Christian ---and she was a healer at one time –yet she is unable to trust God for the healing. Has he brought her to this place? To see her go through the choices she has is agony. She called me to talk about it because she believes my faith is what keeps me from being ill and is what has healed my dog. Of course, I had a dog die four years ago from cancer too but that she overlooks.

Now the second time I had a dog that was ill, I also could not afford the vet debt and so trusted God. However, I did everything I knew to help my dog while trusting God to heal her. She got better.

We have to do our part within our own ability and our level of faith, not someone else's. Faith is one of my spiritual gifts and I exercise it every chance I get. Then doing our best while praying for God's will, and nothing changes, it's time for other choices.

Spiritual gifts are to be used according to the degree of our faith. Thus, we fix our eyes on Jesus, the author and perfecter of our faith, who for joy endured the cross, despising the shame, and sat down at the right hand of the throne of God. - Heb 12:2

If we have not through prior experience built our faith in healing or any other gift then a life or death event is not the time, unless other healers or people of faith are present! Very likely this is the reason we have doctors and veterinarians. God uses their talents and skills when our faith is insufficient.

Having a dream, belief and faith in God, and a support network helps you to pursue the dream. So, what natural talents and skills do you possess that will help ensure your success? Who are in your support network?

David believed in God and loved him with a passion that sent him to slay a giant, yet he was also aware of the talent and skills he had needed to accomplish the job. God had prepared him over the years in a way that provided for that very day, as well as the days to come.

Had David used unfamiliar implements, unskilled in its use, in trying to defeat Goliath with a sword and shield, he would likely have failed. After all, the giant had the same implements of war, and was better skilled in their use, and had greater size and strength.

David overcame these intimidating odds with his faith, god-given talents, and learned skills to confront the odds and obtain victory.

So, consider significant events and people in your life that have provided you with strengths and skills that may be of use now and in the future. Many times we do not realize that we have any strengths or skills but everyone has some. Con men are smooth talking able to convince people to do something not in their best interests. How we use our talents and skills and gifts to serve or not is a choice we make every day.

CHOOSE TO SERVE

There are many choices and most important is the choice to serve God. If married, you have the choice to serve our spouse. Then of course, there we have our children, employers, neighbors, and the list goes on. Within these choices is the attitude we have toward any person, and the choice to communicate well and to behave a certain way in spite of temptations.

While some choices are difficult and rebellion easier, obedience is far simpler when we realize it is God we desire to please not ourselves. Thus, our choice is made not because we have to but because we desire to please the one who first loved us, and gave his all for us.

Choosing to serve and to please God means we make choices to overcome attitudes and behaviors and styles of communication that are unloving and unwise. Attitudes, behaviors and/or communication can have serious consequences when we do not follow in the way of the Lord.

Now, begin to confront the choices you make to alter the consequences you now endure in order to enjoy God's peace.

20. THOUGHT FOR TODAY

The day is sunny and it's hot sitting in the car, yet I wait for my son who has stopped to see a friend. The reason isn't important. Then I see him. Tall and muscular with long brown hair and bell-bottom trousers. I haven't seen anyone wearing those for years. He walks toward me with confidence unusual for most men. Only years later, would I realize that like everything else in his life it was all a bluff. At the time, though, I wouldn't have cared. All I saw was a strong young body and hearing his voice, deep and soft as warm butter, I was captured.

CHOICES: WHAT ATTRACTS YOU?

Initially, Samson is attracted to Delilah for her looks. Some say that men can tell all about a woman's heart too after they meet them for the first time so how come Samson didn't know Delilah was a greedy shrew? She pestered Samson to learn the secret of his strength because the Philistines offered her money. Exasperated he finally gave in and told her, which led to his immediate downfall and eventual death.

Have you been tricked into revealing something about yourself and then, later, you were hurt badly by someone because of it? Describe

Lot saw the well watered plains of Jordon and set his tent toward Sodom. Back in Egypt he had gotten a taste of the good life and he wanted more of the tasty things life in the big city offered. God eventually destroyed Sodom and Gomorrah because of the immoral life in those cities.

In which direction is your life headed? Have you gone as did Abraham to serve the Lord, or to serve an immoral worldly life style? Describe

Ruth followed Naomi and her God because she was attracted to her faith while Boaz was later attracted to Ruth because of her kindness to Naomi. Both women had fine qualities that made them attractive to others, none of which seemed to be greed and petty selfishness.

What attracts you to people, a kind and generous heart or other things?

What attracts people to you, a kind and generous heart or other things?

Martha had a sister, Mary, who sat at Jesus' feet and listened as he talked. But Martha was busy and distracted with serving, and she went up to him and said, 'Lord, don't you care that my sister leaves all the work to me? Tell her to help.' Jesus answered, 'Oh Martha, don't be such a worry work about all this stuff. There's only one thing that's important, and Mary has chosen that good thing [a relationship with God] - she will always have to rely on' " (Luke 10:39-42).

Do you get so busy with the 'stuff' of life that you have no time for Jesus? Describe

What's your relationship like with Jesus?

    1. Warm and cozy   2. Warm then cold   3. Cold and distant

What reason did you rate this question as you did? Describe

How would you rate yourself to the following?

    1 –Agree   2 –Neutral   3 –Disagree

My relationship with Jesus might improve if I read the Bible more.

My relationship with Jesus might improve if I prayed more.

**ELIGHT IN THE LORD**

"Delight yourself in the Lord and he will give you the desires of your heart." (Psalm 37:4)

Many Christians think this verse means God will give them what they want and satisfy their every desire, if they delight in him. But in this context here, the Scripture means to be dependent on God, to receive pleasure from him. Do you get pleasure being in prayer with God? Would you like to spend more time with God in worship, in the Word, in prayer, or with other people playing sports or watching television? There's nothing wrong with watching television or enjoying sports as long as God comes first in our life.

How does one take delight in the Lord so the Lord delights in that person? Do we sternly discipline ourselves to do what *must* be done? Perhaps we put our effort into trusting God's love to forgive even our wishy-washy attitude?

Initially, this chapter was about discipline to achieve a certain end result. But I knowing that discipline if too rigorous --an 'I have to' rather than an 'I want to'—can become a burden. When that happens, my self-defeating behaviors kick in and failure soon follows. "I have to lose weight" turns into an immediate gain of five pounds, or so it seems. "I have to be nice to not-very-nice-people, and I'd find myself annoyed with minor things, and then, become angry. It was a losing battle.

In reading Scripture and thinking about what it genuinely means to be a delight to the Lord, I soon took great pleasure in doing what was needed. Often that means disciplining my attitude, behavior, and communication, not because I 'have to' but because I want to please God. This does not always work well because I let certain things bother me in the extreme.

One of the strategies I often use to 'remind myself' to be more loving is a "love poster" for my fridge, and as a reminder to not swear or be critical, I've posted Philippians 4 on my wall "whatever is true, noble, just, pure, and lovely, whatever things are of good report, if there is any virtue and if there is anything praiseworthy think on these". (See Appendix F)

Yet, when I fail to 'perform' —though I feel my own failure acutely —God does not feel distress because he knows me better than I know myself. God forgives my shortcomings and sins when I sincerely repent. My goal, then, is to accept his forgiveness and truly delight myself in the Lord, for God delights in our sincere efforts done in faith.

Being a delight to the Lord is an experience for true believers throughout the Old and the New Testament.

One thing have I asked of the Lord and will I seek after: that I may dwell in the house of the Lord all the days of my life, to gaze upon the beauty of the Lord and to inquire in his temple. (Psalm 27:4)

As a deer pants for flowing streams, so pants my soul for you, O my God. My soul thirsts for God, for the living God. When shall I come and appear before God? (Ps 42:1-2)

God, you are my God; earnestly I seek you; my soul thirsts for you; my flesh faints for you, as in a dry and weary land where there is no water. (Ps 63:1)

Indeed, I count everything as loss because of the surpassing worth of knowing Christ Jesus my Lord... (Philippians 3:8)

Do you desire to dwell with and gaze upon God's beauty? Does your soul, like the deer, thirst for God, and your flesh faint for lack? When we say this and mean it, then we are a delight to the Lord, and blessings follow such as:

"My heart rejoices in the Lord; my horn is exalted. I smile at my enemies, because I rejoice in your salvation" (1Sa 2:1-10)

Hannah spoke of her joy in the Lord who helped her achieve satisfaction. Horns were used by animals for defense and attack, and they symbolize strength. Thus, Hannah's horn was the strength that came to her from the Lord because he had answered her prayer.

> *God blesses those who refuse evil advice and won't follow sinners who sneer at God. Instead, the Law of the Lord delights them, and they think about it day and night. They are like trees growing beside a stream, trees that produce fruit in season and always have leaves. These people succeed in everything they do.* (Psalm 1:1-3)

This Psalm describes the person who leads an untarnished and therefore a prosperous life in obedience to God and contrasts him with the ungodly, those who will perish (v4). Our friends and associates can have a profound influence upon us, often in very subtle ways. If we maintain friendships and follow those who mock God, we may become indifferent to God's will and sin. True friends will help you draw closer to God.

> *Commit your way to the Lord and trust also in him; and he will bring it to pass. He will bring forth your righteousness as the sun (Psalm 37:4)*

To *delight* in any person or in God is to experience pleasure and joy in their presence. To delight in the Lord we must know him well; that knowledge comes by his Word as well as the stories of others who have experienced God. Knowledge of God's great love for us will indeed give us delight. Thus, to devote ourselves to the Lord is to trust everything to his care. We trust our lives, families, jobs, possessions—to his guidance. We believe he cares for us better than we can; that is being a true disciple of Christ.

Often, we devote ourselves superficially. We say that everything we do is for the Lord yet, we do it for our own benefit. Or we devote our life to God then take it back when we want to control whatever does not go our way. Often, we are so devoted that we act as if everything depends on God, which it does, however we must work as if everything depends upon us.

Many have found that when focused on God, in the revelation of his Word, spending large amounts of time in prayer, remembering the joy of salvation in Jesus Christ, then their delight in God is always greater. So the key is to spend time in his Word, in prayer and in worship thanking him for his son and that great sacrifice. Are you completely devoted to God and fulfilling his purpose in your life, as a disciple of Christ?

How Devoted are You?

The steps of a good man are ordered by the Lord and he delights in his way. Though he falls, he shall not be completely cast down; for the Lord upholds him with his hand --1Corinthians 6:18-20.

The person in whom God delights is one who follows him, trusts him, and is devoted to obeying his will. God watches over and makes firm every step that person takes. If you would like to have God direct your way, then in devotion, seek him before stepping out in faith. All too often we expect God to speak directly to us and give us what we ask for or explicit instructions, and yet ignore the open doors, running head long into them, or we cry and struggling uselessly, then give up. Yet Lord says,

"Let not the wise glory in their wisdom, nor the mighty in their might, nor the rich glory in their riches; but let them glory that understand and know that I am the Lord, doing loving kindness, judgment, and righteousness... in these I delight."(1Sa 17:37)

Being a Delight

Scripture says we delight ourselves in the Lord if we keep the Sabbath holy, and honor it by not doing our own thing or gossiping then we are a delight to God. Jesus said, "Everything and everyone that the Father has given me will come to me, and I won't turn anyone away. I didn't come from heaven to do what I want! I came to do what the Father wants... to make certain that none of them will be lost (John 6:37-40). If this is not enough reason, know that God always has our best interests at heart; he is always with us; he never fails us; he leads, guides, and directs us.

When confused and uncertain, then, "In all your ways acknowledge him and he will direct your paths" (Pro. 3:6). Instead of aimlessly wandering through life, call upon the Lord, and you will "see the works of God, he is awesome in his doing towards the sons of men". All of our thoughts are known to God... God is always at work for the good of everyone who loves him. They are the ones God has chosen for his purpose, and he has always known who his chosen ones would be. (Rom 8:27-29).

Confused and uncertain describes most of my life. When confused and uncertain now, I trust in the Lord, even when I do not entirely understand how it will make a difference. I trust anyway and it does make a difference, yet it brings the peace of mind I seek. Faith with God is vital.

The greatest blessing we can receive is to know God and have pleasure in knowing him. Eternal life is ultimately all about knowing God and the Christ, whom he sent (See John 17:3.) The greatest blessing imaginable is for God's face to shine upon us (Numbers 6:22-27.) in delight. Paul was willing to give up everything (See Phil 3:8.) Are you? If not, are you delighting yourself in the Lord wholeheartedly?

Often, things begin smoothly, and it is easy to delight in God but then, when life seems to go awry, it becomes harder to delight in God. At times, I become angry and resentful. Because I am very aware of God and of the example I set for others, I always return to the Lord and keep on trusting that if I delight myself in him, everything works out.

So, be anxious for nothing, but in everything by prayer and supplication, make your requests known, thanking God for answering prayer before it has been answered, at least as far as you can see. Then the peace that passes all understanding will keep you through Christ Jesus. (Phi 4:6-7)

The word "delight" often is used to describe the relationship that we are to have with God but also to describe God's relationship toward us.

Delight yourself in the Lord (earnestly desire him alone) and he will give you the desires of your heart (Psalm 37:4)

I will delight myself in your laws; I will not forget your word (Ps 119:16)

Your testimonies also are my delight and my counselors (v24)

You light a lamp for me. The Lord, my God, lights my darkness. (Ps 18:28)

21. THOUGHT FOR TODAY

One day, I took a group of people whitewater rafting. These folks did not expect to even get their feet wet and some of the females came in high heels while the men were in blue jeans and sweatshirts. A real no-no!

We put them in plastic waste bags to stay as dry as possible in their swimsuits and issued booties since most of them came without tennis shoes. (No one had given them information about this trip) One asked if they were in over their heads. I looked at them--they were in their 40s and 50s-- and saw that they were all in good physical shape.

So then I drew a picture of waves and rocks and showed them how we maneuver the boats through the obstacles and the rapids. I warned of possible capsize and talked about falling in. Some groaned because they did not want to get wet and I offered to let anyone who wanted opt out, but no one did!

We prepared them with lifejackets and safety talk as we got in the boat. As I reassured them, the river, in a gentle flowing motion, caught us, rocking and lulling us ever so smoothly towards the first rapid.

I shouted "forward paddle!" Everyone was flailing. I steered towards the wave, missing the boulder and smoothly entered the "V" splashing the entire group. Soon everyone was laughing and one woman tossed teasing comments forward about the "weak" paddling skills of others. It was clear they had conquered their fears.

When we stopped for lunch, the group came over to me and thanked me for an eye-opening experience. The river trip ended and I know they will never forget that trip in their lifetimes. --James—

The Scriptures prepares you for life's troubled waters. However, rather than garbage bags we put on the whole armor of God.

Do you feel prepared to continue your journey?

Are there still waves that toss you about now and then? Describe.

What about the rocks you smash against now and then. Have you become more adept at steering around them? Describe

Life is not an encounter or bonding group. Life is a battlefield, and we must be armed for battle. You can stand against Satan's demonic forces - only if you're clothed with the whole armor of God.

____ Do you test everything by the truth of God's Word?

____ Are you void of offense toward God and other persons? Then the devil has nothing to use against you. Jesus wore it at all times (Isa 59:17).

____ Are your feet prepared with the gospel of peace? Following the Savior, bearing glad tidings and peace keeps you safe (Isa 52:7; Rom 10:15).

____ Do you wear the shield of faith, confidence in God and His word? With temptations, with adverse circumstances, faith says, "I believe God."

____ With God's helmet of salvation the Christian is undaunted for the final victory is won; "If God be for us, who can be against us?" (Rom 8:31)

____ Do you have the sword of the Spirit, the word of God to defeat Satan? Three times Jesus quoted the word of God—verses the Holy Spirit gave for that occasion (Luke 4:1-13). The word of God is not the whole Bible, in this instance, but that portion which best suits the occasion.

____ Prayer is not part of the armor but the spirit in which we don the armor and face the enemy; it is inspired and led by the Holy Spirit.

What do you need to better defend against the demonic forces in your life?

Rivers of Life

How do we negotiate the rivers' rapids?

One way is to learn to better manage our attitude, behavior, and communication. Arguments often become walls of rock that we stubbornly run up against and often have trouble getting around. Getting through the difficult situations requires a plan of action and follow-through. First design a plan, after prayerfully deciding what needs to change. Seek guidance from a knowledgeable person to help guide you.

That's where a biblical counselor helps. Then, discipline your actions to do whatever is needed to put your plan into action and complete it. Trust God to lead you. When you turn to the right or to the left (enticing sights along the river distract you), you will hear a voice saying, "No. This is the way! Now follow it." [This is your river guide in action] (Isaiah 30:21)

Also, perceive your idols of silver and gold as garbage [cluttering the boat]; throw them away like filthy rags. Things you see as being precious may need to be changed [high heels for tennis shoes) so your attitude or behavior, and how you respond to the rapids can carry you on without mishap.

Those who are faithful to the Lord and call upon him for help he will answer and get them through the whitewater rapids. But a person must be sensitive to God's Word and heed his leading. Prioritize your life and put God first, then your spouse, children, career and friends.

Setting Priorities:

"Seek first the kingdom of heaven and its righteousness...."

Setting priorities helps our focus. Seek first the kingdom of heaven, and all else will be given to you; this is God's promise.[19]

God formed us before we were even born and purposed a plan for our life, but we chose our attitude, behavior and how we communicate with God and other persons. Do you know where you are going - your purpose and what to do so you have a walk worthy of the Lord? God shows the way and leads us on, but we must be prepared to follow his lead.

---

[19] Zach 11:12-13, "If you think it best, pay me; if not, keep it." So they paid thirty pieces of silver. The Lord said, "Throw it to the potter "the handsome price at which they priced me! So I took the thirty pieces of silver and threw them into the house of the Lord the potter. Psalm 41:9, Even my close friend, whom I trusted, he who shared my bread, has lifted up his heel against me.

SEARCH ME OH LORD

Search me, O God, and know my heart; try me, and know my thoughts, and see if there is any wicked way in me; and lead me in the way everlasting. (Psalm 139:23)

We ask to be searched but we must be willing to listen and hear his answer. Scripture says to examine our ways (See Matthew 26:41). We examine our attitude, behavior and how well we communicate. How do you behave, wise or unwise? Examine yourself. This is for all believers because God says that *"if my people,* who are called by my name, will humble themselves and pray and seek my face, and turn from their wicked ways, I will hear from Heaven and will forgive their sin and will heal their land. (2Ch 7:14, italics added)

The well-being of our home, our family, and our nation is the responsibility of God's people. Being a delight to the Lord and a living example of love is not a matter of discipline but faith at work. Do you focus on your needs or on the needs of other people? While we should care for our self, we should not be so self-focused that we cannot see beyond our own needs, either.

Often being self-focused leads to anger, resentment, and depression while an outer-focus not only helps others but also ourselves. Many people have come to counseling depressed, focused on one problem after another of their own that they cannot see anything but their own misery.

Many a problem lifts as soon as a person gets out of their misery and into someone else. Thus, focusing outside ourselves running straight for our goal and achieving Gods will is the key.

In Paul's race to achieve the goal, he ran with certainty straight for the mark - *to win souls for Christ.* For this purpose each one of us are born into Christ. To achieve this goal requires discipline, so we put aside not only that which is innocent and above reproach but whatever can distract us from our goal. Paul's strength was in Christ but he was also a man after God's own heart, therefore, he subdued his flesh to resist temptation.

Therefore, we also need obedience to God, self-knowledge, and the will to discipline our lives. While discipline can be difficult, those who deny self for God's higher purpose find it is easier to lay aside their own desires in favor of Christ's. Thus, we change our sin behavior for more godly behavior.

PATTERNS OF OUR LIFE

Often, the patterns of our life are not everything we desire. Over the years, habits develop that lead to undisciplined behavior. The commandments are to love God and love one another yet, we are harsh and critical, rather than loving. Love, then, becomes a habit to be instilled within us, especially when we feel justified in being impatient, angry, harsh and critical.

How to love varies? "Silver and gold have I none", Peter confessed, but what he had, he gave, healing in love (Mark 3:32-35). We might think that to give up and sacrifice our needs for others is a marvelous thing, but without love, we gain nothing. Great sacrifice often results from the desire for pride, power, and prestige. We deceive our self as to our genuine intentions. Deep down, sacrifice is for the attention, the applause, and the authority we truly love. Only a loving heart can profit. 1Corinthians 13 describe Jesus' kind of love: "love one another; as I have loved you, you also love one another."

Love is kind and patient, never jealous, boastful, proud, rude, not selfish or quick tempered. Love does not keep a record of wrongs but rejoices in the truth, not in evil. Love supports, is loyal, hopeful, and trusting (vv 4-7).

Jesus himself is an example of love, he who came not to be served, but to serve and he showed love by teaching, feeding, and healing in all the ways described in 1 Corinthians. Jesus responded to the needs of the people, not always giving what a person wanted, but what their overall health required, body, mind, and soul so they could become spiritually mature.

The apostle, Paul, knew he was not perfect, but Christ had a hold of him, so he ran the race and pursuing the eternal prize. So too, God will bless you if you pursue Godly perfection though you have not yet achieved it. In our struggle toward spiritual maturity, as we put the skills we learn into practice, we become more like Jesus, and light the way for others.

LIGHT OF THE WORLD

Jesus was the light of the world while here on earth (John 9:5). He also said, *"You are the light of the world. A city that is set on a hill cannot be hidden. Nor do they light a lamp and put it under a basket... and it gives light to all who are in the house. Let your light so shine before men, that they may see your good works and glorify your Father in heaven"* (Mat 5:14-16).

As we read the Scripture, convicted of sin, we must take action to correct our behavior. What we cannot accomplish, alone, God can. This is not about making a list to slavishly follow rather, obey your heart desire to follow God.

Legalism over rules is the very thing Christ abolished so we live in obedience to God on a personal level. So, believe that with God all things are possible; communicate belief in thought, word, and deed; and then, discipline your attitude, behavior and speech so that you are truly a reflection of Christ.

"Train yourself to be spiritually fit. Physical discipline has little value, but spiritual discipline is of value in everything" (1 Tim 4:7-8, paraphrased)

In obedience to this command, every Christian should pursue intimacy with Christ through the practice of the spiritual disciplines found in Scripture, but not measure this pursuit by rules that aren't in the Bible.

While the Scripture encourages us to engage in the spiritual disciplines, we don't want to pursue them legalistically. Legalism is the emphasis on works in our relationship to God. It measures our spiritual growth by the number, frequency, duration, amount of time we spend in prayer, and so forth. This has no scriptural basis. To believe that we must read four verses in the Bible on a daily basis is legalism.

The opposite of legalism is license. We live as though our freedom in Christ has *no* measurable standards.

"Stand fast therefore," says Galatians 5:1, "in the liberty by which Christ has made us free, and do not be entangled again with a yoke of bondage."

On the other hand, the same heart-changing grace of God is at work in us "both to will and to do for His good pleasure" (Philippians 2:13). As such, we sincerely *want* to discipline ourselves toward more godliness. Thus, biblical disciplines (i.e., Bible study, prayer, worship, fellowship, and fasting) we can measure in one way or another for that purpose.

To measure some aspects of our disciplines to simplify our spiritual life or to hold ourselves accountable to certain goals, then there are some benefits. Even the most painstaking practice of the spiritual disciplines is not legalistic when the motive is to increase our spiritual maturity, for the glory of God so as to be more Christ-like. [20]

---

[20] Donald S. Whitney, *Simplify Your Spiritual Life* (Colorado Springs, Colo.: NavPress, 2003). Accessed 20Jan2011 from http://biblicalspirituality.org/wolegal.html

22. THOUGHT FOR TODAY

Read the priorities for non-Christians and Christians and Rate yourself both as a non-Christian and as a Christian - even though you are a Christian!

1. Always   2. Usually   3. Sometimes   4. Rarely   5. Never

The Non-Christian's Priorities are usually:

1. Leave home, get through school and choose the right career.
2. Earn a good income and accumulate wealth and property, etc.
3. Meet and choose the right marriage partner; first, date and often sex with various partners until the right one comes along.
4. To raise children properly is an increasingly important priority while moving along a career path is important for the newly married.
5. Go to church and/or community involvement is a lower priority.
6. Retirement, old age, dying---and cease to exist ultimately. Nothing is known about an after-life, and today very few people believe we are accountable to God and will face judgment.
7. Life is a battle just to survive and the individual must win to survive!

The non-Christian's world-view is about success, happiness and pleasure based on worldly values. Each one has their own dreams, unconcerned for God's plans.

CHRISTIAN'S GOALS BY CONTRAST:

1. To know God better daily through personal time within the Word as is defined throughout the Bible.
2. To develop a solid prayer life for growth and know what God is doing in the world nearby and at large.
3. Be available to God for the work of His kingdom without question. God is giving in love, which is dying to self and set aside worldly pursuits
4. Have fellowship with other believers and do not neglect assembling with one another together..."
5. Be as salt and light in this age, (flavor the world wondrously).
6. Love God with all our heart, mind, soul, and love our neighbors as our self. "Love covers a multitude of sins." "Love is fulfilling of the love."
7. Our battle is spiritual. We must discern between flesh and spirit and forsake worldly ways of dealing with evil

How did you rate yourself, primarily non-Christian or Christian? What is it you would like to change about your rating and how would you do it?

A Disciplined Life

For a Godly life we live a well-disciplined life in obedience to God's will and ways. Discipline is not about a fixed routine. Discipline is about putting your life in order to where health, work, study, celebration, and relationships etc. are in balance.

Benefits of discipline:

Rate these statements true or false

1. Well Organized. You manage your time well and take time to enjoy yourself and celebrate life. Your life is less chaotic and it makes sense.   T   F

2. Well Done. Chaos and stress are limited and work is doing 100% of whatever you are supposed to do at home, at work, or at play. You love to study or do what you do because you are good at it and you enjoy it.   T   F

3. Well Celebrated. Your mind is free from clutter. You celebrate responsibly, sleep well at night and you, mostly, enjoy getting up mornings.   T   F

When discipline becomes routine:

As discipline becomes routine, involvement in life may come to a halt

1. You hate life, are not interested in work, studies or home, and have lost interest in doing what you have always wanted and enjoyed doing.   T   F

2. Boredom has entered your life and you don't like the atmosphere at work, home, play, or at school where before you once were so happy.   T   F

3. Everything is messed up in your life. Chaos reigns supreme.   T   F

1.   Do you live a well-discipline life?

2.   Do you live a routine boring life?

3.   What would you like to change?

Discipline is not about following a set of rules but arranging your life so you enjoy the well-rounded world God created for us to enjoy and not to become caught up in routines that destroy creativity and joy.

Christ Fulfills The Law

"Do not think that I came to destroy the Law or the Prophets. I did not come to destroy but to fulfill (Matt 5:17). "Bear one another's burdens", Paul said "and so fulfill the law of Christ" (Gal 6:2). What is the law of Christ? Jesus said, "A new command I give you, that you love one another; as I have loved you…" (John 13:34).

Jesus showed attitude and actions how the law was intended to be applied; he loved people, emphasized the importance and the rewards of following these commands, and he taught others to do the same. He did this, not just by his word, but as a heartfelt act of obedience.

Discipline in devotion to God is a delight to the Lord and is what is needed to change one's attitude and behavior. However when discipline fails and our inadequacies do not measure up to the task, we can humbly turn to God, and know his sufficiency brings us to the mercy seat and his grace.

Regardless of our deficiency, God is always sufficient and is the answer to all our prayers. Thus, we need never have an angry resentful attitude that leads harsh words. Words can cut the heart, and a slamming door hits hard as it reverberates in our lives and puts us in danger of judgment

Danger Of Judgment

"If you know someone is angry with you, leave and go make amends so you can return to God and your gifts be received" (Matt 5:22-25). If you fail to resolve the anger, often this is the first stone thrown into the pond. Those ripples then, can lead to murder. Often Christians believe anger itself is a sin but Scripture does not say so. What we do with anger is the problem. Jesus looked at the people with anger, *grieved by their hard hearts* (Mar 3:5).

Anger expressed in violence toward oneself or another is sin. Depression is repressed anger (anger we deny); bitterness and resentments are anger also expressed inappropriately. Thus, we quickly bring about resolution.

Mercy and Love

Numb now. The agony from the whip has lessened. He cannot feel pain or the pull of nails upon his hands that hold him to the cross. Blood trickles, still, a slight and almost annoying irritant upon his cold sensitive skin. So focusing beyond the pain and Jesus' annoyance at such a petty thing, he looks at those who stare, or play dice below.

A rush of compassion fills his heart as Jesus realizes, 'they do not know nor understand what it is they are doing'. If he could have wept yet said "Father, forgive them for they know not what they do" (Luke 23:34).

Jesus' kind mercy is a love that most of us cannot even imagine, never mind loving those who would misuse us given half a chance. Nonetheless, being like Christ we resist evil and give no harm, rather we give more than is taken or asked of us; we even go the extra mile and in our agony, to forgive them, for truly, *they know not what they do.*

The question, then, is: "Am I to forgive and tolerate abuse from my friends, or spouse?" While we are to forgive --forgiveness is covered in chapter six--- always, this does not mean we allow people to destroy us. On the contrary, it is expected that we will express righteous anger at the hardhearted and confront their lack of compassion as did Jesus, or even leave the situation (See Luke 4:28-30).

A roommate had an emotional crisis after moving into the house. His behavior was anxiety provoking and abusive. In the past, I would have become angry, argued with him then called the police, and evicted him from the house. However, over time, I have grown some with the Lord and believed he was here for a purpose. Thus, I dealt with the situation by stating the facts as I observed them, did not discuss the situation, insisted he calm down, and gave a conditional eviction notice.

The condition was that if he chose to calm his emotions, and behave responsibly, he could stay. He became upset and I removed myself from the situation without further discussion. The next day, he was very quiet so I waited to see how things progressed. A day passed and another night. The second day, he arrived at my door apologetic and repentant. Better yet, his behavior changed for the better and he became an excellent roommate.

Lest you think I was calm, cool, and collected throughout, let me disavow that notion. I remained on edge. Yet, I managed the situation calmly.

The Scripture was Psalm 27:14: "Wait on the Lord: be of good courage, and he will strengthen your heart: wait, I say, on the Lord". Thus, in patience and kindness we are able to show others God's love.

TO LOVE, HONOR AND OBEY

Love – The New Testament (Greek) defines love using two different words. The most commonly used Greek word translated "love" in the New Testament is "agape." The Greek "phileo" is a "brotherly love" or a soul love (where we connect through our emotions), experienced both by believers and non-believers. This love is represented by God's love for us. It is a non-partial, sacrificial love best exemplified by God's provision for our rebellion:

"God so loved the world that he gave his only Son, that whosoever believes in him should not die, but has eternal life. (John 3:16)

The gift of God's son was a provision for sin and was given to all, regardless of who they are. God's love is unconditional. In contrast, human love is usually about how a person behaves toward us.

Agape love is founded upon familiarity and direct interaction and it requires a relationship with God through Jesus Christ, since the non-regenerate and unsaved soul is unable to love unconditionally. Agape love sacrifices self and gives to others, unconditionally, expecting nothing in return.

People often insist their love is unconditional yet, more often than not, they expect something in return. When no reward is forthcoming, feeling hurt and unappreciated, many become angry and seek revenge. Even believers find agape love difficult, until they gain a measure of spiritual maturity.

Our Lord asked Peter, "Do you love me?" Three times he asked him. In asking a third time, he pushes Peter to really consider the state of his heart. Peter maybe wondered 'what does he want from me?' But Jesus is merely clarifying Peter's love so that when he gives him instructions, later on, Peter will remember. Because of his deep affection for the Lord, Peter desires to obey Jesus' commands. If we genuinely recognize God's love and affection for us, we also will strive to obey him.

To obey means to listen attentively; by implication, to heed or conform to a command or authority: to be obedient to someone whom we perceive to have authority over us or to whom we assign authority and, thereby, obey.

Whoever controls our actions is the authority we obey. Following the voice of authority from a friend with a low opinion of our clothing or activities may result in our modifying what we wear or what we do; our goal is to gain that friend's approval. To follow a voice of authority into illegal activities is to follow an illegitimate authority. Yet, many people make the choice to honor the authority of another person whose actions are questionable.

Honor -to place value upon; and by implication, revere. Value is determined by, with whom, or where we spend our time.

We all understand the value of time. But how do we spend our time? We may say we value God, our spouse or children, yet spend most of our time and energy elsewhere. So then, what are we truly saying? If we spend the family money on alcohol or drugs rather than food and housing we devalue our family. When we do not take time with God to sit at the feet of the Lord listening attentively, we also show a lack of value. Often people fail to spend meaningful time with their spouse or children, their family, being too busy 'doing' whatever it is that person believes has greater value.

Jesus commanded us to love God and one another but how can we truly love if we do not value God or other people; if we do not believe they are worthy of our love? If we are a Martha or a Marty (Being a Martha type is not limited to women) we often are too busy doing 'things' that we say are for God or our family. However, we are only promoting our own self-esteem or personal worth. Generally, we do this in an effort to feel valued because we do not honestly belief we have value. Our being busy, then, provides a sense of purpose or meaning, at least to the world or ourselves.

Jesus valued God and all people and showed this by putting both first; and he gave his life for our life.

So, to *obey (value) God commands* is to "listen attentively, to conform to [his] command or authority" Children are to obey their parents in *all* things yet, the Word also says, that to love mother or father more than [God] is not worthy: and they that love son or daughter more [than God] is not worthy. Therefore, we must put God and his commands before all else.

> *When a conflict exists between our human expectations and God's commands, God's commands always comes first.*

Because we love and respect God means we should not enable (devalue) any person by allowing them to continue in sin doing nothing when he or she persists especially when that person will not address or acknowledge the error or their ways. We must respect or honor that person enough to attempt to turn them from the sin but do so in a respectful manner.

23. THOUGHT FOR TODAY

The Rechabites are a clan whose manner of life symbolize their renunciation of the agrarian and urban culture their nation had long since assimilated, and who expressed their loyalty to Yahweh and to their ancestor's wishes by clinging to the simple semi-nomadic life of their remote forefathers.

They kept a way of life rooted in their faith, intentionally countercultural, and separated. None would drink any wine; they did not own houses or fields or vineyards; they lived in tents.

In Jeremiah's time, he invited all the men of the Rechabite clan to meet him in one of the rooms in the Temple and there he offered them wine ... cups and bowls full of wine! Was the Lord testing the Rechabites to see if they would keep their vows? No. For the Lord knew exactly what they would do; they would reject the wine.

This invitation is not meant as a test, but to give Jeremiah and the people a sign ... a living and breathing example of people who keep faith. They had been instructed by a distant ancestor to live a certain way and abstain from drinking wine ... and they obeyed!

The faithfulness and obedience of the Rechabites is in stark contrast to the unfaithful disobedience of those of today who call themselves Christian. Jeremiah delivers the Lord's indictment of such people:

"Jonadab's descendants have obeyed his command not to drink wine ... but I have kept on speaking to you and you have not obeyed me.

"You [do] not listen to me or pay any attention to me."

When it comes 'to honor and obey', we place value on someone or 'thing'. To revere or value someone, in honesty, is determined by and with whom, or where we spend our time and other factors.

Considering where and with whom you spend your time and describe how you demonstrate that you value or revere the following?

    ____ in relationship with God

    ____ in relationship with Spouse, if married

    ____ in relationship with Children, if a parent

    ____ Care you give to your home - where you live

    ____ in relationship with your employer and/or career

    ____ Other ______________________________________

DISHONORING RELATIONSHIPS

Honor is not:

- Staying in relationship with someone who will hurt me
- Never confronting another person about their 'faults'
- Enabling sin by remaining silent and not confronting
- Thinking a person is "wonderful" when they are not
- Have feelings of love rather than behave with love

UNLOVING RELATIONSHIPS

- Scripture says much about abuse, though opinions how to identify and deal with abuse varies. Scripture addresses marriage relationships and abuse however. Husbands are to love their wives as Christ loved the church. To harm someone, physically, mentally, or emotionally is sin.

- Regardless of whether rape or another abuse in or outside of marriage, it is a crime and against God's commandments. While husbands and wives are to share their bodies with each other, it must not be by force but by honoring each others desires; the husband is to love his wife as Christ loved the church and *gave his life for it.*

- Abuse and/or exploiting other people is sin, whether it is by a husband, wife, child, or any other person (Luke 1:46-55).

For a study on abuse see Appendix A.

Abusing or exploiting another person in any way, is not love. Confronting the abuser in love, being patient and kind is one way to initiate change but not always does change occur. Consequences for behavior are imperative. No one, parents and/or spouse should be immune from these consequences.

When a parent or spouse has a pattern of abuse, it is important to sever that relationship so they do not have the power to continue causing pain and suffering. Thus, the one offended must discipline their attitude and actions to provide consequences for the abuse and the abuser.

We all fall short of the glory of God but this is not an excuse for abuse. Everyone, including Christians who abuse, do so by choice. It is never God's will for a man or woman to abuse anyone. The Old Testament is filled with stories of violence but not any was condoned by God.

> *For evildoers shall be cut off: but those that wait upon the Lord, they shall inherit the earth* (Psalms 37:9)

Violence is condemned throughout the Bible in passages that address battering, violence, rape, incest, stalking, twisting another's words, threats and intimidation. Scripture condemns violence. Every Christian should know this truth. Abuse is hate and therefore not of God. (See Appendix A)

If asked, could you describe an instance where you were abused and/ or where you were the abuser? Abuse is not simply rape or another violent assault. Often, we abuse people in subtle ways: angry hurtful words spoken to a person or to someone else about them (gossip). Perhaps you cut in front of people in the grocery line or traffic. Possibly you strike out at your children with harsh looks, hurtful words, and/or criticism.

> *"Oh come on. Stop acting so stupid!" She watches him for a few minutes as he struggles to get it right then in frustration she yells, "Give me that; you are too damn stupid. Don't you know anything? I can't believe that God gave me such a miserable dumb kid."*
>
> *Had she taken a good look and remembered when she was eight years old she would have realized she was repeating a similar scenario between her and her father when she was eight and didn't know just as her son who is struggling now to get it right and please mom.*

Abuse within the home is shameful and God is not happy with a parent who treats their child with such distain. While he may have compassion on this mother, let us hope he opens some door of opportunity for her to learn better parenting skills. Fortunately, she does not have a position of authority within the church. Yet, it is likely that her friends at church do not know that she behaves thus, toward her children. At least that's been my experience; abuse is often kept silent in the sanctuary.

While abuse in the home disqualifies a person from a position of authority in the church (such as with pastors or elders), the church must first be aware that abuse is occurring. A leader's family must live an exemplary life. If not, they are to step down until they restore order. Of course, this does not always happen today; it depends on the church and if its leaders believe in and lovingly obeys the word of God.

> *A couple of years ago, I rented a room to a homeless lady that had been referred by her pastor's wife. She was in my home for several months and in that time was a fairly good roommate. However, she liked doing things her way, which is okay most of the time except when I've told a person otherwise. I've try to communicate well and talk over rule changes and that usually works but not this time.*

When it came to a conversation and the mere mention of a problem sent this woman into a defensive rage. Before long both of us were out of control. Then, a days or so later, she came to talk about what had happened. Rather than a peace-making scene she simply had to prove that she was right and I was wrong!

At this point, though I was not a member of her church, I contacted the pastor's wife who had referred her to me and, using Scripture as a reference, suggested she and the pastor meet with us so the issue could be resolved. They refused to even acknowledge my attempt at reconciliation, and in the end, I had to evict her from my home.

She finally left and had to move into a storage room in the back of her church because no one was willing to take her into their home.

Consequences are difficult when we do not honor those in authority, who have some say over our lives. Because it was my home she was under my authority, and she suffered the consequences for challenging my authority in an improper or unjust manner.

Nowadays I do not rely on church leaders but have my own rules for everyone along with firm guidelines from the state law for landlords. All the rules are in black and white in an agreement that must be read and signed before a new roommate moves in. As a result of these experiences I now follow Scriptures guidelines for leaders, being a leader within my home.

1Timothy 3:2-7 lists specific qualifications for church leaders who must be motivated by love not control, gentle, not harsh or abusive in their use of authority; humble and disciplined with their time and resources. The person has a vision for God's plan for them, wisdom in applying God's Word, and uncompromising obedience. Loneliness, criticism, rejection, pressure, and disappointment, weariness, failure, and self-sacrifice are part of the job. This we must accept and live with. In living to please God, believe what he says is true, and the fruit of your faith will be seen is in your life.

24. Thoughts for Today

"My family moved around a lot. We five kids lived with grandparents, aunts and uncles more than with our parents, especially after the divorce. My sister was a lot of fun and we played together as children. I was her little brother and was not like her at all. She was popular and very cool.

When we were with mom she wanted instant obedience or the fists flew, and no one avoided her rage. I tried to avoid her by retreating into my own head, lay low, and pretend that nothing was wrong but look for a way out. Just when I thought I had it figured out —how not to make mom mad —she was mad again and hitting at everyone.

I ended up drinking even as a child, to hide the best I could.

All of us learned to not be around if we wanted to avoid mom's anger and rage toward anything that irritated her. 'I'll give you something to cry about.' 'Wipe that look off your face, or I'll wipe it off for you.' Then came the fist in the face or the ironing cord, whipping across whatever flesh was exposed, or any place handy, really.

My sister read a lot to become invisible and free from the wrath. She even seemed invisible to us sometimes. Still, I remember how scared I felt when she ran off and I didn't see her for a couple of days.

We were at our grandparent's house that summer and mom and dad were together, still, when she was carried in with blood all over. We never knew what happened; they kept it real quiet. Something in her changed after that and my brave fun-loving sister was closed off, and angry a lot, or else she told jokes when things got tense.

==

Have you ever been in a similar situation? Describe

How you did you recover?

Who helped you get through it?

Describe how it felt dealing with the situation.

Describe how it felt dealing with the after effects, later on.

Describe a success you had and the steps you took to achieve it.

Use the following scale to rate yourself as a spiritual leader

1. Always   2. Often   3. Sometimes   4. Rarely   5. Never

____   I am motivated by love not control
____   I am gentle, not harsh or abusive using of authority
____   I am well-disciplined in use of my time and resources
____   I have a vision for achieving God's purpose for my life
____   I am knowledgeable and wise regarding God's Word
____   I am uncompromising in my obedience to God's authority
____   I well-manage the loneliness, criticism, rejection, pressure, disappointment, weariness, failure, and self-sacrifice in life
____   I live to please God, and believe what he says is true
____   Faith's fruit is seen in my life: Love, Joy, Peace, Patience, Gentleness, Goodness, Meekness, and Moderation

There is no good or bad score, but your answers may suggest that work is needed in some areas? Pay attention to those and decide on needed change. Describe

EFFECTIVE EXPRESSION

If you [show] love to each other, all will know you are my disciples.
(John 13:35) and the love of God is perfected in [you]... (1 Jo 2:5)

Imagine having that kind of passion and expressing God's love at all times. What feelings surface, fear or anticipation? Augustine described love as:

"...a temporary madness. It erupts like an earthquake then subsides. And when it subsides you have to make a decision. You have to work out whether your roots have become so entwined together that it is inconceivable that you should ever part. Because this is what love is: Love is not breathlessness, it is not excitement, nor is it the promulgation of promises of eternal passion. That is just being "in love" which any of us can convince ourselves we are.

Love itself is what is left over when *being in love has burned away*; it is an art and a fortunate accident. All the pretty blossoms have fallen from our branches and we find we have become one tree not two."[21]

---

[21] Captain Corelli's Mandolin, "Love is the beauty of the soul." —St. Augustine

Scripture defines love, in a way somewhat similar to Augustine's but not as an emotion, as a way of expressing ourselves that we develop, over time. In Neither the Scriptures nor Augustine's is the standard many think of as love, such as a warm fuzzy feeling, passion, or other common view. In Scripture, as in life, we experience difficult emotions[22] and express them not always in loving ways. Love is an attitude and behavior that is God in us who is love, and whose love is sacrificial; God is love in action.

God expresses love in many ways, through his patience with people, through the many gifts he has given those who believe in Jesus, and through his vast patience waiting for unbelievers to believe.

"The Lord God, compassionate and gracious, slow to anger, and abounding in loving-kindness and truth (Exodus 34:6); and who once were disobedient, when the patience of God was kept waiting in the days of Noah, during the building of the ark, in which ... eight persons, were brought safely through the waters [of the flood] (1 Peter 3:20).

The Lord is not slow about fulfilling his promise, as some count slowness, but is patient toward you, not wishing any to perish but for all to come to repentance [and belief in him] (2 Peter 3:9). Or do you think lightly of the riches of his kindness and tolerance and patience, not knowing that God's kindness leads to repentance? (Romans 2:4) 'I gave her time to repent of her immorality, and she does not (Rev 2:21).

God also expresses his love in anger toward our disobedience and sin when we do not repent, as any parent who loves their children. God is merciful, quick to forgive; loving, kind, and patient. He never turns away... not even when his people worshipped an idol... (Nehemiah 9:17-18). God also loved by giving his son, Jesus as a living sacrifice, so we would believe and accept Jesus as Lord and have our sins forgiven.

Jesus lived without sin, which is hard for most of us to image, but even more so imagine expressing your love by sacrificing your sinless life [if you were sinless] for everyone who is a sinner, and willingly commit to the sacrifice beforehand. Often we become angry at people and want retribution.

Most of us cannot understand God and his forgiving sinners. This is beyond imagination. We tend to react emotionally to whatever is happening, and become angry, resentful and, sad, or tearful. People can only sacrifice their self interests for another by learning to love, genuinely.

---

[22] See page 152

Love is the pure expression of our emotions no matter how we may *feel* at any moment. When anger is expressed as love perfected, others believe that God's love is in us. "Whoever abides in love abides in me" God confides, and "I in them" (Galatians 6:4). Rather than anger and bitterness we should be at peace. Love for God means confidence in God. David describes his confidence and his knowledge of God's love for him in Psalm 27.

"The Lord is my light and my salvation; whom shall I fear? The Lord is the strength of my life; of whom shall I be afraid?" (Ps 27.1)

The most common word for "love" in the New Testament is "agape", which is God's love for people and is sacrificial love. God's expressed his love for us by providing for our sinful rebellion through Jesus' sacrifice on the cross.

"For God so loved the world that he gave his only son, that whosoever believes in him should not perish, but have eternal life. (John 3:16)

Those who love as God know no fear, because perfect love casts out all fear. Believing in God's love, we have perfect trust in that love, and we trust that God has everything under control regardless of the situation. We know that he works all things together for our good therefore we have no need for anxiety, sadness or depression, or anger. Instead, we pray and ask for God's mercy and grace and accept the peace Jesus left us (John 14:27).

Jesus knew how to be at peace. He had many emotions and responded to those emotions appropriately. When angry, he directed his anger at those with whom he was angry managing his emotions with clear thinking. Thus, he expressed himself as a sweet fragrance, pleasing to God. This behavior is exactly what the world should be seeing in us. Read these following verses and consider what they say and how God speaks to you through them.

Thanks to God who always leads us in triumph in Christ, and through us spreads the *fragrance of His knowledge* in every place. We are to God the *fragrance of Christ* among those who are being saved and among those who are perishing. To the one *we are the aroma of death* leading to death, and to the other *the aroma of life* leading to life. And who among us is sufficient for these things? (2 Corinthians 2:14-16)

In an ancient triumphal procession, the Roman general would display his treasures and captives in a cloud of incense priests burned for the gods. To the victors, the aroma was sweet; to the captives, it smelled of death slavery. When Christians preach the Gospel to some unbelievers it has the nasty smell of death while for others it is a sweet fragrance.

Fragrance Of Christ

Scripture speaks about pleasing fragrances several times. After the flood, Noah offered sacrifices to God that was a pleasing aroma; and in Leviticus we see that God commanded the Israelites to put oil and frankincense on their grain offerings; also New Testament offerings were as a sweet savor to the Lord (Eph 5.2; Phil 4:18).

John recounts the story of Mary anointing the feet of Jesus shortly before his crucifixion (Matthew 20:28) where the aroma filled the whole house. Ephesians 5:2 says, "You must live a life of love as Christ loved, and gave himself as a fragrant offering and sacrifice to God." It is hard to imagine how God could enjoy such a sacrifice but it was the love expressed that God found fragrant, not the suffering and death endured. Paul saw his gifts as a "fragrant and acceptable sacrifice pleasing to God" (Phil 4:18).

Which of your attitudes and behaviors are fragrant and pleasing to God? By contrast which are offensive and less than pleasing? Would you like to be a sweet fragrance to God? If so, do you sacrifice self for others? Are you after the look-good, being outwardly pleasant with unhealthy sinful thoughts? Is God pleased with the words of your mouth?

> *Today I was attempting to do something new and in frustration my temper caused me to spew garbage from my mouth. It was definitely not a sweet smelling fragrance or sound.*

There are days when my fragrance is sweet as a rose, but on others, I am an offense to God! Most of us know when we are offensive. The Holy Spirit is not shy in convicting us of our sin. We may blame others for our attitude or behavior, but being accountable for how we feel in-the-moment and choose to responds, allows clear thinking to dominate instead of emotions. The more we discipline or moderate our emotions appropriately, the more fragrant we become and more pleasing to others.

> *I discipline my body and bring it into subjection, lest, when preaching to others, I myself should be an offense* (1Co 9:27).

Offenses

There are a lot of angry offensive Christians in the world today. While it's okay to be angry Scriptures says not to sin in our anger (Ephesians 4:26).

Some of us are so overly sensitive to the least slight, real or imagined that we become filled with irritation, resentment, frustration and bitterness and simply refuse to let go. Then, it becomes a habitual response.

Jesus taught us to be at peace with all men, at all times. The New King James uses the term peace over ninety times (See Appendix C).

BEING AT PEACE

Heman, the Ezrahite, cried to the God day and night. In his misery he despaired of life itself because his life was getting steadily worse.

"I cried to God with my voice, God *is* my voice and he heard me."

Asaph cried out for courage when in distress when he was in doubt. Later, after making requests to God, Asaph's focus changed:

"Lord, I will remember what you have done, your miracles of long ago. I will think about each one of your mighty deeds. Everything you do is right, and no other god compares with you. You alone work miracles and you have let nations see your mighty power; you rescued your people" [Psalm 77].

This Psalm gives no answer other than hope that God will rescue him. Thus, no matter how low we get we can always take our problems to God and express our anguish, though he may do nothing to relieve the situation, yet, he understands. Recall Jesus' anguish in the Garden and on the cross.

Psalm 138 encourages, saying, "In the day when I cried you answered me and made me bold with strength in my soul." (v. 3)

Only after Asaph puts aside his doubts about God's holiness and readiness to care for him did he eliminate his distress. As we pray and praise God our attention is focused on him not on self, and our distress is relieved.

25. THOUGHTS FOR TODAY

One day, some time ago, when online checking my bank account I noticed there was a $950 problem. In shock and disbelief, I immediately checked to see if the bank was open. It was 7am, too early, and two hours until I could deal with a situation that seemed to need 'immediate' attention.

Recalling other unpleasant experiences with banks, I instantly became irritated feeling the bank only cared about their money not my loss. Fear and anger surfaced and before long my dogs that felt the anxiety and tried to provide comfort by being close. The emotions of anger caused me to push the animals away and refuse their love and attention.

I tried to reason/think through the emotions and the situation by remembering that God would take care of things; everything would be all right. Then while praying [I considered later, Satan's demons of despair doubtless spoke to me] "Remember yesterdays' sins, those that persist? You're a real disappointment to God. Perhaps, he is punishing you now for those sins? After all, how can God truly care for you a persistent sinner? If you were truly God's child you would not repeat the same sins, would you? Just give up and walk away".

Despair and futility swept over me. "If I just let go and walked away, leave it all behind, I would have no money, no debts, and live on the streets or in my car without a thing to worry about!"

That last thought brought to mind that as a Christian, I already had nothing to worry about, if I walked by faith and chose to be at peace and not give into the emotions like I was doing now, and had done years ago when drugs and suicide had been the answer. Yet, I now knew that was not the answer; there was only one answer – my God. My emotions calmed and I instantly feel better.

I began to write about the experience to later share the events as I'm doing now, thinking it would be a great example. By the time the writing was finished, it was 9:30am and the bank was open!

How time flies when we are not focusing on problems! By responding to the prompting of the Holy Spirit, rather than the anger and despair, the trauma event proved relevant and likely, useful.

What's your soft spot? (Rejection, finances, making mistakes, rudeness)

Describe a situation that you managed poorly and well.

What made the difference?

BE ANXIOUS FOR NOTHING

Philippians suggests we be anxious for nothing, but in all things by prayer and by asking, with thanksgiving [For we know God has already answered], make your requests known. Then, the peace of God that surpasses all understanding, will keep our heart and mind through Christ. Thus, we give praise to God for answered prayer. Amen.

By him let us continually offer the sacrifice of praise to God, that is, the fruit of our lips, giving thanks to his name. (Hebrews 13:15)

This theme is seen throughout the Psalms. As we praise and thank God for material and spiritual blessings, we should also thank him for our answered prayers before they are even seen.

Remember when you asked for protection, strength, comfort, or patience, and God provided? Do you take God's answered prayer for granted, or do you think you must always be cheerful and positive? That is a mistake. Grief takes time to heal and being positive when we are hurting is to deny our feelings. Denial does harm and leads to anger and resentment. Learning to manage our emotions well takes time and patience; it's a learning process.

OUR EMOTIONS

Emotions are not easy to manage, but clear thinking helps the Holy Spirit to lead instead of our emotions. Thus, we express the true fragrance of Christ. When we allow our emotions to determine our respond, it makes obeying the prompting of the Spirit difficult.

Being a slave to emotions or will of God is a choice we make daily, in every situation, and it requires reverence for God because we desire to obey him. When we obey, we walk by the spirit not the flesh, in service to God. Choose this day whom you will serve (Jos 24:15); be a slave to your emotions, or to Christ and be free.

Emotions are god-given, but we must listen to God rather than the emotion so we acquire skills and attain sound counsel [to live rightly] (Heb 11:6).

To increase learning and attend to wise counsel we must listen! Even the wise must stop and listen instead of talking, so they become wiser. We learn from wise counsel, by listening and hearing! If our mouth is moving, our ears cannot hear. Be swift to hear, slow to speak (1John 4:17). The unspiritual live by human nature; their impulses control their actions (Ephesians 5:2). Thus, Fruit of the Spirit are not as evident.

FRUITS OF THE SPIRIT

We receive spiritual gifts but the fruit of the Spirit comes by the Word and life experience that develops our character, the character of Christ. The fruit is manifested in the life that is transformed by Jesus.

Love –"Love is patient and kind. It does not envy, nor boast, is not proud. It is not rude, nor self-seeking, it is not easily angered; and it keeps no record of wrongs. Love does not delight in evil but rejoices in truth. Love always protects, trusts, hopes, and endures. Love never fails" (1 Cor. 13:4-8).

Joy - "The joy of the Lord is strength" (Nehemiah 8:10). We keep our eyes on Jesus, who leads us. He endured the shame of being nailed to a cross, because he knew that he would be glad he did one day, when as now he is seated at the right side of God's throne! (Heb 12:2)

Peace - "Therefore, since we have been justified through faith, we have peace with God through our Lord Jesus Christ" (Romans 5:1).

"May the God of hope fill you with all joy and peace as you trust him, so you may overflow with hope by the power of the Holy Spirit" (Ro 15:13).

Longsuffering (patience) -- "strengthened with all might, according to his glorious power, we have all patience and longsuffering with joyfulness" (Col 1:11) "In lowliness and meekness, with longsuffering, forbearing [putting up] with one another in love" (Ephesians 4:2).

Gentleness (kindness) -- Live "in purity, understanding, patience, kindness and in sincere love, and truthful speech and in the power of God; with weapons of righteousness in the right hand and in the left" (2 Cor 6:6-7).

Goodness - "We pray always for you, that God would count you worthy of his calling, and fulfill all the good pleasure of his goodness, and the work of faith with power" (2 Thess 1:11). "For the fruit of the Spirit is in all goodness and righteousness and truth" (Ephesians 5:9).

Faith (faithfulness) - "O Lord, my God; I exalt you, I will praise your name; for you have done wonderful things; your counsels of old are faithfulness and truth" (Is 25:1). "I pray that out of his glorious riches he strengthen you with power through his Spirit in your inner being, so that Christ may dwell in your hearts through faith" (Ephesians 3:16-17).

Meekness "...if one be overtaken in a fault, you who are spiritual, restore that one in the spirit of meekness; considering yourself, lest you also are tempted" (Gal. 6:1) "With all lowliness and meekness, with longsuffering, forbearing [putting up with] one another in love" (Eph 4:2).

Temperance (self-control) - "But also for this reason, giving all diligence, add to your faith virtue, to virtue knowledge, to knowledge self-control, to that perseverance, to perseverance godliness, to godliness brotherly kindness, and to brotherly kindness love" (2 Pe 1:5-7).

When we seek the fruit of the Spirit God tests us and bring trials so that we may develop these traits. Thus, as we are able to respond with the Spirit we become more mature and it is evident to others.

TO READ THESE EVERY DAY, THEN MY TEMPER DOES NOT GET OUT OF HAND.

IN THIS WORLD

The world of full of difficulties; it's inevitable. Jesus said "In this world you will have troubles but cheer up, I have overcome the world" (John 16:33). So we believe what Jesus said and respond to encounters with people with fruit of the Spirit, which decides the kind of life we will lead.

To be harsh, unforgiving, resentful, angry, bitter, and self-pitying Satan then controls that relationship or situation and we have chosen darkness and rejected the light. Those who respond so often blame God and lose their joy and peace while the fruit of the Spirit bring a different outcome.

With peace and joy in our heart, we are forgiving and pray God to work in the heart of an offender, and have an even temper, so they are at peace. We walk in the spirit with meekness, we do not take the issue personal thus, self-pity or bitterness is avoided. Instead we have compassion.

Which habits of responding would you like to change?

Breaking a habit is a struggle where we cry out to God, "Lord help me"; and know that the Holy Spirit is always with us to help at all times. Yet, we must make the choice to do whatever is right in God s sight.

Ask and it will be given to you; seek and you will find; knock and the door will be opened (Luke 11:9). God expects us to take action while asking for what we need, while seeking to find the doors he opens. God gives us the ability to do what is needed but we must choose wisely. So get wisdom! With everything, get understanding (Proverbs 4:7).

When emotions arise, test it to see if it is of God. If it is not of God, resist it. Thus, we struggle against emotions, and turn to Jesus who understood, having been tempted and overcame. Jesus was tempted just as *are we, yet* he was without sin. He experienced every emotion do we, yet did not give in to his feelings. The Word of God sustained him.

26. THOUGHT FOR TODAY

The Abyss

When thoughts take wing and
Fly to insurmountable heights
When like a wet-slick umbrella
Shedding emotions like rain
When laughter peaks reaching
The utter depths of despair
When the anguish of soul is
Smothered by flames of passion
When I knock at the door and enter
Because no one answers
When the fear in my heart echoes
The loneliness of my being
When I enter the abyss - sucked
From the vortex of existence

March 1984

In 1984 my emotions ran rampant and I had no healthy ways to cope whatsoever. Suicide was a common reaction to my despair and hopelessness. 1978 saw the start of these troubles and for a while I gained the care I needed. The first time when I woke up in ICU on a respirator being given a warm sudsy bed bath, it was almost like going back to infancy. It was a wonderful feeling. Thus, began my suicide cycle; my goal from that point on was for someone to take care of me.

Of course, after the first couple of times they figure out what you're up to and the care and nurturing stop. In emergency room, crying in the depths of despair, once, a part of me stood back watching the mental health worker and I could see her sense of helplessness. She didn't have a clue what to do with me. Now that was frightening, and my own sense of helplessness mounted.

What difficult emotions do you often deal with?

How do you respond to each of these, disciplined or not?

In saying, "I love you" to someone do you behave lovingly?

Have you felt the depths of despair, and if so, how did you deal with it?

Are the fruits of the spirit clearly evident in your life? Describe

Describe an instance where you experienced an agony of the soul?

CRY OUT TO GOD

King David was in agony as he endured a great trial, but in his suffering, he gained victory. David cried out to God:

"My God, why have you forsaken me? Why are you so far from helping me and from the words of my groaning? O God, I cry in the daytime, but you do not hear; and in the night, and am not silent. (Ps 22:1-2)

Yet again he sought God when troubled

"This is my anguish; but I will remember the years of the right hand of the Most High." I will remember the works of the Lord; (Psalm 77:11)

David's was not a cry of doubt, but an urgent appeal to God. Often, we expect to be relieved of our discomfort or even the trial itself but that is not what God does when we call on him.

Many believe that in being comforted, God relieves us of our troubles. But if that were so, people might turn to God only to be relieved of suffering and not out of love. Being "comforted" is receiving strength, encouragement, and hope in our troubles. The more we suffer the more God comforts. Do not expect to be freed from the trial, rather understand that every trial will help you be stronger and more at peace. Through trials and understanding you will then be able to comfort to others who endure similar trials.

We often respond to trials impatiently, rather than waiting on the Lord. But God says we are to stop being angry, and not do evil. People easily angered behave foolishly, and troubles often follow. Yet, problems can also follow boredom, which can lead to laziness or depression – such as the deep sleep of which Proverbs speaks (19:15).

When we have little or nothing to do people become idlers and tattlers, gossips, and busybodies; they mind everyone's business but their own. Those who have faith, knowledge, self-control, patience, love, godliness, and kindness, however are not idle; they usually are busy doing God's work. We avoid trouble when we fear the Lord enough to seek work adequate to keep ourselves busy being productive.

"Do you not fear me?" asks God. "Will you not tremble at my presence, which set the boundaries of the sea that it cannot pass: though the waves are tossed, yet can they not prevail; they roar, but cannot pass over it?"

Jeremiah questions our attitude when we are in God's presence. How do we behave? Do we "come with respect, trembling because God is all-powerful and can strip away all the blessings?"

Like Judah and Israel we often grown to expect God's blessing and rather than reverence for God, no longer are we in awe of his divine might. Thus, God can strip away our blessings. We then suffer the consequences of our actions but rather than whine and cry, return to him.

Do not wait until God removes your blessings before you commit yourself or you will be grieving. Often, we experience grief with any great loss, and to lose God is a profound loss. God's anger, though, is short lived, particularly toward the repentant heart. Proverbs reminds that while a merry heart makes for a cheerful countenance a sorrowful heart breaks the spirit, which can lead us back to God

While we may weep for a night [in repentance], joy comes in the morning. God is mercy and his grace comforts those who keep his commands and abide in his love. Jesus said this to give us joy, not a brief joy, either. Jesus did not want us to despair.

There are times when we feel despair. Life's trials press down sometimes, beyond measure. At times, even Paul despaired: "we were pressed down, more than our strength, so that we despaired even of life itself; troubled on every side, *yet not distressed*; perplexed, but we were *not in despair*. Jesus also cried out in despair "Eloi, Eloi, lama sabachthani?" which is interpreted as, "My God, my God, why have you forsaken me?"

While we despair, we should never doubt God. Jesus taught that to have faith we can say to the mountain "Get up and jump in the sea" and it will. He questioned, "Why are you so frightened? Why do you doubt?" We ask God for something and in faith do not doubt. Thus, we are not tossed about in a storm like the ocean wave, but at peace.

Call upon the Lord when in distress and have faith that he will answer and bring you peace. When in sorrow David felt confined that he had no room but when the Lord set him free, he gave him a large space and the freedom to move about without hindrance. "The Lord [is] on my side; I will not fear" David said (Ps 118.6).

We all experience fear, anger, and grief, at times, there is also joy and peace that surpasses all understanding. Scripture says to make a joyful noise unto the Lord. Serve him with gladness: come into his presence with singing. Then, abiding in God's love we sing joyfully unto the Lord.

If you keep my commands, you will abide in my love; even as Jesus kept the Father's commands, and abided in his love. Thus, in God's love we find joy and the peace Jesus leaves with us.

"Peace I leave with you, my peace I give to you: not as the world gives. Let not your heart be troubled, nor be afraid" (John 14:27).

"God blesses those who refuse evil advice and won't follow sinners or join in sneering at God. Instead, the Law of the Lord makes them happy, and they think about it day and night" (Psalms 1:1-2).

Jesus experienced sorrow, *"My soul is exceeding sorrowful even unto death: stay here, and watch [with me]?"* (Matt 26:38).

God's answer is a promise that one day he "will wipe away all tears from our eyes; and there shall be no more death, sorrow, crying, nor any more pain: for the former things are passed away" (Rev 21:4).

Take a look the emotions listed below and identify those with which you are most familiar? Some are more a mental state than an emotion however we often think of them as emotions.

Common Emotions		
Confusion	Doubt	Fear
Frustration	Jealousy	Loneliness
Rejection	Revenge	Sadness
Weariness	Disappointment	Procrastination

GOING TO THE CROSS

Jesus did not feel like going to the cross; [*in an agony He prayed earnestly*]; and subjected his will to the will of God, "Father, if you are willing, remove this cup from me. Yet not my will, but yours be done". And an angel appeared, strengthening him. His sweat was as great drops of blood falling to the ground (Luke 22:42).

Jesus' righteousness was established when he was tried in the fires of affliction by God who tries the hearts and minds.

In this Psalm God *searches our minds (thoughts and purposes) and hearts [emotions],* and tries us until purified (Psalm 7:9), until we can manage our emotions with love not anger or despair. Should God search your mind, emotions, and purposes, what might he find?

TRYING TIMES

How can we learn to discipline of our thoughts and emotions unless God allows us trying times? While we may resist these trying times, eventually we must come to accept them to find peace. God never allows more than we can bear and it is through this testing that we learn to deal with greater afflictions. Thus, unbelief is purged and faith strengthened for the greater glory of Christ. Trying times are learning times and so God trains us to fulfill his purpose.

Certain emotional states can provide trying times (i.e., bi-polar mood disorder), but even when emotions fluctuate from one extreme to the next, we can learn to resist the lows and the highs and find a healthy balance. The choice we make makes the difference!

There are always days when a person is up and days when they are down. The key is to balance the emotions by keeping our thoughts in check, disciplined. Anyone who has seen the film "A Beautiful Mind" about John Knox, a Noble prize winner who had schizophrenia knows that he chose to overcome his disability by making choices, and with the help of family, friends and co-workers. Stability and honesty are both important.

Scripture says that if we have sinned, we are to tell each other what we have done; that we can pray for one another and be healed; and that the prayer of a righteous person—one innocent before God--is powerful, making a difference. So, talking about our faults helps, and with prayer can bring healing and peace of mind.

Slamming the cupboard door, mouth a hard slash of frustration with teeth clenched, and immediately suspect - "She took it; I know she did; where else could it have gone?" Cursing harshly under my breath and abruptly yanking open then slamming the drawer shut. "Damn her!" About that time I see the lost object of my rage —where I put it just the day before – and my dogs slink from the room, tail between their legs looking anxious and fearful - my heart breaks.

Have you experienced mood swings that hurt innocents and perhaps overcame through faith by disciplining your thoughts while recognizing the strong emotions and choosing not to react? I'm better than I use to be and talking to a friend – confessing my faults – does help but has not resolved all the issues with my out-of-control emotions and mouth.

When angry over situations that stir up emotions, we redirect our thoughts by reading Scripture, self-talk and prayer. Sadly, reciting Scripture or prayer that would help redirect my anger, is sometimes the last thing that comes to mind when anxiety, rage, or fear surface in the heat-of-the-moment.

The key is to practice awareness of emotions in-the-moment then not react, which takes even more practice. To respond thoughtfully and considerately to an event is not always easy. It's not something I have learned as yet, and I have fifty plus years of a disabling habits to overcome.

While we may not do away with an emotional disability overnight, anyone can learn to deal with it in a godly way, learning new skills. Also, family and friends often can sense our struggles, and if we are honest with them, they can offer encouragement. We must be receptive to their help regardless and not perceive them as a threat. Bring it into the open and be healed!

Whatever we hide has power over us, so bring everything out of the dark into the light of day so they lose their grip. John 8:32 says that the truth will set you free and James advises that we "confess our faults to one another so that we may be healed and restored to spiritual health (James 5:16). Pretending we do not have a problem or that we are in full control of our life brings trouble. Are you able to confess your sins and faults to others?

My friends and I talk about situations and emotions and often in the telling and resolving of problems we end up laughing and enjoying the foolishness of our all-too-human frailties. Not that we think the sin involved is funny but it gets us out of the pity party and into a more praiseworthy situation.

The trick is not to cater to our emotions. God helps if we continually trust him and follow the lead of the Holy Spirit not the flesh. If we follow our emotions, we pay a price. The carnal mind is hostile to God and does not willingly submit to God's law.

27. Thought for Today

People can be fearful, funny, faint-hearted, or faithful in our emotions but, sometimes, we become angry or anxious when fearful. We feel defenseless and unable to cope with a situation so become angry or anxious. Fear and anxiety are two emotions the Bible speaks of often. Be not afraid; fear not; be not anxious; where is your faith? However, many other emotions are also found in the Bible, such as those listed below.

Confess your faults to one another, and pray for one another, that you may be healed. The effective, fervent prayer of the righteous man or woman avails much. (James 5:16)

Are you able to identify your emotions and faulty reactions, those that create problems between you and other people?

Rate your emotions and how often you experience each one, and situations that typically bring those emotions to the surface. Use the back of the page.

1 = rarely   2 = infrequently   3 = moderately   4 = frequently   5 = daily

___ Anger	___ Anguish	___ Anxiety	___ Confusion
___ Doubt	___ Fear	___ Frustration	___ Jealousy
___ Loneliness	___ Rejection	___ Revenge	___ Sadness
___ Weariness	___ Disappointed	___ Procrastinate	___ Paranoia

How do you manage each emotion when they arise?

Write about the emotions and/or situations where they surface and how you express yourself and then, how you can express yourself differently.

Untrusting:

Feeling anxious and untrusting; "someone moved my toothbrush therefore, they must have done something to it". Suspicious, I rummage through my other things ... but then call to mind that m*y roommate has never done me harm before so this might be imagination and I can choose not to overreact this event. Thank God I have a trustworthy roommate.*

This is an extreme example but many experience a lack of trust or paranoia, and have to learn to deal with it, and the consequence of not trusting. Like any other emotional issue, a person must learn to manage them if he or she hopes to live in the world and remain sane.

Emotions cause us problems often because we express them in immature ways. The following lists several examples of immature expression.

Anger	=	emotional/mental immature expression of fear
Anxiety	=	(see anger) immature expression of personal concerns
Alcoholism	=	emotional and mental immaturity and repression
Blaming	=	self-focused, unresponsive to personal responsibility
Dependent	=	clinging to other people rather than to God or self
Depression	=	repressed anger or grief; immature self-focused pity
Drug use	=	(see alcoholism and/or dependent) immaturity
Bi-Polar	=	immature awareness; not express honest emotions
Resentment	=	self-focus; unforgiving spirit; (see anger & blaming)
Paranoia	=	extreme self-focus; lack of trust; lack of awareness; immature expression of fear (see blaming)

None of these are intended to minimize or hurt a person's feelings rather, the intent is to help create awareness so that healthy change can occur.

We deal with life to the best of our ability, but with these and other issues, we need to improve our coping abilities and use them more effectively just as we must learn to use our spiritual gifts according to the level of our faith.

Because of the Lord Jesus, however, we can choose emotional maturity that comes with spiritual maturity as we learn and grow in the Lord. So, don't stress out over these. Simply see them as a point of awareness and a place to initiate change and personal and spiritual growth.

The key is not to cater to our emotions but use our Spiritual Gifts in order to harvest mature fruit of the spirit so that we have a mature spiritual life.

THE PRICE WE PAY

Part of the price we pay for catering to our emotions, is not being able to live the Spirit-filled life. Those ruled by the flesh or their emotions think only of themselves. When ruled by the Spirit we think of spiritual things what is pleasing to God. As such, if we are followers of Jesus then we walk as did he and do what pleases him. This is not easy, when emotions are seen as a weakness and we feel guilt experiencing anger, sorrow, or grief. Or we have detached from emotion and do not feel anything particularly if we suffered severe abuse and/or have become abusers. While this happens all too often, neither is a godly solution.

Jesus was not overly emotional nor was he detached from emotions but had a full range of emotions he expressed in the moment as was appropriate. He was not always calm and pleasant, without variation in mood or emotions. Rather, Jesus was appropriate to the situation, expressing how he felt, and he was not ashamed to be seen being emotional.

> At Gethsemane; [Jesus] took Peter, James, and John with him, and *being troubled and deeply distressed*, said, "My soul is overwhelmed with sorrow, to the point of death" (Mark 14:34)

No matter our emotions in the moment, Jesus knew and understood for he experienced them all, but, he chose to respond with peace. "Anyone who desires to come after me, must deny [their own self interests], pick up their cross daily and come follow me" he said. Thus, to express emotions as Jesus is to deny our emotional displays or its denial and instead respond thoughtfully, with love.

EMOTIONS OF JESUS

HE FELT SAD AND WEPT

As Jesus entered Jerusalem, he wept, "If you had only known on this day what would bring peace—now it is hidden from you. The days will come when your enemies will build a wall against you and hem you in on every side. They will dash you and the children to the ground and not leave one stone unturned, because you did not recognize God's coming to you."

Jesus saw [Mary weeping after the death of Lazarus], and the Jews who had come with her also weeping, he was deeply moved in spirit and troubled. "Where have you laid him?" he asked. "Come and see, Lord," they replied. Jesus wept.

HE FELT JOY

"I'm telling you," Jesus says, "so that you might be filled with joy." The Lord wanted them to know that when things are going well, we feel elated. When hardships come, we sink into depression. But joy in its full sense transcends the waves of circumstance. Joy comes from a consistent relationship with Jesus Christ. Our lives are so intertwined with his that he helps us walk through adversity without sinking into waves of despair and manage prosperity without moving into highs that can crash harshly. The joy of living with Jesus Christ daily keep us levelheaded, no matter how high or low our circumstances.

HE FELT INDIGNANT

Jesus saw [the disciples stopping the children], indignant, he said, "Let the little children come to me, and do not hinder them, for the kingdom of God belongs to such as these".

Mothers usually brought their children to a rabbi for a blessing, thus these mothers gathered their children around Jesus. The disciples thought the children were unworthy of his time. Jesus however welcomed them because little children have the faith and trust needed to enter God's Kingdom.

HE FELT COMPASSION

More than any other emotion Jesus felt compassion for the suffering of others. When Jesus heard what had happened, he withdrew by boat privately to a solitary place. Hearing of this, the crowds followed him on foot from the towns. When Jesus landed and saw a large crowd, he had compassion on them and healed their sick.

Jesus called his disciples and said, "I have compassion for these people; they have already been with me three days and have nothing to eat. I do not want to send them away hungry, or they may collapse on the way."

As Jesus and his disciples were leaving Jericho, a large crowd followed him and two blind men shouted, "Lord, Son of David, have mercy!" The crowd rebuked them and said to be quiet; they shouted louder, "Lord, Son of David, have mercy on us!" Jesus stopped and asked. "What do you want me to do?" "Lord, we want our sight."

Jesus with compassion touched their eyes and immediately they received their sight and followed him.

HE FELT DISTRESS

They came to Gethsemane; and Jesus said to his disciples, "Sit here until I have prayed." And He took with him Peter and James and John, and began to be distressed and troubled. He said to them, "My soul is deeply grieved to the point of death; remain here and keep watch." He went a little beyond and falling to the ground and began to pray "If it is possible, let this hour pass me by". He cried, "Abba! Father! All things are possible for you; remove this cup from me; yet not my will, but your will."

HE FELT FEAR

He admitted to his fear and gave it to God; and instead, chose courage. Courage does not mean you never experience fear rather courage is doing something in spite of the fear experienced. Yet the things that brought fear to the heart of our Lord were not the same things that make us fearful.

Jesus was afraid on two occasions in the Gospel. On each of the two he prayed to his Father and in prayer he got the strength to continue and face the situation. In Gethsemane, the night before his crucifixion he prayed to his Father to let the cup pass. His prayer was answered, though in a different way to that we would expect. The answer was in his response, "Not my will, but yours be done."

Another time, Jesus said, "Now my soul is troubled." (John 12:27) Here Jesus prayed and recovered his strength in prayer. When troubles come, our best approach is to pray, and God provides strength to continue.

God is with us always, whether or not we *feel* him near. Jesus chose to serve God not his emotions. And like Jesus, we also can choose to serve our emotions or God. Like Joshua we must *'Choose this day who you will serve* [your emotions or God].

God gives us the ability to do whatever is necessary but choosing wisely is necessary. No matter the emotions in the moment, being human Jesus knew and understood, and responded very different from the way many of us often respond. When we learn from Jesus, we are at peace and our emotions do not get out of control.

Paul's love and affection (see Philippians 1:7-8) was based not only on experience but on the unity that comes when drawing upon Christ's love. All Christians are part of God's family and share equally in the transforming power of his love.

Do you love fellow Christians, friends and strangers alike? Let Christ's love motivate you to love others and to express that love in your actions toward them rather than wayward emotions.

One friend is always saying, "I love (you, a neighbor, or my friend) *in Christ*. So, I asked her, "What exactly do you mean? Is that love different than what you have for your sister or your husband?" She said, "Well, it's God's love." "But," I persisted, "What does that mean, exactly." My goal here was not to be unkind, rather it was to get her to think about what she was saying, and if she truly meant it, or was it all for show or an obligatory thing.

When people tell me that they love me *in Christ* I feel that their love is more an obligation, and not heartfelt. The problem from my point of view is that we often view love as something other than attitude and action. For me to profess that I love someone means that I need to get my act together and behave as though I love that person. Thus, I choose to be patient and kind, generous, long-suffering when it comes to their faults, and not to be envious when good things happen in their life but not in mine.

∞

On the next page are a series of emotions that can be found in Scripture so, take a look and circle those with which you are most familiar. Note those that you have great difficulty managing. Then, meditate on the Scriptures and ask God to reveal the answer for you.

At night I pray, Lord search me and know my heart and see if there be any wicked way in me and lead me in the way everlasting. Now, included in this prayer of Psalm 139 is the awareness that I want to know any sins from the past that are not yet forgiven so I can deal with it.

For instance, this morning God a memory from the past —a twelve year old sin needed to be addressed, one I had long forgotten. I've noticed that God doesn't come at me with every single sin, which is why I pray for awareness, so God will continue to bring them and I can ask forgiveness and make amends whenever possible.

"Beloved, I wish above all things that you may prosper and be in health, as your soul prospers" (3John 2) God wants you emotionally stable. Do you want to be emotionally stable or do you prefer a life of emotional drama?

Think on this as you review the emotions from Scripture on the next page. Learn to rule your spirit and be in good mental and emotional health.

∞

Anger	Discouragement	Rejection
• Proverbs 15:1 • Matt 5:21-26, 43-48 • Eph 4:26,27,31,32 • James 1:19-21	• Psalms 42, 43, 62	• Psalm 38 • Isaiah 52:13-53:12 • Matthew 9:9-13 • John 15:18-16:4 • Ephesians 1:3-14 • 1 Peter 2:4-10
Anxiety/Worry • Psalm 25 • Luke 12:22-31 • John 14:1-7 • 1 Peter 5:7 • 1 John 4:13-18	**Doubt** • Psalms 8, 146 • Proverbs 30:5 • Mark 4:35-41 • John 14:8-14; 20:24- • James 1:5-8	**Revenge** • Leviticus 19:17,18 • Isaiah 25:1-5 • Mat 5:38-42 • Ro 12:17-21
Confusion • Psalm 37 • Ephesians 4:14 • Colossians 2:8 • 2 Thess 2:1-17 • 1 Jo 2:3-6; 4:1-3 • Jude 3,4, 17-25	**Fear** • Psalms 27, 46 • Luke 12:4-7 • John 6:16-21	**Sadness** • Psalm 34 • John 16:16-24 • 2 Cor 1:3-6
Depression • Psalms 16, 130 • Lam 3:18-24 • Ephesians 3:14-1 • Hebrews 4:16	**Frustration** • Job 36:1-33 • Matthew 7:7-11	**Stress** • Nu 6:24-26 • John 14:27 • 1 Corinthians 1:3 • Philippians 4:8,9 • Col 3:1-4, 15
Disappointment • Psalm 55 • Jer. 15:10-21 • Matthew 5:1-12	**Jealousy** • Exodus 20:17 • Proverbs 23:17 • Ro 13:11-14 • 1 Cor 3:1-3 • James 3:13-18 **Loneliness** • Psalm 22 • John 10:14-16 • Matthew 25:1-13 • Titus 3:14	**Weariness** • Is 35; 40:28-31 • Mat11:28-30

After reviewing these emotions and noting those that are indicative of you, after considering the follow Scripture, complete "Thought for Today".

Take a moment to consider the following.

Anger   A soft answer turns away wrath, while a harsh word stirs up anger. Proverbs 15:1

Anxiety   ...which of you by being anxious and troubled with cares can add [a moment to your life]? Luke 12:25

Depression   Sorrows are multiplied for *who* run after other *gods*. Ps 16:4

Disappointed   Every word of God *is* pure; He *is* a shield to those who put their trust in Him [he never disappoints] Pro 30:5

Fear: Please listen and answer me, Oh Lord, for I am overwhelmed by my troubles. Ps 55:1-2

Discouraged: Blessed *be* God, even the Father of our Lord Jesus Christ, the Father of mercies and the God of all comfort, 2Co 1:3

Doubt: In a storm at sea, fearful, his disciples woke him. Jesus asked "Why are you so timid and fearful? How is it that you have no faith (no trust in me)?" Mark 4:40

Jealous: Don't be jealous of sinners; honor the Lord. Pro 23:17

Lonely: I will not leave you alone. I will return. John 14:18

Avoidance: Being lazy is being a troublemaker. Proverbs 18:9

Rejection: Come to Jesus Christ the living stone rejected, but which God has chosen and highly honored. 1Peter 2:4

He said,   "Never will I leave you, nor forsake you!" Hebrew 13:5

He's our lifesaver

28. THOUGHT FOR TODAY

Those ruled by the Spirit think of spiritual things, what is pleasing to God who desires that we love others putting them before ourselves.

Read page 203 and think about each emotion; read Scripture for those that are relevant to you. Now answer these questions.

When the emotion [anger] is present, what is going on in my mind?
"I'm stressed out and blame my roommate or boss for [a certain problem], because I don't know what to do about it; it's easier to blame her."

Do I will to think this way and feel miserable?   Yes   No
"Yes. I have not taken the steps to relax and talk over things with someone, and try to figure out a solution. My pride is getting in the way. I find it hard to admit that I can't take care of this by myself."

Is this a habit that can be changed?   Yes   No
"Yes. I've gotten into the habit of being independent, self-sufficient. I know that I need help though. My anger and frustration can change with effort".

Describe how you can replace the one habit for a healthier habit.
"The next time I find myself getting angry or frustrated and tense, I'll go to a new location, relax, and calm down. Then, I can talk about it with a friend or counselor and figure out a better way to manage the situation."

What emotions do you need help with most? (Anxiety, fear, or grief)

How does it affect you physically? (Tension, sharp focus, humor)

How do you manage your [tension] now? (Avoid it; joke around)

What would you do different? (Deal with whatever makes me anxious)

When you fail to respond well (we all do) how do you feel about it?

  I feel (despair and want to give up; I'm feeling hopeless) I feel (joy and hope, knowing God is with me showing mercy)

How do other people respond when you disagree with them? Give an example: (what they might say and how they behave)

One thing I fear more than anything else is . . .

List eight things that make you smile and/or give you joy:

1.

2.

3.

4.

5.

6.

7.

8.

 **FORGIVE AND FORGIVEN**

The Bible begins with the purity of creation. Sin enters with Adam and Eve, followed by spiritual death and separation from God. God wants to forgive us for he is merciful. So, centuries after Adam and Eve, Jesus is born sinless, suffers and dies for our sins still sinless, and is the means to forgiveness for all people, for all sin, and, absolutely, for all time. The problem occurs when we do not accept Jesus sacrifice, his forgiveness.

The Old Testament reveals that for a person to have their sins forgiven, a goat was sent into the wilderness to symbolically carry off the peoples sins. Also, a lamb or dove without spot or blemish could be sacrificed so the one bringing the sacrifice had their sins washed away in the lamb's blood.

In the New Testament, Jesus carried the people's sins into the wilderness symbolically when he first started his ministry; on the cross he became the sacrificial lamb with his blood sacrifice. Jesus is the ultimate sacrifice for sin. However, one *must* accept Jesus Christ as their Lord and Savior, and his sacrificial death as a substitute for their sins.

Sin is disobedience against God's will (1John 3:4); the result is death (Romans 6:23). Having sinned we are all under the penalty of the law, which is eternal death. But God is merciful and wants us to have eternal life, to live with him forever in heaven (Revelation 22:5).

God gave his son, Jesus that we might have that forgiveness. Jesus paid the ultimate penalty for sins so that we might have eternal life with God in heaven (Romans 5:8, John 3:16). If we turn to God and repent of our sins he is just to forgive us (Acts 3:19, Col 1:13, 14).

Only God has the power to forgive sin (see Mark 2:7 and Luke 5:21). Yet when we confess and genuinely repent of our sins, he does forgive and cleanses us from all unrighteousness (Psalm 32:5).

Jesus and Forgiveness

- Peter asked, "Lord, how often should I forgive someone who sins against me? Seven times?" "No, not seven times" Jesus replied, "*seventy times seven*! (Ma 18:21-22, italics added)

- "Take heed. If your brother sins against you, rebuke him. And if he repents, forgive him. And if he trespasses against you seven times in a day, and seven times in that day turns and says, 'I repent', you *must* forgive him." (Luke 17:3-4)

- They came to Calvary, and crucified Jesus who said, "Father, forgive them, for they know not what they do..." (Luke 23:34)

- "If we say we have no sin, we deceive ourselves... If we confess our sins he is faithful and just to forgive us our sins, and to cleanse us from all unrighteousness." (1John 1:8-9)

Ephesians 4:31-32 instructs us to "Let all bitterness and wrath and anger and tumult and evil speaking be put away from you, along with all malice. Also be kind to one another, tenderhearted, forgiving, as God for Christ's sake has forgiven you."

Forgiveness is essential to a godly and a loving life, but it takes time and willingness. It would it be great if we always walked by faith and never doubted, and our lives were filled with peace and contentment knowing that God saved us and we are forgiven. That is not reality.

Regardless of what was done to us we must humble ourselves, and forget about holding an endless "grudge" and, instead, "choose to hardly notice" when we have been wronged. Rather than being "harsh and unforgiving" we are "patient and kind." This is God's love.

Numb, now that the agony had lessened, he no longer felt the pain or the pull of the nails that hold him to the cross. Blood trickles down still, rather slight, an annoying irritant upon his cold sensitive skin.

Jesus focuses beyond the pain and his annoyance at such a petty thing. Seeing those who stare or play dice below, he feels a rush of compassion, suddenly realizing 'they do not know nor understand what it is they do' "Father," He cries. "Forgive them, for they do not know …" (Luke 23:34).

Flogged, a crown of thorns woven and thrust upon his brow, and crucified on a cross, Jesus forgave those who tortured and murdered him. He realized that understanding the immediate, long term, or the eternal consequences of our actions is truly not within our human grasp. Intent upon our own pain and revenge, for hurts thrust upon us and now lie in a heart turned to stone, we simply stare at the world, unfeeling, and return to our game or television or other device. Yet, were someone to accuse us of such a cold heartless attitude, would we deny?

Joseph, son of Jacob and Rachel had older brothers who in jealousy and envy, after having nearly murdered him, they instead sold him into slavery. Denying their part, they lied to their father. Then later, an innocent man in Egypt Joseph found himself in prison for many years, yet when released, he became second in command only to Pharaoh himself because he kept faith and did not despair. Perhaps, that was all a learning process for Joseph, for he was human, after all. The Bible does not tell all the details.

In spite of all that happened, when he faced his brother's years later, Joseph did not avenge himself for the wrongs done to him. Rather, he forgave them because while they had intended evil, he knew that God had intended good would come of it. As a result of his magnanimous or attitude, rather than renew the hurts he restored the relationship.

MEMORIES

Yes, I can imagine memories that rush to the surface, indescribable hurts against body, mind, and soul. Outraged, you cry out, "What about when …?" Then, describe a tortuous memory from your childhood or your adult years. Believe me when I say, I know of those injuries having been a victim myself, both as a child and an adult.

Still, for those who survived to tell about it, God does have a purpose. He did not want that terrible thing to happen--remember free choice we spoke of earlier--but people do terrible things to each other. Yet, God works all things together for good *to those who believe.* When in the midst of trials –no matter how painful –it is difficult to believe, and often we do not want to wait on God. What other option is there, other than misery?

Most of us refuse to wait twenty seconds to be vindicated when someone wrongs us, much less wait twenty years or more. Waiting and trusting that God will vindicate us, or not caring whether he does, is the answer. Simply waiting on the Lord because we know all things work together for good to those who love him keep our mind at perfect peace. Those who are called for his purpose find this a real test of faith, but one that strengthens them.

If one who offends you is hungry, give that person food to eat, if he or she thirsts, give that person water to drink, for you will heap coals of burning fire upon his or her head. The intent is not to punish with literal fire but to bring a sense of guilt, so they person repents, as did Joseph's brothers. Thus, God will reward you for the good you do your offenders. Romans instructs, if possible, be at peace with all; not avenging yourselves, [leave that to God] for it is written, "Vengeance is Mine *I will repay*," says the Lord. "So, do not be overcome by evil, overcome evil with good." (Ro 12:21, italics added)

In this day of lawsuits and legal rights, this sounds almost impossible. But when someone hurts you, instead of giving the person what they deserve, forgive. Perhaps reconcile, but certainly end the revenge, and bring a sense of guilt so that person will change. By contrast, repaying evil with evil hurts you as much as it hurts your offender. Even without repentance, forgiveness frees you from anger and bitterness.

Though we confess, are forgiven, and cleansed from unrighteousness we are not relieved of the consequences. God may forgive a theft or even murder, but that does not mean you or another person will not go to prison for the crime. The laws of humankind must be honored Scripture says, yet there are laws that seem to go against God's laws (See Appendix B).

While all are subject to the governing authority, not only for God's anger but for conscience' sake, there are laws that oppose God's laws. Today believers must be careful of the law for we are not to have fellowship with sinners for evil corrupts.

"Don't be deceived; evil companions corrupt good character" (1Cor 15:33).

Be patient and kind with those of corrupt character for your kindness may draw them to the Lord (just as I was drawn many years ago). Nonetheless, do not associate with the sexually immoral (fornicators and/or adulterers). In 1Corinthians Paul instructs the church to cast out a man who was having sexual relations with his father's wife. The intent was order to bring him to repentance and save his soul. Paul encouraged the church, later, to reunite with the man after repentance had occurred so he did not become deeply depressed and give up.

Scripture is clear that believers must be careful with whom they associate. 1Corinthians 15:33 says, "Do not be deceived: 'Bad company corrupts good morals.'" Psalm 1 says, "How blessed are they who walk not in the counsel of the wicked, stand with sinners, or sit with scoffers!" We are in the world but not part of it. Yet, Paul says in 1 Corinthians 5, we will never be able to be totally separated from evil people as long as we are alive on this earth.

It is the professing believer who makes a practice of sin is, according to Paul, that we need to avoid. While we all stumble, God is willing to forgive us an infinite number of times. The person to avoid is not the humble, struggling Christian but the arrogant, unrepentant. Those who care less about sin and yet claim to love Jesus have no place in Christ's church. The person must be disciplined, removed from fellowship (Ma 18:15-18, 1Tim 1:20). Scripture is adamant that the church is not to tolerate sin (Revelation 2:20).

Jesus associated with prostitutes and tax-collectors, people recognized as corrupt and sinful. Yet Jesus came to be known as the friend of sinners (Matthew 11:19), which He didn't mind for he came to save the lost (Luke 19:10). It was the sick, not the healthy, who needed a Physician (Matthew 9:12). However, Jesus never compromised his integrity by mingling with the sinners, but preached to them.

Jesus gave sinners the truth, confronted their sin and offered them grace. We should not view sinners as "untouchables" as if they would corrupt our hearts. Instead we should fellowship with them, telling them the truth, and offer them God's grace. However, we should get as far away as possible from a professing believer who lives as a sinner; we should have nothing to do with these people. They wreck our testimony, they lead us astray, and they corrupt our minds. They are the true danger.

29. THOUGHT FOR TODAY

Sacrificing Family

A man should never neglect his family for business once said Walt Disney for he had "been there, done that" and was not proud of it. The sad part is that wives and children are the ones affected. Today, single parent families and two-parent family find mothers working to support their life style. Often, just to survive but also to provide unnecessary excesses.

Most times, a man's or woman's intentions are not a conscious sacrifice of the family yet, it happens. As head-of-house these providers of the home may spend much time at work providing a constantly improved lifestyle that requires more and more time on the job. On any given day, however, it is up to that person whether he sacrifices family for business or anything else. Can he turn it off, shut it down, and walk away in the knowledge of what he has accomplished this day is sufficient?

God did it in creation; he looked at what he created and said "it is good". While he could have said, "Maybe just one more little thing before I quit", but instead he stopped and acknowledged a job well done each day.

What do you sacrifice for (business, personal happiness, or an addiction)? (Your family for a career, friends for an addiction, adultery for a marriage)

Rate these questions

1. Always   2. Frequently   3. Occasionally   4. Hardly ever   5. Never

___ Do you believe you are without sin?

___ Are you able to rebuke someone who sins?

___ After rebuking someone, do you forgive them?

___ Do you forgive other sinners *seventy times seven?*

___ Do you not know what you are doing when you sin?

___ Do others not know what they are doing when they sin?

___ Do you confess your sins on a regular basis? (Daily, weekly or other)

___ Do you accept forgiveness, God' or another person's when forgiven?

___ Do you feel people should be cast out of the church for immorality?

___ Are the Christian you associate with involved in sin life style (addiction, sexual immorality of adultery/homosexuality, or ...)?

FRIEND OF SINNERS

1. What did Jesus do in Mark 5 that showed he was "the Friend of sinners"?

2. What in Mark 2:13-17 showed that Jesus was the Friend of sinners?

3. Mark 12:37 says what about Jesus' relationship with many of the people to whom He spoke?

4. What in Ephesians 2:1 shows Jesus is the Friend of sinners?

5. What in 1 John 3:1 shows that God loves us?

6. According to Mark 2:17, why did Christ come to Earth?

7. What information in Hebrews 4:15 shows Jesus is the friend of sinners?

8. According to Psalm 119:11, what is one way to keep from sinning?

9. According to John 14:15, how do we know that we love Jesus?

THE SOLUTION

So what is the solution? Forgiveness is an absolute if a sinner repents of their sin and even if they do not, for on the cross Jesus asked God to forgive those who crucified him though they were unrepentant. And his instructions on forgiveness can be established in four simple steps: "When you recognize someone has anger against you, leave where you are (one way to interpret this is to leave the bitterness and resentment, or ruminating on the offense); and forgive and release your anger."

Paul instructed the church to cast out the sinner who was involved in sexual immorality, yet forgive once repentance occurred.

The result of forgiveness is that we are freed from the bondage to hatred and anger, thus we are also free to love others without painful constraints. The question is, are you willing to forgive and be forgiven? If you are, the next step is to forgive those who have wronged you. If you do not, then, beware, for God will treat you the same as you treat another.

Forgiven but Not Forgiving

The kingdom of Heaven is like a king ... one man owed ten thousand talents but he had nothing to pay, and was going to be sold along with all he possessed so payment was made. He asked the king for patience and promised to pay him. The king, moved with compassion, forgave the debt. But this man did just the opposite with someone who owed him a very small amount by comparison, and he demanded payment. The one who owed him begged for patience. Rather than forgive the debt as his was forgiven, he threw the man into prison until he paid in full. When the king heard, angry, and delivered the man to the tormentors until he paid all that was due.

You may not want to forgive someone, and want to see them punished. But forgiveness does not release them from the consequences of their sin! Still, God says that vengeance is his, not ours. The person must answer to God for the sin, whereas by forgiving we are set free from our emotional bondage.

HAIR TRIGGER

At times, there may be triggers that activate your anger. When this happens, you can always remind yourself that you forgave the debt, and you don't have to be angry anymore. You have a choice to be in bondage or free. Personally I'm on the side of forgiving and forgetting and I've had some horrendous things happen to me in my life.

Several years after a difficult relationship ended I had forgiven the sins against me and resolved my anger. At least I thought so. Then, one day, driving down the street, I turned onto a certain street and, suddenly, I was assailed with a flash of rage at this man.

To this day I have no idea what triggered that particular event, but it happened in the blink of an eye. Sometimes situations occur that create a 'flashback' and emotions surge. We may not understand the cause. In these instances, the same solution applies; remember that the debt was forgiven (if it was) and that emotion is not an appropriate response.

My response to that memory was to remember that I had forgiven and did not need to be angry. Then let it go and thank God it was over!

Even so, there are triggers that bring forgotten memories usually when I'm talking with a friend about my relationships and suddenly, I realize, from my words and emotions at-the-moment that I'm angry and have not forgiven that one incident. So then I pray, "Lord, I forgive them, help me forget". Generally, that is the last time that incident comes with so much emotion attached to it. And if it does, it's easier to put aside.

MAKE THEM PAY

Sometimes, we refuse to forgive, to "hold it over" a person; we make them pay with our silent outraged anger however this attitude can and often does affect all other relationships. If someone has hurt us and we do not forgive them, our lives may be wasted as we try to make them pay for the wrongs they did, or we make someone else a surrogate or replacement and project our anger onto an innocent person such as a spouse or a friend, etc.

When I succeed, in my mind I see how my father handled success: with pleasure and a drink in his hand. With failure, I remember how he handled failure: with despair and a bottle of gin. Now I've learned to at least make different choices in that area. (Contributor unknown)

How we are in a committed relationship --both marriage and close friends – often is how we experienced relationships in our families-of-origin, largely. We talk, walk, eat, think, and even drink like our parents and not realize how influential they have been in our lives. For some of us, we become aware when dealing with our children and first recognize these similarities, in the counseling office, or at work with authority figures.

In a relationship, remember, we carry our family from childhood within us, a family culture made up of expectations about the world, other people, and how to act in it and with them. Our past impacts our present life.

We do not have to let the past prevent us from achieving our peace of mind in the here and now! Jesus said that heaven was within our grasp. Thus, we must reach out and grab hold. We often choose future mates and friends who resemble our parents in certain ways. Conflicts inevitably develop when we choose to not accept them after a time simply because they remind us too much of our parents behavior – though we may not recognize it.

The main thing is to *give up the need of trying to have your mate or friend understand.* Also, give up the idea of changing your spouse. Accept them are they are, and they just might change. You married him or her for who they were then and still are now, so what's not to love?

Allow that person to be as they "are"- accept "what was and still is" and allow yourself to forgive them (and your parents too) because in reality they never did anything to you. No one does anything to us; as Jesus said, *they do not understand what they are doing.*

It is incredibly liberating to not waste any more time and energy in trying to have someone understand and instead, you simply forgive!

Forgiveness means you are willing to abandon your right to feel resentment, negative judgment, and behave indifferent toward a person. Instead, you choose to feel compassion, generosity, and love. Forgiveness should not be done as grim obligation either but replace the resentment with compassion, condemnation for generosity and/or respect, and indifference and a desire for revenge with a sense of goodwill toward that person. It is a choice!

With this understanding, you have a starting place for remembering what needs forgiveness and you have a means for forgiveness. At first, it may require an act of will where you imagine yourself forgiving the offender even when you do not 'feel' like it. As you realize the freedom gained, then the act itself becomes more willing or heartfelt.

While Jesus offered a simple forgiveness process, many people, including myself, do not find it that easy. I had to get past my past and the people who had offended me, and those whom I offended. Some offenses I had no memory of and I did not understand what had happened. Thus, I struck out at everyone in anger. I had to gain knowledge before I could forgive. There was one Scripture in particular that I found helpful, Psalm 139:23-24.

THE KEY TO FORGIVENESS

When I came out of jail in 1989, I never wanted to go back. Nonetheless, in order to have a godly life, I had to be healed of the past; that meant finding a way to forgive. Most of my life I had idealized my father and blamed my mother for everything. When it came to forgiveness, I had to honestly deal with everyone in my past. We can make excuses for not forgiving a person, but that does not solve our problem. Forgiveness does.

1. We have to humbly admit that we are sinners too, therefore, no different than our offender for God sees all sin the same. "If we say we have no sin, we deceive ourselves, and the truth is not in us. (1 John 1:8)

2. We believe that forgiveness is possible as long as we have forgiven those who have sinned against us, and behave as such, by actually forgiving them, and accepting God's forgiveness for the part we play. (See #3)

3. We confess our lack of understanding, careless words, and/or impatience that contributed to the abuse. Honestly confess any doubts of an offender's sincerity, as well, otherwise distrust will continue.

5. We establish clear guidelines of discipline to ensure genuine repentance: restitution, financial accountability, maintain a job, or stop substance use, and discipline ourselves not to go soft on them too soon.

4. We express our pain and suffering honestly to the one who hurt us but not to manipulate and punish them. The hope is for them to gain awareness of the pain they caused so they can honestly repent and be restored.

5. We forgive our offender, though we may not restore the relationship yet. Change often requires time and hard work. Periodic failure does not always indicate an unrepentant heart. Proceed with caution. If he or she sins, confront, confess, then, forgive, repeatedly. Don't give up too easily.

6. We give God's grace for "No temptation has overtaken you but what is common to everyone of us; and God is faithful, who will not allow you to be tempted beyond what you are able, but with the temptation will provide the way of escape also, *that you may be able to endure it*" (1 Corinthians 10:13).

 "We know that God works all things together for good for those who love him and are called according to His purpose" (Romans 8:28).

7. Do *not let Satan have an opportunity* (Ephesians 4:27)"Let all bitterness, wrath, anger, clamor and slander be put away from you... and imitate God, as beloved children; and walk in love, just as Christ also loved you, and gave himself for us, an offering and a sacrifice to God" (Ephesians 4:29-5:2).

30. THOUGHT FOR TODAY

How do you score in the following areas? How true are they of you?

1.   Always 2. Usually 3. Occasionally   4. Sometimes   5. Never

____ I am a sinner, and I am no different than my offender(s).

____ I believe in forgiveness and I have or will forgive my offender(s).

____ I confess that my lack of understanding, careless words, impatience, or rebellion against authority may have contributed to the problem.

Examples:

As children, we sometimes rebel against a hardworking single parent who then feels pushed to the limit, and beats us. This does not excuse abuse, but is simply a confession of the part we <u>may have</u> played.

As adults, our careless words or rebellion may get us fired from a job, which does not excuse an employer who may have acted in haste.

____ I have doubts about my offender's sincerity, and can honestly tell them.

____ I have clear guidelines for the offender to ensure genuine repentance: restitution, financial accountability, maintain a job, or stop substance use.

____ I am willing and able to discipline myself to follow through on discipline.

____ I express my pain and suffering honestly to my offender not to manipulate and punish but so they gain awareness of the pain they caused.

____ I am willing to forgive my offender(s)

____ I am willing to restore the relationship(s) when appropriate

____ I have forgiven my offender but have not restored the relationship

____ I am willing and able to confront, confess, then, forgive repeated sins.

____ I give God's grace because I understand we all fall short of God's glory and "know that God works all things together for good for those who love him and are called according to His purpose" (Romans 8:28).

____ I study Scripture so as *not to let Satan have an foothold (*Eph 4:27)

∞

OPTIONS

Not all crimes are forgiven by victims and not all offenders apologize or ask forgiveness. When an offender repents there are options available if they desire to reconcile the broken relationship. Those options depend on the circumstances of course. Parents may remove the car keys from a teenagers grasp for traffic offenses. When the teen shows through repentance and transformed behavior that they are responsible, the parents may return the keys and let them drive again. This illustrates responsible parenting.

Nonetheless, abuse is not the only problem we run into even among Christians. Scripture illustrates a scenario where a person was having sexual relations with their fathers' wife, and Paul advises that he be cast out of the church and given over to Satan in the hopes of saving his soul. Once repentance occurs and the immoral behavior altered the person can then be brought back within the fold.

> Only when the man or woman who has been abused recognizes the harm they do by staying with their abuser and participating in the abuse will this be resolved!

Similarly, in domestic violence situations whether a woman or a man has been abused/violated in some way, that abuser's right to have contact is removed --until the abuser shows with transformed behavior that they are now a non-abusive person.

Sadly, many return to the abuse situation in spite of restraining orders. I did.

It's about setting firm boundaries on the abusers behavior to save that person from their sin and eternal damnation!

As a result, a person can say with confidence and a clear conscience that they have lived with God-given holiness and sincerity in all their dealings, depending on God's grace, not human wisdom; this is how we have conducted ourselves before the world (2 Corinthians 1:12). Paul later encouraged the church to bring the repentant back into the fold.

ELEMENTS OF FORGIVENESS

There are two parts to forgiving: (1) the offender who desires to be forgiven, and (2) the offended one who chooses to forgive. Sins needing forgiveness include addiction, anger, abuse, anxiety, and physical, mental, emotional and spiritual abuse and other behavior that one must learn to express with love not hate. Any action that does not show love of God or another and that does any harm is sin.

Psychology believes there are psychological defenses that protect people from repeatedly reliving a traumatic experience so they can function in the world. Yet these defenses hinder a person's growth. Defense mechanisms include denial, rationalization and repression. Yet, the Bible does not excuse or allow us to rationalization for sinful behavior or for not forgiving.

GOD'S PATIENCE

Nonetheless, God has always been patient and forbearing, giving the people time to see the error of their ways and repent and then seek forgiveness. Some writers believe that for forgiveness to take place a victim must see an offender in the context of the offender's own life and develop compassion for them as a person, as well as consider the circumstances that may have contributed to the offense---*not to excuse the offense*. God has compassion on all people though they still pay the consequences of their sin.

The goal of many forgiveness interventions similar to the 12-Steps have participants seek to make amends (they do not necessarily forgive or seek forgiveness). In the process, the person lists the hurts they did to others and attempt to make amends when appropriate and possible. Next, they make an inventory of the hurts done to them and forgive their offender.

Not everyone finds this forgiveness process helpful and many end-up revisiting the amends process repeatedly. My belief is that when amend or repentance takes place without forgiveness they are doomed to repeat the process until they make a decision to forgive their offender.

AMENDS VERSUS FORGIVENESS

Amends is defined as the offender accepting responsibility for their offense, offer sincere apology [not the same as asking forgiveness], and sincerely repent. Making amends however, is not forgiveness yet perpetrator amends do promote forgiveness in the following ways: First, it exerts beneficial effects on a victim's mind and emotions. Amends enhances the likelihood that a positive change in the victim's attitude and behavior toward the offender will occur.

For example if an offender were to discuss the offense in a concerned and apologetic manner the victim often feels some empathy toward the offender. When this occurs, a more positive emotional state is created; the victim is more willing to consider forgiveness and cease to harbor anger and resentment or continue to be fearful.

Second, the immediate outcome for the victim provides a sense that some partial debt repayment has been made, which helps overcome the fear and distress. When an offender responds to a victim's righteous indignation with heartfelt apology, rather than anger and defensiveness, the victim also may experience positive benefits that reduce a tendency toward retaliation. Third, in admitting their guilt and accepting responsibility an offender then creates a better future outlook for both their self and the victim. Their heartfelt amends acknowledges the debt the offender wishes to repay. With offender amends the victim is more likely to offer forgiveness.

Have you ever made amends as the 12-Steps suggest? If so, did you find the process helpful? And were you able to then forgive?

OLD TESTAMENT FORGIVENESS

Forgiveness is evident throughout both the Old and New Testaments: Esau forgives Jacob (Genesis 33) - with trickery he robbed him of his birthright (Genesis 45, 50); Moses forgave the Israelites (Numbers 12); David forgave Saul (1 Samuel 24-26) who hunts and tries to kill David; Solomon forgives Adonijah (1 Kings 1); God forgave David for his adultery, getting Bathsheba pregnant, and scheme to have her husband killed. And the ultimate forgiveness was Jesus who faced the crucifixion and said, "Father forgive them..." (Luke 23)

The Bible is clear that we must forgive whenever we carry anger or any bitterness and resentment toward someone. Jesus warned that anger without just cause must be dealt with; that if we know someone is angry with us (they carry bitterness and resentment toward us) then we must go to them and be reconciled with that person.

Bitterness hidden in a person's heart is troublesome. The bitter fruit of such causes us trouble: malice, strife, contention, covetousness, pride, jealousy and oppression. Ruminating leads to mental, emotional and physical health problems. Thus, we must deal swiftly with these and receive the benefits found in forgiveness. So cease to ruminate and forgive instead!

The Old Testament offered one method for forgiveness through the sacrificial ritual. Here the priest made atonement before the Lord so that the person was forgiven for any sins of which they were guilty. The sacrificial ritual centered on the blessing of forgiveness.

There were two offerings in particular: a sin and guilt offering for the purpose of dealing with guilt. While animal sacrifices are not offered now benefits come by working through this process. First, recognize that your sin that needs to be forgiven and that it is a failure to meet God's standards and no one else. This offering confronts you with the reality of your sin and brings it out into the open.

Often we try to relieve our guilt by denying its reality, but right and wrong are God's standards and they were established long ago. Freedom from guilt is only possible once we have accepted the fact that we have sinned then, ask God to forgive you and be relieved of the guilt by accepting his forgiveness. So dig into the dark and secret places where your sins are hidden, bring them into the open, and deal with them!

James advises:

"Confess [your] faults [they are not always sins] one to another, and pray for one another, that you may be healed."

> We may say to a person, "I am so sorry" but we never ask for their forgiveness by saying, "Will you please forgive me?"

Confession is not for our restoration or for God's sake; it is for our sake, so we can be set free. It is difficult to imagine being set free if our sin and repentance remains hidden, perhaps, out of shame and guilt. Thus the sin and guilt offering serves a valuable purpose.

Fasting and Forgiveness

Fasting was required for the people only on the Day of Atonement. However the Pharisees fasted twice a week simply to impress people with their "holiness." Jesus distained this public fasting and encouraged the people's self-sacrifice be done quietly and sincerely for God's alone.

Jesus wanted us to adopt spiritual disciplines for the right reasons, not for praise or a look-good to improve our appearance of holiness.

JESUS, THE WAY

Jesus entered the wilderness to start his ministry and in doing, took the sins of mankind upon his self. Later at his sacrifice on the cross his blood was shed, similar to the sacrificial lamb in the Old Testament. Like sheep we have all gone astray, each of us turned to our own way and the Lord lay on Jesus the iniquity of all, which he accepted. It is not just that Jesus died for sin but that he died for each of us personally; it has to be personal.

By faith the people of Israel accepted the sacrifice as effective for their sins personally. By faith, we must believe Jesus died for us personally and accept his sacrifice as effective for our sins. Scripture advises: confess your sins, be forgiven and purified, but also repent and change your ways, and pray for one another to be healed. A similar process is in the Gospels: admit to and confess the sin, accept responsibility and repent, then accept Jesus' sacrificial death on ones behalf.

Scripture makes it plain we are to forgive. "Love [your] enemies"; Jesus said, "Pray for those who persecute [you]" including your self-abuse. There are reasons why people abuse of course, and just as many for self-abuse.

ABUSE

Some learned to abuse from their parents. Receiving abuse themselves or seeing others abused (one parent abusing the other or the sibling, etc.). Abuse teaches them to abuse. Rather than being an out-of-control victim, some choose to be the abuser and in control. They get a sense of control over their lives and not being at the mercy of someone else. That they hurt another person in the process may not fully register with them.

Abusive behavior results from mental health disorders such as poor anger management and a drinking or drug problem that get out of control perhaps during an argument (e.g., the drug and alcohol use affects, at the brain level, a person's ability to inhibit themselves) so they strike out at another person.

Others abuse because they have brain damage, or because they were so abused as children that their innate empathic abilities never developed. Sometimes abuse is inflicted upon oneself and there are many reasons for why a person chooses self-abuse and that has to do with self-love!

SELF-ABUSE AS SELF-LOVE

What are people trying to accomplish when they harm themselves?

Jesus said we are to love our enemies *as we love ourselves*, which suggests people love themselves. Ephesians says, "For no man hates his own flesh; but nourishes and cherishes it..." Thus, people self-abuse out of self-love; they want to feel better and the emotional pain and/or emptiness to end.

- Self-injury helps *regulate strong emotions* and bring the person to a baseline state helping to calm and balance their emotions.

- Self-harm can *distract from emotional pain; it expresses what cannot be put into words* (anger, shocking others, seeking support/help).

- Self-injurious behavior can *exert a sense of control over your body* if you feel powerless in other areas of life.
- When you hurt yourself the behavior can be manipulated so people feel guilty then they either care for you or go away.
- Some have a *history of abuse* and blame themselves for the abuse, feeling they deserved it and so punish themselves.
- Self-abuse is *self-soothing that is used* to calm intense emotions. This self-care often occurs if a person never learned healthy self-care.[23]

COMPASSION AND UNDERSTANDING

Clearly, these are all ways we are loved and cared for especially when one does not feel loved and cared for in the world. Once understood, a person can then learn new ways to express pain or get a need met rather than self-abuse. Compassion while encouraging change is also preferred over condemnation. The self-abuser must ask forgiveness of God and accept the same, yet also understand the reason behind but not ruminate on the abuse or its various causes.

RUMINATION

The word "ruminate" is from the Latin for chewing cud, wherein cattle chew, swallow, then regurgitate and re-chew their feed. Similarly, human ruminators reflect on or mull over an issue to insane limits, continually "bringing it up" in one's mind.

Mental rumination, of which we speak, is a brooding and harboring of resentment ongoing. Rumination impairs thinking and problem-solving and drives away essential social support – friends get tired of hearing us complain continually. People do not want to be near someone who complains bitterly, ruminating on past events constantly; it drives both family and friends away and depression can then deepen.

A bitter, complaining, resentful, unforgiving person brings suffering and misery upon themselves and those who live and work with them. So rather than ruminate on the wrongdoing, meditate on the divine and ask God's forgiveness and get better.

---

[23] Deborah Cutter, Jaelline Jaffe, and Jeanne Segal, contributors, "Self-Injury: Types, Causes and Treatment," http://www.helpguide.org/mental/self injury.htm (25April2009)

FORGIVENESS PROCESS

1. AWARENESS (31)

Read Psalm 139:23-24 and meditate on it:

Search me God, and know my heart; try me, and know my [offenses], and see if any wicked way is in me [such as not forgiving]; and lead me in the way everlasting [to forgive offenses against me and those whom I have offended] (Ps 139:23-24)

Having asked God to reveal your offense and the offense of another do not minimize and/or deny the reality but admit to what you did and to what was done to you. Accept that forgiveness is possible.

Describe how not forgiving has encouraged abuse of self and others. These might be self-inflicted injuries, food and/or eating disorders, substance abuse, and hurtful thoughts (rumination), and emotions (i.e., anger, bitterness, resentments) that stress the body and mind and contribute to physical, mental and emotional health problems.

Describe how not forgiving damaged relationships with family, friends, or coworkers, (being harsh, critical, physical abuse, avoiding contact, etc. pushed people away and alienated them).

THE PRODIGAL SON

Read the Parable of the Prodigal Son, Luke 15:11-32

In the story of the Prodigal Son in Luke 15 forgiveness is given the repentant son who returns to the father and has the relationship restored. See yourself as repentant returning and receiving forgiveness. How does that feel?

Write 5 Bible verses on forgiveness, and how you would apply them.

Now read Luke 15:11-32, 19:1-10, 23:33-35, Mat 5:38-40, 6:9-15, 18:15-35, Ro 12: 14-21, 2 Cor. 5:16-21, Gen. 33:1-11, 50:15-21, Num. 14:17-20.

Comment on any of these Scriptures that give you pause for thought.

Describe the difference in amends and forgiveness? (See pg 226)

On a separate sheet of paper draw a time line, and at the beginning write those events that you remember and/or ruminate on and want to put in the past. At the end, write your hopes for the future.

Mark where you are now and where you would like to be.

Example:

1949 sexual assault; 1951 parents divorced; Dad was absent from that point on until his death 1966; etc. Currently, I am stuck in 1951 when Dad left and so, I do not trust men to be there for me, thus am uncommitted in romantic and/or enduring relationships, etc.

I would love to be right now in a committed romantic relationship of trust, genuine love and consideration for one another.

Remember a time when someone forgave you and/or you forgave someone. What made that event possible (or could have)?

Describe a time when you wanted forgiveness but it did not happen.

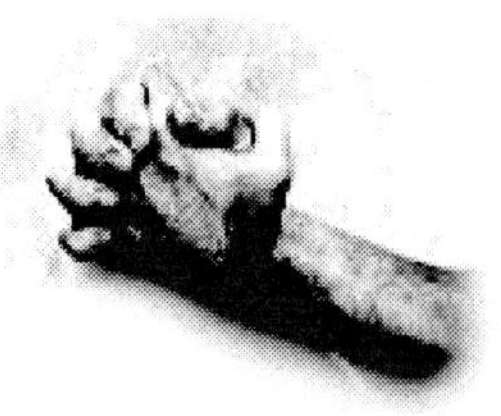

2. BARRIERS AND BENEFITS OF FORGIVENESS (32)

Our beliefs (attitudes and behaviors that express what we truly value) can create barriers and reveal its benefits; it's our deeply held beliefs.

David as a young boy went before the giant Goliath to defeat him, being outraged that the Philistine had defied the army of the living God and perhaps, because no one had done a thing to challenge him. But, he also asked about rewards for slaying the giant, Goliath.

What benefits do you see in forgiveness? How will you or your life be better as a result of forgiving someone?

List your barriers and the beliefs surrounding them.

He knew what he was doing; he is just mean and irresponsible. There is no way I'll forgive him; that encourage him to do it again. Men cannot be trusted; they always end up cheating on you.

For what purpose did God bring you to this place?

He probably wants me to learn to trust again and find a decent man and have a real committed relationship; that's what I pray for.

Explore and describe the benefits to forgiveness for all concerned.

Hopefully, I won't be as angry or bitter all the time. My friends get tired of hearing me talk about it. If I didn't remind him all the time of his failure and forgave him, perhaps he would be more open to God.

What do you believe about the benefits, especially for the offender?

Read Luke 5:21; 5:24; 6:37; 11:4; 17:3-4; 23:34;

What do these Scriptures say about forgiving?

List the beliefs behind your resistance to forgiveness.

Explore the source of any bitterness and resentment.

What keeps you from forgiving and from accepting forgiveness?

What do these obstacles teach you about the process of forgiveness?

In Luke, the elder son observes his father and brother. Perhaps, the elder son resents his brother, distrusts his motives. He resists forgiving him. Many of us can see ourselves in the older brother.

Can you see yourself?

Do you resent him?

Why do you resent him?

How easy or difficult would it be to forgive him?

3. COMMUNICATE YOUR INTENT TO FORGIVE (33)

Who do you chose to forgive? Now tell someone about it.

Write a scenario where you forgave or asked God's forgiveness.

Verbally express forgiveness for those whom you intend to forgive.

What are the benefits for you in obtaining or granting forgiveness?

There are reasons we choose not to forgive. Forgiveness involves risks and being vulnerable. Jesus asked God to forgive those who had persecuted him and were in the midst of crucifying him. Gregory Jones remarks that the Christian message of a God who forgives without repentance is too easy. Why should someone be let off so easy, by forgiveness? But God does not let them off the hook that easily. Jesus tells us that we must repent, and change our ways before forgiveness is forthcoming. Confess resentments and explore the beliefs in them --we fear our offender will take forgiveness as an invitation to resume the relationship or that what they did was all right, or we believe it's just not fair.

Perhaps the brother believes "It's not fair" and his sense of justice demands punishment. The father reaches out to forgive and not punishment perhaps because he understands the conditions that brought his younger son home was punishment enough. However, the elder brother is angry and resentful.

Anger is not bad. Jesus was angry for injustices, and Ephesians 4:26 instructs us to be angry but sin not. Anger tells us that something is wrong, but sin is an inappropriate response to that anger. The task of forgiving is to direct our anger appropriately, be reasonable.

Forgiveness is an act of will, not an emotional response. We will ourselves to respond to the anger with forgiveness and move towards justice.

Our desire for revenge can lead us to retaliate against those who offend us because we believe that punishment is required. The elder brother wants to get even with his brother so, like many of us the elder rejects his younger brother and refuses to join the celebration.

He wants his younger brother to be held accountable for his behavior and he wants his father to recognize the wrong done. But as the father knows, the answer is forgiveness not retribution.

In granting forgiveness, the sin is acknowledged for if sin did not exist, forgiveness would not be required.

Read Joshua 24:15 and 1Samuel 17:22-50. Write about the choices these men made and how each responded to the problems.

4. DEVOTED TO FORGIVE (34)

Design a plan for persons you intend to forgive and how you plan to accomplish it. Include the offense, how you felt, how you offended someone similarly, and if they forgave you, any resistance and/or resentments you still experience, and your sense of compassion for your offender, if any, and your intent to forgive.

Read Luke 23:34

Now write about Jesus' last moments on the cross.

Now, imagine yourself forgiving your offender.

What are your emotions?

We address these in the next step, so just write them for now.

The question now is how can we forgive?

We have explored resistance and resentments to forgiveness and chose to forgive and join the celebration. We also looked at the times when we wandered and still returned to the grace of forgiveness.

Look at Luke 15:11-32 and consider this story encourages us to be like the forgiving father reaching out with compassion.

How can you see yourself in the father's role? Describe.

The realization that we are not God but his children, who have also strayed and come home to forgiveness, is monumental. We also are created in the image of God, and in Jesus we are reconciled to God; thus like Jesus we can love, have compassion and forgive.

Often we hear, "what would Jesus do," when the question we should ask is, "what will I do to behave more like Jesus?"

What Jesus would do is vastly different than anyone else. We are each unique individuals and the most that we can hope for is to use our understanding of his love and mercy and then behave based on that understanding, which may look different from Jesus'.

To think and behave as Jesus could likely set us up for failure. We are striving for the ultimate perfection and that alone comes from God. So, keep it simple and let God lead you along the way.

Read Isaiah 49:15-16; Matt 23:37-38; Psalm 91:1-4; Ps 23; Ps 18:1-3.

How did each of these persons express God's love?

Which of these Scriptures speak to you of Gods forgiving love?

Read Matthew 18:21-23 and Genesis 4:23-24.

What pattern of violence would you like to break?

Whom will you forgive and how will your life change as a result?

How do you feel about forgiving, and change that may take place?

5. EXPRESS EMOTIONS (35)

Often as we plan a change of attitude and behavior and to forgive, we are suddenly beset with fear and anxiety the prospect of succeeding or failing its weight presses down. You may feel vulnerable at the thought of forgiving your offender, or hope that forgiveness will succeed and bring results not experienced previously, perhaps restore and even change the relationship. But a deeply rooted fear surfaces because formerly when you have forgiven, nothing changed, and the offender repeated the offenses.

Faith is the substance of things hoped for and in the face of fear we must put our faith in God and trust that he will bring it to pass according to his will and his purpose. In the meantime, we can set boundaries to prevent offensive behavior. The domestic violence victim can choose not to reestablish the relationship until certain behavior changes occur and the offender maintains those changes over time. The question is has the offender genuinely repented; and do they now show love and care rather than anger or violence?

What deeply rooted fears continue to plague you?

What is your fear or anxiety about – from where does it originate?

What emotions surfaced when you imagined forgiving your offender?

Your thoughts:

("I've never forgiven ..." "I never can forgive because..."; "I don't know if it is possible to ..."; "I am afraid that he/she might ...")

The Bible admonishes us 'not to fear' ninety-eight times. Yet in the New Testament, faith is found two-hundred and forty-two times. Thus, it appears that faith is the answer to fear.

Does this knowledge encourage you?

Can you find it in your heart to forgive in spite of your fear?

Behind the unforgiving countenance, the elder son perhaps feels fear.
Can you identify with his fear?

What was life was like for the elder son <u>before</u> his brother left?

What was life like for him <u>after</u> he left home?

What is his fear once his younger brother's return?

While broken relationships bring pain, through experience we learn to adapt or adjust to our fears, and may become trapped in self-destructive patterns that developed. Often we become comfortable both with our fear and our failure. Forgiveness cannot always restore a relationship and does not return what was lost yet it can help a person move forward with hope and bring peace to us and reduce the fear and the sense of failure.

The elder son's resentment is understandable and expresses the anger, desire, need, and fear common to many. What will the elder brother do? Do you think the elder brother is aware of his fears?

In difficult situations are you aware of your fears?

What would you do with your resentments, anger and fear?

Remember a time when you thought justice was done (a relationship, a legal judgment, a political situation, or another conflict).

Remember your desire for revenge and self-destructive rage. Imagine telling your offender that you forgive him or her. Write about your emotions that you feel in that moment, as you remember.

Imagine the Prodigal Son's elder brother. What do you imagine he will do? Will he join the celebration or leave, angry and resentful?

What would you do?

While resistance is natural, most of us do not want to be the elder son and set apart, feeling alienated. No one wants to be estranged from family or friends, enduring our self-righteousness loneliness, missing the celebration.

How can the elder brother move to a forgiving spirit?

How can you?

Read 1 John 4:8. What does this Scripture say to you? Describe.

How do you recognize your emotions and then express them?

How do you express God's love?

Can you express love regardless of how you feel in the moment?

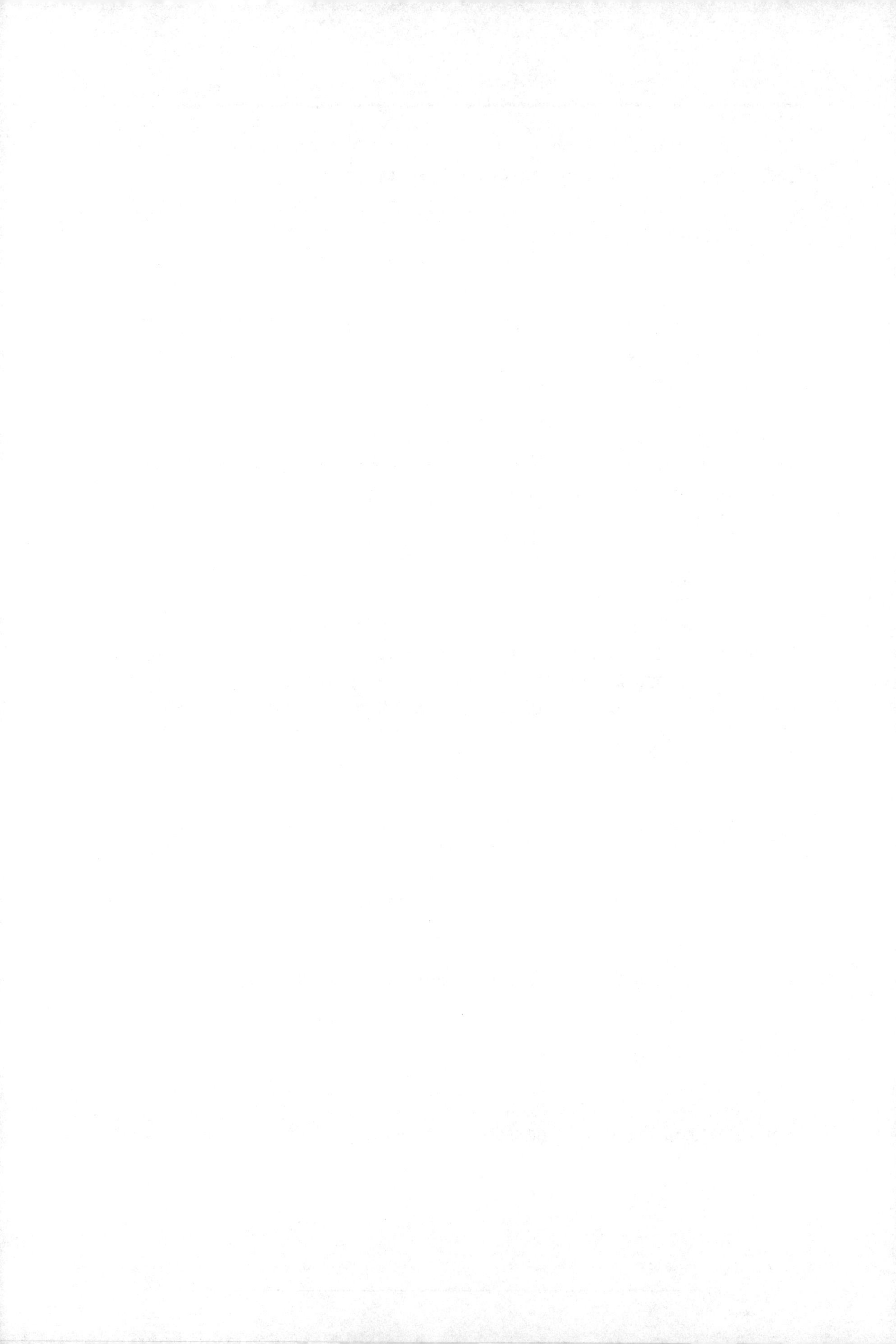

6. FORGIVE AND BE FORGIVEN (36)

Often, having dealt with our beliefs surrounding forgiveness and learning to discipline our harmful thoughts, behaviors and emotional reactions, a person often find that forgiving itself comes easy. Still people need to deal with their own offenses, and the time is coming for them to ask God's forgiveness for the harm they have done. Imagine the elder son actually forgiving his younger brother. Imagine how he now feels and describe it.

When have you forgiven someone?

How did you feel?

In the parable of the Prodigal Son the father's initial response is compassion for his returning son who had demanded his inheritance and left home, which likely gave the father great grief. Nothing the son has done has changed this, yet he receives forgiveness. What an incredible act of loving kindness! Forgiveness leads to "peace of mind" and frees us from the bitterness and resentment that often weighs us down, lifting us out of the misery of depression and other burdens.

Imagine the suffering Christ endured before being crucified and while on the cross, yet at the last his heart went out to the people. "Father," he said, "Forgive them for they know not what they do."

Imagine a time when you offended someone and not have realized the consequences of your actions. Later you felt guilty about the offense. How much sweeter would forgiveness taste to receive it now?

Can you imagine other people who hurt you that they may not realize your pain, or the significance of their action? Imagine how being forgiven will feel, particularly if they do know, yet are still forgiven.

Describe how you feel about this possibility.

1John 1:8-9 says: If we say that we have no sin, we deceive ourselves, and the truth is not in us. If we confess our sins, He is faithful and just to forgive us *our* sins, and to cleanse us from all unrighteousness. First we forgive others so that we can confess our sins then ask and accept God's forgiveness. Now forgive those you imagined forgiving.

Now write your thoughts and feelings throughout this experience.

Ask forgiveness of God and those whom you have offended against. Write about your thoughts and feelings throughout this experience.

7. GIVE UP THE MEMORIES (37)

Ruminating on offenses delays forgiveness and is difficult to stop. When memories surface at odd moments and we begin to ruminate on them, the anger and resentment resurface. Thus, we must be prepared to continue forgiveness and not allow ourselves to be tempted returning to the old hurtful ways. Scripture ruminated upon and kept in one's mind and heart however is a sound method for resisting temptation. This seed grows and bears fruit when you need it most. "Man [or woman] does not live by bread alone" Jesus said "but by every word of God."

Explore how you intend to protect your clean heart so you do not ruminate and continue to renew the resentments.

While Jesus does not tell the end of the elder son's story, he shows a forgiving spirit in the father who forgives the younger son. We are more likely to identify with the elder son than the younger, but we are both. There are no innocents for all have sinned, and come short of the glory of God.[3] Not just victims, we are also victimizers. Thus, to forgive we have to empathize with others and that empathy is based on the ability to see ourselves as forgiven as well as forgivers. To see the younger son and welcome the forgiveness we must also see ourselves as the elder son and be open to forgive and to be forgiven.

Write an ending to this parable.

SUMMARY

In choosing to forgive, we must also apply that knowledge. Unless we use the knowledge we have gained, it profits nothing. Forgiveness for Christians begins with God and is extend it to another as an act of freewill. Rumination inhibits forgiveness while forgiveness improves overall health thus reducing depression and anxiety that resulted from not forgiving.

God's command for us to forgive is clear. Scripture describes God's forgiveness, and provides models of interpersonal forgiveness that is evident in the parable of the Prodigal Son and Jesus dying on the cross. But it also offers a vision of grace and responsibility in forgiveness. While knowing about forgiveness can help motivate people to forgive, Christians should be motivated to forgive in obedience to God, and because he first loved and forgave us.

Animal sacrifice showed the carrying away of sin. Ultimately, Jesus' sacrifice took away the sins of those who believe and repent. God's forgiveness through animal sacrifice was an act of mercy, not purchased by the person bringing the offering, while Jesus' sacrifice purchased our forgiveness.

The New Testament also shows the need for humility, prayer, and a right relationship with God by repenting, turning from a sinful way of life. God wants to turn people from darkness to light. In teaching the disciples to pray, Jesus restates the need for forgiveness, "forgive us our debts, as we forgive those who are indebted to us". In saying, forgive us for we forgive them, this is not a onetime event, but ongoing without limits.

We are to forgive, but it is conditional. Repentance is required. God's forgiveness says, "I will remember their sins and iniquities no more". Thus, for Christians to know God will remember our sins no more, and being in the image and likeness of God are we not to 'choose to forget' another's offenses likewise?

IFT OF GRACE

Go into the world and proclaim the gospel to all creation. Those who believe and are baptized will be saved, but those who do not believe will be condemned. Miraculous signs will follow: *in my name they will cast out demons; they will speak new tongues; they will take up serpents; and if they drink anything deadly, it will not hurt them. They will lay hands on the sick, and they will be well. (*Mk 16:15-18*)*

God has a plan and as disciples we are reliable teachers of the Word. Thus, we do our part and pass on only what is honest, true, pure and lovely by living a life of grace and truth to be a reliable messenger.

Jesus came to show us the way to life through God's Word, and the behavior he modeled he expected of his disciples, his followers. Thus those who choose to follow Christ must be grounded in the Word. As teachers of the Word, we prevent troublesome and/or sinful behaviors with a thorough study of Scripture and knowing those things that are true, honest, right, pure, lovely, and of good report. Anything of virtue and praise, we must think on.

That which disciples have learned and received [godly behavior] we must do so that the God of peace will be present with us (Phil 4:4-9). We must give up our life as God *who did not spare his own Son, but delivered him up for us all"* (Romans 8:32) Moreover, Jesus gave his life so that he might express his life in and through us.

As we follow, Jesus pours his grace on us, and in him we are complete for in him "are hidden all the treasures of wisdom and knowledge" (Col 2:3) to choose this way of life is self-denial and submission.

The life that Jesus offers is different than that offered by churches. His servant leadership is distinct from society and too bold for today's Christian community. Is it too bold for you? What will you choose?

To choose the life of Christ is to commit to doing the following.
- Accept and follow our god-given purpose
- Believe as Jesus believed
- Commit to live as Jesus lived
- Devote to training as did Jesus
- Express ourselves in love as Jesus
- Forgive as Jesus forgave on the cross
- Minister and lead others just as Jesus led

Choosing to be a Disciple

To *choose the life* is to choose *his* life. George MacDonald said:

"Because we come out of a divine nature, which chooses to be divine, we must choose to be divine, to be of God, loving and living as he lives. Man cannot create this life, it must be shown him, and he must choose it.

We are not and cannot become true sons [daughters] without our will willing his, our doing following his making. He was not the Son of God because he could not help it, but because he willed it to be."

Becoming a Disciple is a journey toward Christ, following in his footsteps. Jesus sought disciples in a call to repentance.[3] The call to salvation is distinct from the call to follow Christ[24].

---

[24] Charles Bing, "Making of a Disciple", *Journal of the Grace Evangelical Society*, Autumn 1992—Vol 5:2 from http://www.faithalone.org/journal/1992b/Bing.htm, accessed 25January2010

38. THOUGHT FOR TODAY

Have you chosen to be a disciple of Jesus Christ?

How do you see that in your life, now and/or in the future?

Rate yourself

   1= always   2= frequently   3= occasionally   4= hardly ever   5=never

☐   I accept and follow God's purpose for my life

☐   I believe as Jesus believed

☐   I am committed to live as Jesus

☐   I live a well-disciplined life as did Jesus

☐   I am able to honestly express myself in love

☐   I am able and do forgive as Jesus forgave on the cross

☐   I am to minister - lead others to the best of my ability

Do you believe the modern day 'prosperity gospel'?

What about it appeals to you aside from the money angle?

BEING A DISCIPLE

A disciple of Jesus totally surrenders to his way of seeing and doing things. As such, we come with a desire to conform all of our life to the authority and Lordship of Jesus Christ. To Jesus, righteousness is a matter of the heart and not a code of behavior. Jesus came to reveal "who God is and how God does things."

As a disciple of Jesus we always ask Jesus more about who God is and what is God's will and ways as revealed in Scripture.

- As his disciples, we should come with a deeply rooted desire to want to surrender to his authority. He is our rabbi as well as The Rabbi and it is to him that we surrender. Disciples of Jesus today cannot explicitly or implicitly transfer any authority to a pastor, teacher, or well-known author, and thus taking any authority away from him in the process.

- In Matthew 28:20, Jesus says he will be with us always. Thus, with the continual indwelling of the Spirit of Christ within every believer, there is no need for anyone else to assume his role as rabbi of his disciples

- Jesus revealed who God is and how God does things in his encounters with people. His disciples learned what it means to be his disciples by studying the entire context of Jesus' explicit and implicit teachings in these encounters. The role of the teacher-preacher author as a co-disciple with certain spiritual gifts helps open the depths and riches of Scripture, thus further revealing to all disciples more of who God is, his will and his ways.

- Being a disciple is to: surrender and submit for a lifetime your life totally, ones worldview, paradigms, career, personality, character, ethics, desire, motivations, values, family, ego, sexuality and attitudes to the authority of Messiah Jesus and his teachings?

- Groups and one-on-one relationships can consistently ask and explore what it means to surrender every aspect of one's lives to the Lordship of Christ. It is important that groups and relationships define what they are about and their purpose. The difference between various groups can be vast in respect to their impact on the daily, personal holiness of a disciple.

A CERTIFIED DISCIPLE

We develop certified physicians and psychologists and place our lives under their care more easily than God simply because they have the education and proficiency in an area. So whom do you serve? If it be the world then serve it, but if it be Jesus Christ, then follow him on his walk and do it well.

There comes a time in everyone's life when they must make a choice: do we serve the gods of this age, or serve the living and true God? Do we serve the god of our fathers that held us captive, a slave to sin and who oppressed us, or serve the God who forgives, heals, and grants us his favor and blessing? Joshua challenged the people of Israel to choose saying, "But as for me and my household, we will serve the Lord." (Joshua 24:15)

CHRIST'S WALK

Jesus came to deal with the problems that afflict all humans:

Poverty: To preach the gospel to the poor
Sorrow: To heal the brokenhearted
Bondage: To proclaim liberty to the captives
Suffering: And recovery of sight to the blind
Oppression: To liberate the oppressed

Jesus proclaimed a new era for the world's suffering and presented himself as the answer to all the troubles of life. Whether you view these in a physical or a spiritual sense, Christ is the answer and he shows us the way through the life he lived and what he taught.

1. PRAYER

Jesus said by way of a parable that we always ought to pray and not lose heart. A parable was told about a widow who appealed before an unjust judge for help but he was not interested in helping her. However, when she persisted, he relented. "Though I do not fear God nor regard man, because this widow troubles me I will avenge her, lest by her continual coming she weary me."

This judge was not motivated by fear of God nor compassion for the woman– rather it was his own selfish interests that he served–yet he helped the widow. God is motivated to help us out of compassion.

Jesus contrasts the motivations of God who responds to the needs of those believers who call upon him, persistently in prayer. "Shall God not avenge his own who cry out day and night to him?" Therefore, prayer is foremost in Jesus' recommendations to a godly life.

Jesus' call to prayer is by example. "In the morning, he rose long before daylight, and he went out and departed to a solitary place; and there he prayed." Jesus was up before dawn in prayer with God. Once, He prayed throughout the night. "He went to the mountain to pray, and continued all night in prayer to God."

Following in the footsteps of Jesus is to follow in the manner of his prayer life as well as other ways. Jesus had a full prayer life, as did Paul. "Since the day when we heard, I do not cease to pray for you, and to ask that you may be filled with the knowledge of his will in all wisdom and spiritual understanding; that you may have a walk worthy of the Lord, fully pleasing him". We also need an attitude of prayerfulness: "Praying always with all prayer and supplication in the Spirit" thus, the Holy Spirit guides us into all truth. However, we must have our eyes open to see and our ears so they hear God.

2. Meditation

The Bible commands us to meditate. We are to meditate on his word day and night (Joshua 1:8), and our "delight is in the law of the Lord, and [and on his law] we meditate day and night" (Psalm 1:2).

The Old Testament uses two primary Hebrew words for meditation: *Haga*, which means to utter, groan, meditate, or ponder; and *Sihach*, which means to muse, rehearse in one's mind, or contemplate. Also translated as dwell, diligently consider, and heed.

Some describe meditation as *focused* thinking. A person selects a verse and reflects on it repeatedly. Those who know how to ruminate already have the skills to meditate but need to apply them in this better way.

In *Satisfy Your Soul*, Bruce Demarest says that meditation helps us focus beyond ourselves and the world and "reflect on God's Word, his nature, his abilities, and his works. Thus, we prayerfully ponder, muse, and 'chew' the words of Scripture. The goal is to let the Holy Spirit to activate the life-giving Word of God" within each of us (p133).

The best times during the day we can actively turn our minds over to God's Word in Christian Meditation is just before we fall asleep; have God's Word be the last thing that occupies our mind. Upon awaking, have God's Word be the first thing to fill our minds at the start. Finally, set time each day to meditate on God's Word so it can speak to us throughout our day. Our meditation focus' on "Whatever is true, honorable, right, pure, lovely, of good repute... anything of excellence and if anything be worthy of praise, dwell on these" (Phil 4:8, NASB).

God's will is that we "increase in knowledge of God". We get to know the Lord by receiving knowledge of God by his Word and "count all things loss for the excellence of knowing Christ Jesus my Lord."

In Ephesians Paul desired: "that the God of our Lord Jesus Christ, the Father of glory, give to you the spirit of wisdom and revelation in the knowledge of him," (Eph 6:18 41 Eph 1:17 42)so that we would be strengthened, according to his power."

With the Lord our strength, all things are possible for "I can do all things through Christ Jesus who strengthens me." (Phi 4:13). The power of this possibility brings "patience and longsuffering with joy," all of which is necessary not only for waiting on the Lord, but for enduring trials, and for living among varied people.

Another way to increase in knowledge of the Lord is to notice his voice even in the night. God speaks to some perhaps in sleep, of those things they need to hear. To listen and obey is the correct response. While we may question whether it is God or not, yet we are reminded of our omissions, those things we are called to do but have not done. Dreams may at times bring foolishness but when God speaks his voice is clear and intended not only for our instruction, but to teach us how to help others who otherwise could not understand the hidden things, and be helped.

3. SOCIAL SKILLS

Jesus left the wilderness to begin his ministry. One of the first things he did was gather a group of people about him. Social support is important for many reasons. When God made the heavens and the earth, no grass or plants were growing. God had not sent rain, and there was no one to work the land. But streams came up from the ground and watered the earth.

Then God took a handful of soil, made a man and breathed life into him.

God made a garden in Eden, in the east, and put the man there then, he placed all kinds of trees and fruit trees in the garden. Two other trees were in the middle of the garden. One the trees of life--the other the tree of knowledge, knowing between right and wrong...

God put the man in the Garden of Eden to care for it but told him, "You may eat from any tree in the garden, except the one that lets you know right from wrong! ..." Then God said, "It isn't good for the man to live alone. I will make a suitable partner for him." So the Lord took some soil and made animals and birds. He brought them to the man to see what names he would give them. ...

None of these were the right partner for the man... God put the man in a deep sleep and ... made a woman from a rib. God brought her to the man.

God achieved many things in the creation, he gave man a purpose, to care for the earth; he created animals to fill a need for but it was not companionship. Yet when God brought the woman Adam exclaimed: "Someone like me!" He recognized her likeness to him. The fact that God made a woman for the man we might deduce that the man is therefore complete, however this was not God's purpose for creating a woman; it was so the man would not be alone (Genesis 2:18).

Jesus did not live alone, but initially gathered a group of men and women about him, people with whom he could share his purpose, his beliefs, as well as teach them to share his hope for and with the rest of the world. Do you have people who support your dream?

A social group provides support, people with whom we can share our vision, and who will provide encouragement, but also accountability. Confessing our faults to another, repenting and being forgiven brings us deeper into the fold, no longer astray, we have a sense of belonging and companionship, community, which leads to improved overall health of the mind and emotions, all of which has a positive influence on our physical well-being.

3. CELEBRATION

On the everyday of creation, God celebrated his work as "well done". When a single sinner is saved, the angels in heaven celebrate[25] Jesus first miracle was turning water into wine at a wedding celebration. Clearly, the Lord understood about joy and celebration.

God's will is to have an attitude of gratitude: "giving thanks to the Father..."

---

25   Luke 15:1-7 (the lost sheep); 8-10 (the lost coin)

Since God's grace comes through humble, trusting prayer, and obedience to his will, then celebrating with a grateful heart all that God is and has done would be in order.

4. GIFT OF GRACE

Giving is the foundation of God's grace. Paul said in a letter to the Corinthians, "*I thank my God always concerning you for the grace of God which was given to you by Christ Jesus.*" The work of God does not come by what we do. "*For by grace you have been saved through faith, and that not of yourselves; it is the gift of God, not of works, lest anyone should boast*" (Ephesians 2:8-9).

Grace is in everything God desires to do in a person. "Every good gift and every perfect gift is from above, and from the father of lights." Ja 1:17. Whatever God does by grace is given by him to each of us (1Cor 12:7 and Eph 4:7); this also applies to spiritual rest and peace.

"*Come to me, all who labor and are heavy laden, and I will give you rest ...* (Matt 11:28); *Peace I leave with you, My peace I give to you; not as the world gives do I give to you*" (John 14:27).

Thus, when it comes to having a deeper relationship with the Lord, God gives us what is required for growth so we labor not in vain or grow weary: "*God, the Father gives you the* Spirit will make you wise so you understand what it means to know God (Eph 1:17)

God prepares us disciples to pass on the message of hope to others no matter who they may be. Men and women from jail or treatment or simple ordinary folks all have problems and we often fail to help because the one thing that helps we do not give, and that is sharing the good news then turning their lives over to God.

5. THE WORD

Armed, you keep your home in peace, otherwise, though you sweep and clean demons will return, seven times stronger (Luke 11:21-26). Thus armed, put the Word into practice and you have nothing to fear.

Encourage others to do what is right. We have to understand their needs and if they want to be saved. They may be comfortable in their misery and the attention it brings and just need a shove in the right direction.

Jesus met a man at the Pool of Bethsaida, who had been crippled 38 years. That is a long time to be there and not find a way into a pool. Jesus asked, "do you *want* to be healed?' To which he replied, "I can't" (John 5:1-24)

"Stand up, roll up your mat, walk home" Jesus said to him (John 5.8) then left. Instantly, he was healed! Jesus did not enable his helplessness, but gave the man a practical solution and a choice to walk or not.

After 38 years, this man's problem likely had become a way of life. No one had ever helped him before so he had no hope of ever being healed. The man's situation looked hopeless. Perhaps yours does too.

No matter how trapped you feel in your infirmities, God can minister to and heal your deepest needs, and forgive your worst sin. Don't let a problem or hardship or sin cause you to lose hope. Once you have your life well in hand —in the hand of Christ Jesus —you will be better prepared to help others who suffer in like manner, sometimes in prison.

There are many opportunities for disciples in prison ministry to help and encourage those who live in a culture of the despair and hopelessness. While not every Christian will have the desire to minister to prisoners, for those who are the called, there is a need to share the love of Jesus Christ to men and women who are desperate to know and experience that love.

Matthew 25:31-46 describes Jesus separating the nations at his return and he says, "I was in prison, and you came unto me" (v. 36). But then the nations ask when they had gone into the prisons to minister to Jesus, He answers, "Surely you know that whatever you have done for one of the least of these my brothers/sisters, you have done it for me" (v.40).

And the author of Hebrews 13:3 admonishes, "Remember them that are in bonds (in prison), as though bound with them."

In Acts we see Peter and Paul both imprisoned. Several of Paul's letters close with a list of men who either ministered to him in prison, or they were still there ministering to him while he was in bonds. Ministering to prison inmates can have a powerful impact on their lives.

As a prison inmate comes to know Jesus on a personal level, with support and fellowship from strong people of faith the number who reoffend is dramatically reduced. Prison ministries are about fellowship, mentoring, listening, teaching and caring for jailed and imprisoned inmates as though they were Jesus himself.

Prison ministries are there to give the love of Jesus to society's outcasts, whom Jesus died to save. We allow the Holy Spirit to demonstrate God's love in and through us toward them when we fellowship with them. You may feel inadequate to minister to prisoners, but if you are committed in your relationship with Jesus you can only help them in theirs.

God may have special work for you to do in a prison ministry, or because you have been a prisoner yourself. Many have ministered effectively to hurting people because they themselves triumphed over the same hurts both in and out of prison.

39. Thought for Today

The Life of Christ

Jesus led the way from birth into the wilderness and throughout daily life that he lived in obedience to God and then ended on a cross. What he found important he practiced along the way.

Prayer

What prayer life do you have?

What would you like to have different?

Meditation

Do you meditate?
For what reason do you meditate?

What form of meditation do you use?

How does your meditation differ from the description on page 3?

The Word

How much time do you spend in the Word?

Are you satisfied with the amount of time spent?

What would you like to change about that, if anything?

Social Life

Do you have any kind of social life?

How many friends do you associate with?

How many are close friends you share confidences with?

How would you describe your friends?

Celebration

Do you take a day of rest for the Sabbath? Describe

Do you celebrate a job well done? Describe

How often do you celebrate (not parties or Halloween)?

God's Grace

Describe how you have experienced God's grace in your life.

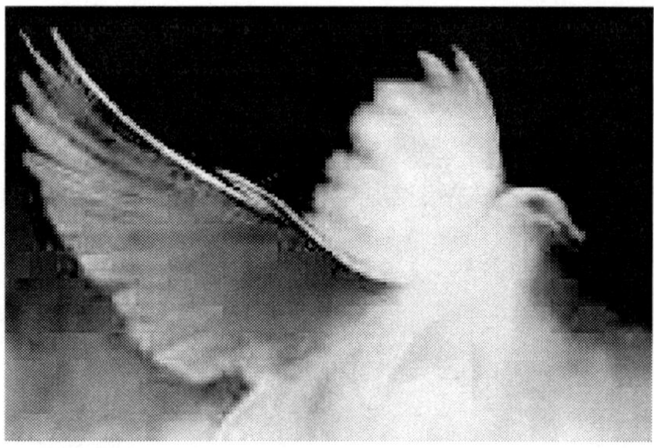

WHO IS MY NEIGHBOR?

Generally, we think of our neighbors as those next door, and thus, we tend to see God's command as including only those who live near us.

When asked who a neighbor was, Jesus responded: "Make no distinction as to either race or creed; but wherever you come across someone who has been stripped, beaten, robbed, and half-dead, don't wait for another to help him, but bind up the wounds; minister to that person, and treat him or her with the natural love of brotherhood."

Thus, we become excellent disciples.

Disciples are people whose lives are not perfect. Yet we must minimize problem areas to be a role model and disciple of the Word so we walk in the way of the Lord our God. Then we are ready to go to the nations; no longer just followers, we are teachers of the Word. Teaching the Word is not giving advice, but to share the gospel's message that Christ taught through the Word and the way he lived. Then the Scriptures become a guide for others who want to follow Christ and live in God's love.

Living in God's love does not mean we believe everything people say and blindly follow anyone who calls themselves ministers of God. Rather, test what they say to see if it is of God, in Scripture. And practice loving one another. If you are not loving and kind, you do not know God who is love. When we love, God lives in us and we are a reliable teacher of the Word. Jude warns about false teachers, to examine what a person says and observe the lives they live so that we approve only what pleases God. As we call upon God to help us in this area, we have the assurance that he will. As a reliable teacher, we must know Scripture and its guidelines.

At the end of each day, God looked at his creation and said, "It is good". Thus, on the seventh and final day, he could rest easy, knowing he had done a good work. We must be able to do the same; at the end of each day, look back and see if it was "well done" and what we must do to improve the results over time. Having done what is possible within our abilities, leaving the rest to God, we must complete Gods example, and take a day of rest.

A day of rest from all the trouble and strife is not easy for some people. Often, we must learn to make an entire day of rest a habit by practicing. When we do not get the rest we need, troubles seem to come easier. We become irritable, tempers flare, and battles begin.

At times, our bodies give out; we become sick or 'sick with despair' and depression can put us into a dismal place of rest. There are many ways our bodies and minds can force rest upon us when we do not take a rest by choice. We must rest from work, school, celebrations, and any other activity that causes wear and tear. But more importantly is the rest that we take to celebrate a job well done that acknowledges our effort.

Genesis 2:1-3 God **rested** from His creative work the seventh day. This is not the rest of weariness but the rest of satisfaction and completion of a job well done. Although God did not command man to keep the Sabbath then, he did teach the principle of one day of rest in seven.

So do not wait for a forced rest, take one by choice and really enjoy the time off. Turn off the phone, the television and stove (fast or eat light). Pick up a good book, play in the yard or take a walk. When you cannot come up with ideas for yourself, ask other people what they do. There are likely a few folks out there who know how to rest and really enjoy life. Learn from them.

Let all who run to you for protection sing joyful songs. Provide shelter for those who truly love you and let them rejoice. (Psalm 5:11)

40. Thought for Today

Everything is permissible –because we do not live under the law–but not everything is beneficial (1Corinthians 6:12)

> What I do (i.e. movies, food, drink, and/or humor), is it helpful, physically, spiritually, mentally, and does my behavior glorify God?

Everything is permissible, but I will not be mastered by anything.

> What has power over me (i.e. television program, internet, time on the computer or with friends in the absence of God)?

If whatever I eat (drink), if it causes another to sin I will not do it again.

> Which of my actions hurt others? (TV, games, or other activity keep me from time with my family, or encourage them to sin)

Whatever I (eat, drink, behave) with others do all for the glory of God.

> Does my behavior glorify God?
>
> Does my attitude reflect the love of Christ?

Giving of Self

List those things that you could do for others without payment (do not include charities and donations)

Why are random acts of kindness never wasted?

What effect do they have on other people?

What effect do they have on you?

Do they have to do with people or solitary pursuits?

Who gave you the best present ever and what was it?

Write one act of kindness done toward another and how you felt about it:

The Truth Revealed

In the Bible the Revelation of Jesus Christ as told to John reveals truth that every Christian needs to know, indeed, every person needs to know to be forewarned. The Bible contains all knowledge critical to know, yet it is the Revelation of Jesus that we are mandated to read and to share with others.

Life Application Study Bible says its purpose is to reveal the full identity of Christ and to give warning and hope to believers. Written approximately A.D. 95 from the Isle of Patmos where John was a prisoner. John was an eyewitness of the incarnate Christ, and had a vision of Christ in his glory. God also revealed to John what would take place in the future—judgment and the ultimate triumph of God over evil.

"God blesses those who read these words of this prophecy to the church and he blesses all who listen to and obey what it says..." (1:3).

Jesus entered the world and was then wrapped in cloth, slept in a manger on a bed of straw. He grew to manhood in Roman-occupied Palestine and his gentle hands grew strong and calloused in Joseph's carpentry shop. As a man, he walked throughout the countryside touching people, preaching to crowds, and trained 12 men to carry on his work.

Along the way he was harassed by those seeking to rid the world of him and his influence. Falsely accused and tried for crimes he did not commit, he was condemned to die a shameful death. He was spat upon, cursed at, pierced by nails and a sword, and hung on a cross for all to mock. Jesus, the son of God born a man, gave his life so that all might live.

At God's own time, the risen ascended Christ will burst one again upon the world with a shout, not of an infant as it takes it first breath but in a shout of triumph. Then everyone will know that Jesus is Lord of Lords and King of Kings! Those who love him will rejoice with songs of praise while his enemies will be overwhelmed with fear.

Revelation is a book of hope but also of warning. Sin did abound in the churches then, as they do now. And so, Christ called to those Christians then as he calls us now to commit ourselves to live in righteousness. We can take heart as we understand John's vision of hope: Christ will return to rescue his people and settle accounts with all who defy him.

Love Perfected

One day certain books will be opened and the book of life is one that will be opened, and whatever is written in the books, we will all be judged according to our works (Rev 20:12-13), which follow us to the grave (Rev 14:13). We have all received the gift if ministering to another (1Pe 4:10), and God provides the means for it is he who prepares us. (See 1Pe 5:10)

"*May the God of all grace... perfect... you*"; whatever we need he provides so that we are equipped. "*Now may the God of peace . . . make you complete in every good work to do his will . . . And he himself gave some to be apostles, some prophets, some evangelists, and some pastors and teachers, for the work of ministry.*" (Hebrews 13:20-21 and Eph 4:12)

"*May the God of all grace... establish... you,*" keep you moving firmly forward in the direction he has. Like Jesus' commitment to complete his purpose, going to the cross, the resurrection, and the ascension. "*Now it came to pass, when the time had come for him to be received up, that he firmly set his face to go to Jerusalem.*" Luke 9:51

"*May the God of all grace... strengthen... you*" in your ministry, one which requires the strength that God alone can and will provide, "according to the riches of his glory, to be strengthened with might through his Spirit in the inner man." Ephesians 3:16

"*May the God of all grace... settle... you*" so you are grounded in God's love: *that you, being rooted and grounded in love.*"Ephesians 3:17

Finally, in gratitude for all God has given perfecting, establishing, strengthening and settling us, we give of ourselves in return (Psalm 116:16) so that we live for him not ourselves because he loved us and washed us from our sins in his own blood (Revelations 1:5).

Christ's concern is that we do God's work. Who we are as a person is not from knowledge alone, but by putting our knowledge of God to work in our lives until it becomes a habit. When we continually turn to sin, our character is that of a sinful person. When we strive to walk in the spirit and resist the carnal, we have Christ's character.

DISCIPLES OF CHRIST

Having learned to walk in the Spirit as disciples of Christ, allowing that Spirit to guide our lives, we are now prepared to pass on Jesus' message of hope and salvation and be a blessing to others.

In Closing, Scripture reminds:

Christ encourages and his love comforts you. God's Spirit unites and we are concerned for the wellbeing of others. Now we live in harmony by showing love to each other. United in what we think as being one. Don't be jealous or proud, but humble and consider others more important. Care about others as much as you care about yourselves and think the same as Christ Jesus: Christ was truly God but did not try to remain equal with God but he gave up everything and became a slave when he became like one of us. Humble and obedient to God, Jesus died on a cross. Then God gave him the highest place and honored his name above all others.

Thus, at Jesus Christ every knee will bow down, those in heaven on earth, and under the earth. To the glory of God the Father everyone openly agrees that, "Jesus Christ is Lord!" Romans 10:13. Whoever calls on the Lord will be saved. How then will they call on him in whom they have not believed and how will they believe having not heard? (v14). John wrote Christ's revelation "*Blessed* are they who then *read* this Word and *follow* the Word" (Rev 1:3).

Blessed means more than riches and wealth as it is often interpreted rather, blessed means highly favored or fortunate (as e.g. by divine grace); blessed to be saved from the consequences [eternal destruction] of our sin; "a saved soul" of which all are blessed who read and hear and learn from Revelation. This blessing is clearly a joyful happiness at our good fortune in knowing that the Lord is coming to take us to heaven for an eternity with him.

We read aloud because hearing the Word keeps *us* focused and engaged! Scripture tells us that faith comes from hearing the spoken Word of God as it is read to the people who then hear and follow it (Romans 10:17).

THE END

CPSIA information can be obtained at www.ICGtesting.com
Printed in the USA
266085BV00004B/551-596/P